THE MEXICAN REFORMATION

THE MEXICAN REFORMATION

Catholic Pluralism, Enlightenment Religion, and the *Iglesia de Jesús* Movement in Benito Juárez's Mexico (1859–72)

JOEL MORALES CRUZ

PICKWICK Publications • Eugene, Oregon

THE MEXICAN REFORMATION
Catholic Pluralism, Enlightenment Religion, and the *Iglesia de Jesús* Movement in Benito Juárez's Mexico (1859–72)

Copyright © 2011 Joel Morales Cruz. All rights reserved. Except for brief quotations in critical publications or reviews, no part of this book may be reproduced in any manner without prior written permission from the publisher. Write: Permissions, Wipf and Stock Publishers, 199 W. 8th Ave., Suite 3, Eugene, OR 97401.

Pickwick Publications
An Imprint of Wipf and Stock Publishers
199 W. 8th Ave., Suite 3
Eugene, OR 97401

www.wipfandstock.com

ISBN 13: 978-1-61097-201-7

Cataloging-in-Publication data:

Cruz, Joel Morales.

The Mexican reformation : Catholic pluralism, Enlightenment religion, and the *Iglesia de Jesús* movement in Benito Juárez's Mexico (1859–72) / Joel Morales Cruz.

xii + 224 p. ; 23 cm. Includes bibliographical references and index.

ISBN 13: 978-1-61097-201-7

1. Latin America—Church history. 2. Mexico—Church history. 3. Catholic Church—Mexico—History. 4. Protestants—Mexico. I. Title.

BX1428.3 C73 2011

Manufactured in the U.S.A.

A mi madre

Contents

List of Illustrations | viii
List of Tables | viii
Acknowledgments | ix

1. Introduction | 1
2. Matters of History | 8
3. Church and State I: The Royal Patronage | 35
4. The Character of Mexican Catholicism in the Colonial Era | 50
5. The Catholic Enlightenment in New Spain | 77
6. Church and State II: The National Patronage (1824–50) | 119
7. The *Iglesia de Jesús* (1859–72) | 130
8. Conclusions | 187

Bibliography | 205
Index | 213

Illustrations

Figure 1:
Jorge González Camarena, *La Fusión de Dos Culturas (The Fusion of Two Cultures)* | 9

Figure 2:
Mestizaje and *Castizaje* Compared | 31

Figure 3:
Diego Rivera, *México en la Historia, Perspectiva: El Campesino Oprimido (Mexico in History, Perspective: The Peasant Oppressed)* | 36

Figure 4:
The Emergence of the Church of Jesus | 192

Tables

Table 1: Examples of *Castas* | 30

Table 2: Baroque Catholicism and Catholic Enlightenment | 79–80

Acknowledgments

> Writing is easy:
> All you do is sit staring at a blank sheet of paper
> until drops of blood form on your forehead.
>
> —*Gene Fowler*

ANYONE WHO HAS EVER written a short story, novel, dissertation, or work of nonfiction can sympathize with the quote above. The attempt to put years of accumulated experience or knowledge onto paper can be simultaneously liberating and torturous. For those of us involved in academia, it can also be described as an act of narcissism and ego. After all, we believe that what we have to say on a particular topic is not only indispensable but that it *must* be disseminated to and fro across the land from academic journals to Amazon's top seller list.

Yet writing is rarely an act of narcissism. Hilary Rodham Clinton quoted an old maxim when she titled one of her books, *It Takes a Village to Raise a Child*. With apologies to the Secretary of State, it takes an entire community to create a book. The months, or in some cases, years-long project requires more than the sole hapless academic shackled to laptop and library, no less so in my case than in all others.

The book you hold in your hands has its origins in a graduate level course on Christianity in Latin America. I became intrigued by the discovery that, contrary to the idea of a monolithic Catholicism in Latin America's colonial past, there existed various expressions of faith at times seemingly contradictory one to the other, some of them serving as correctives to what they perceived was wrong in the Church of their time. I decided to pursue one of them, Mexico's Church of Jesus, into a dissertation. Past treatments, few and often far between, tended to focus on the relationship of the Church of Jesus with the Episcopal Church of the United States. I decided to take a different approach and look at the ideological origins of the movement, rooting it in its socio-political and religious matrix. Naturally the ensuing journey drew me into several libraries and the Archives of the Episcopal Church in search of primary and secondary source materials. As a result, my gratitude must extend to that "great cloud of witnesses" whose long-term help and support has made this work possible.

My deepest thanks go to the libraries and staff of the JKM library at the Lutheran School of Theology, the Regenstein Library at the University of Chicago, and to Chris Higgins at the Archives of the Episcopal Church in Austin, Texas.

I would never have reached the dissertation stage had it not been for the many professors I had the privilege of sitting under during my academic career. I especially wish to thank Michael Shelly of the Lutheran School of Theology, Daniel Rodríguez at MTS, and Gilberto Cavazos-González, O.F.M. of Catholic Theological Union for their participation on my dissertation committee. I promise I will use my degree for good, not evil.

Dr. Jose-David Rodríguez of LSTC served as both Graduate Dean and as my advisor. He embodies the idea that teaching is not merely a career path but a vocation. I am grateful for his watchful eye over my academic and professional progress during and after my time at school.

The staff and editors at Wipf & Stock have been indispensable throughout this process. Their mission in making the work of scholars and academics readily available to the public is a joy and an encouragement.

Though most are unaware of their contribution to this process I thank the pastors and congregation at Holy Trinity Lutheran Church in Chicago for being the Body of Christ and offering a source of joy, service, and spiritual renewal week by week.

I am grateful to my family: to my late father for his support and joy throughout years of tragedy and triumph and to my brother for his part in helping me to get to where I needed to go for research. As I said, sometimes research and writing can become a very ego-feeding endeavor. Every academic needs someone in their lives who inhabits the simpler realities of faith to keep him or her grounded. My mother, Eva Cruz, has been that person. I thank her for her example and love that were always put into action through encouragement, sound advice, and home-cooked meals during the lean times.

Joel Morales Cruz
December 12, 2010
Feast Day of Our Lady of Guadalupe

1
Introduction

From the house across the street, the rhythmic blows of tambourines and the sound of hallelujahs. Shouts to the sky, the ecstasy of a new Pentecost. On the bus, an itinerant vendor of eternal truths. A fistful of incense or a pamphlet of revelations in exchange for some coins. Next to a handsome new temple, a gringo and his local colleague dressed in suits are in search of saints for the "latter days." At the door, two preachers with a copy of Watchtower and a chat if you have the time.

The radio in the hut high in the mountains, a Luis Palau crusade, conquering the countryside in Christ's name. Laminated roofs on the horizon, rural children with foreign grandparents. Small airplanes landing in a North American stronghold in the middle of the Amazon jungle. On the television, the seductive voices of Jimmy Swaggart or Pat Robertson, electronic messages of salvation for a lost modern world. Colorful tents, not of circuses but of evangelical campaigns. A meeting of the redeemed in the Model Stadium, the final showdown between Good and Evil.

The newspapers and magazines show signs of alarm: "invasion of the sects," "cultural penetration," "evangelical explosion," religious contest in the nation, "new imperialist strategy." Worry. Confusion. What is happening?[1]

WITH THIS POETIC PORTRAIT, anthropologist David Stoll introduced his seminal work on the spread of evangelical Protestant religion in Latin America in the latter half of the twentieth century. According to

---

1. Quoted in Stoll, *Is Latin America*, 1.

the *World Christian Encyclopedia*, Protestants may have comprised over 11 percent of the general population of Latin America at the beginning of the new millennium. In some countries such as Brazil, Guatemala, and Puerto Rico, the percentage may be even higher.[2] The phenomenon of Protestant growth, particularly in its evangelical and Pentecostal forms in this traditionally Roman Catholic region, has drawn scholars from diverse fields in an effort to greater understand it. This trend has not only intrigued but has also alarmed some of the hierarchy of the historically dominant Roman Catholic Church to the extent that during an address to the Latin American Conference of Bishops held in Santo Domingo in 1992, Pope John Paul II referred to Protestant churches as "ravenous wolves" while the future Benedict XVI accused the United States "the protestantization of Latin America and the dissolution of the Catholic Church" in 2004.[3]

Behind this fascination or fear of the rising Protestant demographic in Latin America, there is the assumption that Protestantism in its many forms is a foreign import. Whereas Roman Catholicism is perceived of as native to the region (though that faith was itself imported from Europe in the sixteenth century), Protestantism is seen as a recent intruder on Catholic (holy) ground, brought to these countries by immigrants, missionaries, or even with the backing of the United States to destabilize the Catholic presence in the region.[4] These statements have a basis in truth. It is true that some Protestant bodies were introduced

---

2. This figure takes into account the twenty Spanish and Portuguese-speaking countries of Latin America and the Caribbean. Because their early colonial experiences early on have caused them to diverge significantly from the shared cultural and historical legacies of the Iberian-American nations, I have excluded the English (Jamaica, Barbados, etc.) and French (Haiti, Martinique, etc.) speaking countries from this list as well as Dutch Surinam, and so on. Regarding religious identity, I have included both Anglican and "Independent" descriptors under the Protestant rubric. Though many would consider Anglicanism a separate strand of Christian faith, not only have the bodies associated with the Church of England traditionally been understood as falling under Protestantism but the forms of Anglicanism that evangelized Latin America have generally been of the evangelical variety that has more in common with Protestantism than Catholicism. Independent churches are bodies that are independent of historic, institutionalized denominations. These may reflect indigenous movements that have either broken off from other bodies or indigenous charismatic and Pentecostal churches such as the *Igreja Universal do Reino de Deus* in Brazil. Barnett, David B., et al. *World Christian Encyclopedia*.

3. Cf. Jenkins, *Next Christendom*, 156.

4. Magister, "Benedict's First Visit," para. 23, 24.

through immigration—German Lutherans, Italian Waldensians, and Russian Mennonites in nineteenth-century Argentina, Paraguay, and Uruguay, for example. Protestant missions to Latin America from Great Britain and the United States began shortly after the region gained its independence from Spain but increased since the 1950s after the Cultural Revolution in China closed that mission field. The expanding strength of the United States in the nineteenth and twentieth centuries also took the form of a religious Manifest Destiny as evangelical leaders were encouraged to proselytize and Americanize recently acquired territories such as Alaska and Puerto Rico.[5]

This perspective, whether of scholarly curiosity or clerical condemnation, reflects what the historian of Spanish heterodoxy, Marcelino Menéndez Pelayo (1856–1912), once wrote: that "the Spanish language was not created to speak heresies."[6] In other words, to be an heir of the Spanish Empire—the thousand cubs of the Spanish lion, as a poet once declared—to be linked through culture and language to Isabel and Fernando, to Cortéz or Pizarro, to Inca de la Vega, Cervantes, Sor Juana, or Borges is to be Roman Catholic. It is a conviction that literally changed the face of Spain in the dawning decades of the modern era and led to the expulsion of the very Jews and Muslims who helped enrich the Iberian kingdoms both economically and culturally during the Middle Ages. And it was because of this belief that the fires of the Inquisition were stoked against anything that resembled Protestantism, whether in the Old World or the New. The historical reality, however, is not always cut-and-dry as this exploration will seek to show.

This work has its origins in a graduate course on Christianity in Latin America at McCormick Theological Seminary in Chicago. During its progress I discovered the presence of what I playfully referred to as "proto-Protestant" groups in mid-nineteenth century Brazil, Mexico, Chile, and Colombia that antedated missionary efforts from Protestant denominations in the United States and Europe. "Far from being the

---

5. See for example, Berge, "Voices for Imperialism." A. F. Walls also notes, "America is the West writ large, Western characteristics exemplified to the fullest extent. Americans themselves have always been aware that they represent the decisive and ultimate development of the West," Walls, *Missionary Movement*, 223. See also Rodríguez, *La Primera Evangelización*, 5–99 for an introduction to the religious and socio-economic context of American evangelicalism in the nineteenth century.

6. Pelayo, *Historia*, 26. Note: all translations from original sources are done by the author.

first results of U.S. missionary expansion, these associations had their roots in the political culture of Latin American radical liberalism, and in the associative ferment and enthusiasm which those same liberals tried to encourage in civil society in order to give themselves a power-base."[7] Prior treatments on the Church of Jesus, however, emphasize that body's association with the Episcopal Church in the United States, particularly in the latter half of the nineteenth century. This work differs from all other respects as it seeks to root the Church of Jesus movement *within Mexican Catholicism*, both the Enlightened Catholicism of the eighteenth century and the dominant Tridentine Catholicism of the colonial era. I rest my argument on two most basic assumptions: firstly that no movement arises *ex nihilo* but must reflect a prior matrix and development and, secondly, that ideological and social movements, no less than individuals in a society, interact with their progenitors and contexts as they form their own identities and structures. I have titled this work "The Mexican Reformation" to underscore both the emergence of Protestantism in Roman Catholic Mexico and to connect it to the political context of the Reform Era of Benito Juárez.

To use a scientific metaphor, the story of the Church of Jesus movement and nascent Mexican Protestantism is one of evolution and mutation as religious expressions changed and adapted to survive in and meet the understood needs of the social and political contexts in which they found themselves.

The following chapter will seek to sketch a historiographical survey of Latin American Protestantism. It will serve as an introduction to the state of research on early Mexican Protestantism and the Church of Jesus in particular. Here I will discuss my methodology and the particular historical approach I will take to this study in interaction with other frames of thought including social, theological, postcolonial, and Latino/a studies.

The third chapter will survey the religio-political framework that determined the life of the Catholic Church in the colonial era, namely the relationship between the Crown and the Cross as expressed in the royal patronage, or *patronato real*. This backdrop, rooted in the Middle

---

7. Dussel, *Church in Latin America*, 324. Some of these groups were associated with freemasons. Many lost the participation of liberal clergy and, inspired by a burgeoning anti-Catholicism, took paths that led them into Protestant circles. Others veered towards spiritualism or theosophy.

Ages, is necessary towards an understanding of the emergence of the Church of Jesus and its relation to the government of Benito Juarez.

Chapter 4 will explore the nature and expression of Colonial Catholicism in its baroque, Tridentine expressions. In this milieu—in which races, classes, and languages were constantly interacting with one another—the religious universe was an open one though officially within the limits of Tridentine orthodoxy. The divine and miraculous was immanent, breaking through to everyday reality and palpable through a relic, a holy person, and most of all, the miracle of the Mass. Interacting within the multi- and inter-ethnic stew in which it was rooted, colonial, Baroque Catholicism was a faith in perpetual motion as devotions and religious expressions adapted to their contexts, changing and evolving to meet the religious and social needs of the people.

One such mutation will be explored in the fifth chapter, that of the Catholic Enlightenment of the mid-late eighteenth century. This movement emerged from the desire of the Spanish Crown to exercise more control over the devotions and the orthodoxy of the Church. The Catholic Enlightenment, born of the openness to religious experience that was the baroque, turned on its parent like the perennial Greek myth, as reforming clerics and statesmen in Spain and Mexico emphasized a more rationalistic faith, embedded in the Bible and the church fathers. This enlightened faith sought to apply reason to orthodox faith and focused more on individual piety and works of charity than on the extravagant expressions of public faith that it sought to curtail.

The second half of the political contextual frame drawn around the Church of Jesus will be described in chapter 6 with the matter of state patronage over the Catholic Church in the decades following Mexican independence. During these first few decades of the Mexican Republic, the very nature of the nation would be debated as both liberals and conservatives sought to define the relationship between the State and the Church. How would the new government replace the role of the Spanish Crown in defining the role and polity of the Church in society, if at all? Would the Catholic Church in Mexico take on a subservient role to the State and its policies or would it be governed directly from Rome? Would Mexico follow the lead of other nations in enacting religious tolerance or would it maintain the colonial status quo between Church and State albeit with republican, rather than royal, rule? These questions formed the

Sturm und Drang of Mexican policy vis-à-vis the Church and provide the religio-political topsoil for the Church of Jesus movement.

Given these factors—the Church/State patronage context stretching to the beginning of Spain's New World colonies, the open, multiethnic and hybrid nature of baroque Christianity that in turn engendered the more critical and Bible-based pieties of the Catholic Enlightenment—the movement that would become known as the Church of Jesus arose in the mid-nineteenth century when several Catholic priests allied themselves with the constitutional reforms of the Benito Juarez administration. The genesis and development of this movement with be described in detail in chapter 7, including its relationship to other liberal dissident movements of the time. The Church of Jesus, seeking the support it could not or did not receive from the government, sought out the assistance of the Protestant Episcopal Church in the United States (PECUSA). The influence of the Episcopal Church transformed the Church of Jesus from that of a reform movement within Catholicism to that of a distinctly Protestant body. Though not without its critics, this tectonic change, and its ties to the North American church, would form the basis for an indigenous Protestant tradition in and of Mexico.

The final chapter will serve as a summary and reflection on the writing of Latin American Christianity and what this present exploration can mean for our interpretation of Latin American Christianity. Given that some of this historical writing is accomplished by scholars approaching the topic from various Christian perspectives I will, with "fear and trembling," include a brief proposal for an ecumenical historiography of Latin American Christianity.

In the process, as this work will demonstrate, I found the themes and language necessary to make the connection between the Church of Jesus and Enlightened religion. Accomplishing this, I decided to go further, believing that if the Church of Jesus movement was indeed rooted in the Mexican Catholic Enlightenment then logically it would be rooted in the religious movements that gave birth to this one, namely the baroque Christianity of the colonial era. Baroque Catholicism, by its very nature, formed a fertile field for the development and propagation of diverse religious expressions which—though sometimes opposed and sometimes abetted by the hierarchy of the Church—was irresistible given the plural social and ethnic makeup of the American colonies. Rooted in the ideals of the Catholic Enlightenment, the Mexican Church of Jesus was able to evolve, even as it was tossed to and fro by political and cultural waves, into something more akin to nineteenth-century evangelical Protestantism—from reformist group to dissident church body maintaining Catholic identity to anti-Catholic faith to nascent Protestant body under the Episcopal Church.

2

Matters of History

A MEXICAN CHURCH

THE WORLD-SHATTERING EVENTS OF the sixteenth century between the Old World and the New have often been described as an "encounter," as if they were a chance meeting between two entities—a respectful nod and smile of acknowledgement to one another across the waters of the Atlantic. This language of encounter fails to take into account the violence and upheaval experienced by the American, and later African, peoples as the Spanish, Portuguese, and later the English, French, and Dutch sought to carve out colonies and outposts on the continent using the weaponry of war, ideology, economics and religion.

In the National Museum at Chapultepec Castle in Mexico City there hangs a mural that portrays this violence in tragic hues of red, orange and brown. In *La Fusión de Dos Culturas* (The Fusion of Two Cultures) a Spanish conquistador and an Aztec Eagle warrior lock in a death-embrace, each one's weapon piercing the other. In the corner the symbols of their patrimonies burn in the surrounding flames, out of which emerges the eagle of the Mexican nation in decidedly Hegelian fashion.[1]

---

1. Strictly speaking, the Aztecs called themselves *Mexica* (which in time would lend its name to the entire nation). The term *Aztec* stems from the mythological origin-place of the Mexica called *Aztlan*. Since reappearing in the eighteenth and nineteenth centuries among scholars, the name *Aztec* is the generally accepted generic name for the dominant peoples of the Valley of Mexico who, by the sixteenth century were already a syncretistic mix of other peoples, cultures, and religions they had conquered. In this work I use the names *Aztec* and *Mexica* interchangeably. Cf. Townsend, *Aztecs*, 55.

Figure 1: Jorge González Camarena, *La Fusión de Dos Culturas (The Fusion of Two Cultures)*. National Museum of History, Chapultepec Castle, Mexico City, 1963. Author's photo.

Yet even this portrait is only partial. The so-called fusion that occurred across Latin America, including Mexico, involved not only two cultures—the Iberian and the American—but a multiplicity of peoples: the Tainos, the Caribs, Arawaks, Maya, Aztec, Yaqui, Hopi, Inka, Guarani, etc. The language of "two cultures" simplifies the fact that through the course of exploration and conquest there were numerous encounters between the Iberian newcomers and the complexity of indigenous peoples—each with its own cultures, languages, cosmologies, and so on.[2] The fusion that resulted from these clashes; the physical and ideological results of these many encounters (added to by the subsequent addition of African slaves) created the admixture or hybridity that is the basis of Latin American culture, including religion.[3]

2. There exist innumerable works that focus on particular Native American cultures such as the Aztec, Taino, Olmec, or Inca, mostly written by anthropologists. A recent popular work that presents a continent-wide portrait is Mann, *1491*. For information on indigenous worldviews and religions see Gossen, *South and Meso-American*; Sullivan, *Native Religions*; and Andrien, *Andean Worlds*.

3. Immigration during the nineteenth and twentieth centuries by Asian and

Almost three and a half centuries later a group of priests broke ranks with their co-clerics and lent their support to Benito Juarez's Reform Laws and the Constitution of 1857 that, among other things, severely limited ecclesiastical courts and ordered the sale of ecclesiastical properties not used for the immediate uses of the Church. These Constitutionalist Fathers sought to effect reform within the Catholic Church, affirming that Christianity was not incompatible with the new laws. Eventually these Constitutionalist Clerics would receive support from the Juarez government which sought to create a national Catholic Church independent of Rome. Soon after, when Juarez was forced into exile in 1863, the dissident Church sought the assistance of the Protestant Episcopal Church whom they hoped would lend them financial aid and consecrate for them a bishop, thus placing them under apostolic succession.

When Juarez returned to power in 1867 there was a renewed interest in establishing a national Church but this came to naught. Instead, new leaders arose such as Manuel Aguas, the ex-Dominican priest whose anti-Catholic attacks—influenced in part by Mexican anticlericalism and by evangelical Episcopalians from the United States—helped take the *Iglesia de Jesus* (Church of Jesus), as it was now known, beyond the idea of simply reforming the Catholic Church. The Episcopal Church lent much needed financial assistance and administrative assistance but with the consequence of placing the Church of Jesus further under the auspices of that North American denomination in spirit and in authority.

This writer proposes that the origins of Mexican Protestantism, in the form of the Church of Jesus, lie not in the North American foreign mission enterprise but in the very nature of Mexican Catholicism which, from its beginnings, evidenced a plurality of expression. Some of this diversity—such as the use of indigenous languages, the multiplicity and variety of devotion, etc., was tolerated in realization of the variety of peoples in the land (native populations, African slaves, immigrants, peasants, etc.), the differing approaches of the secular Church, and the evangelization efforts of the religious orders. Other expressions, of course, that were perceived to upturn accepted notions of race and gender along with having undue influence of Indian and African religion upon Catholic orthodoxy, worried the Spanish and ecclesiastical

---

European peoples would further add to this cultural stew. Note for example the role of Japanese Peruvians in that nation's politics, sports, and entertainment and the Italian origins of the quintessential Argentinean tango.

authorities.[4] Nonetheless, the pluralist society that was created in New Spain as a result of the intermingling of peoples went hand in hand with Baroque, Tridentine Catholicism that encouraged this kind of plurality in the religious sphere through its emphasis on the immanence of God and the saints in relics, sacred places and holy persons.

The Bourbon Reforms of the eighteenth century brought about changes that challenged the economic and social position of the Church, both in Spain and in her colonies. As the Bourbon monarchs, using the power of the royal patronage, sought to place the Church under their control, Enlightened Catholicism sought to effect change within the Church itself. This educated elite sought to curb what they saw as abuses within the Church—what they perceived as superstitions or over-opulent displays of piety that distracted from the gospel message presented in the Bible. The Bourbon State initiated an effort to modernize popular piety, regulating public religious observances, and limiting confraternities, for example, but in the process alienated indigenous communities and forced the parish clergy to decide between enforcing official enactments and supporting their own flocks.[5] This general effort at reform went hand-in-hand with later forms of Jansenism, which by now had been shorn of most of their Augustinian tenets and emphasized not only a "rational," individual piety but also supported the power of the local bishops and the State over and against papal prerogatives in the administration of the local church, thus paving the way for the advocacy of national Churches.

Thus on the eve of the Mexican Wars of Independence there existed a variety of catholicisms side by side: the popular pieties of the masses (whether they be native, African, Spanish, wealthy, poor, etc.), the official Church of the Bourbons seeking to reform the ecclesial state even while undermining the Church's economic and social privileges, and the undercurrent of priests and laypeople who simply lived within the protean, multiple qualities of colonial Catholicism.

The efforts of the Bourbon Crown to limit the power of the Church, including priestly privileges, the secularization of some parishes, as well as the expulsion of the Jesuits in 1767 bred resentment among the some of the Creole clergy and the people and inspired a nascent nationalism in New Spain fueled by an increased interest in the colony's indigenous

---

4. See for example Jaffary, *False Mystics* and Giles, *Women in the Inquisition*.
5. Meyer, *Oxford History*, 179–82.

past and in the Virgin of Guadalupe whose apparition centuries earlier was seen as validating the equal status of Mexico and any other State. This formed part of the religious groundwork for the struggle for Independence that was initiated and supported by parish priests.

With an end to the Wars of Independence and the ouster of the Spanish Crown the Mexican government took up the debate over the patronage of the Church. Liberals and Conservatives, divided basically over the role of the colonial past in the new nation's future, debated and fought over whether Mexico, as a sovereign nation, was heir to Spain's ecclesiastical prerogatives or whether the right of patronage fell back to the papacy. Whereas that question was never successfully settled in the rise and fall of an emperor and several presidents, the matter of state control over the Church, for various reasons including the need for Mexican bishops and suspicions of ultramontane, Roman control, would remain in the background.

While the early Mexican Republic provided for the exclusive rights and claims of the Roman Catholic Church, the Constitution of 1857 and the administration of Benito Juarez undermined those privileges. These Laws of Reform were strongly opposed by the Church hierarchy and the Vatican who, perhaps rightly, perceived in them the threat of losing power and religious monopoly.[6] The subsequent Wars of Reform would pit Liberals against Conservatives and ended with the latter's (with the support of the Mexican Church hierarchy) appeal to the French who eventually installed the Austrian Archduke, Maximilian, as Emperor of Mexico.

It was obvious to the Juarez government that one of the dangers to a strong, independent State lay in the Roman Catholic Church, whose hierarchy and policies were still dictated by a Rome that was not only distant but antagonistic to his reforms. Thus Juarez began entertaining the thought of establishing an independent national Church that would retain its Catholic faith while distancing itself from the Vatican. A small number of clerics, the Constitutionalist Fathers, seeking to reform the Church's piety, rallied to its support and to uphold the 1857 Constitution. In short, the Church of Jesus, as it would be known, was the result of reformist initiatives that hearkened back to the eighteenth century when Enlightened Catholicism, itself a reaction to and a product of pluralistic Baroque Catholicism, emerged to challenge those traditions. These find

---

6. Meyer and Sherman, *Course*, 380–81.

fertile ground in the heritage of the Conquest, a society formed by the mixture of Africans, indigenous, and Europeans, and their descendants. The Church of Jesus, and consequently, nascent Protestantism in Mexico, is Mexican in its roots and spirit. Like its sixteenth-century predecessor, this Mexican Reformation emerged and evolved from its religious, social and political contexts.

HISTORY MATTERS
Protestantism and Protestantisms

Before embarking upon a centuries-long quest towards the roots and development of our object, the Church of Jesus, it is necessary to clarify and detail several things. From the start, we need to define the underlying question of our topic, namely, what is Protestantism, particularly in a Latin American context? From here we will attempt to describe just how the history of Protestantism in Latin America has been undertaken, namely, its historiography. Lastly, for this section, we will look at the historiography of the Church of Jesus movement.

Protestantism—one of the three major branches of Christianity, along with Roman Catholicism and Eastern Orthodoxy—arose in sixteenth-century Europe as a reform movement within Western Christianity that sought to address alleged theological and moral abuses within the Catholic Church and to return to a purer form of Christian faith shorn of medieval accretions.[7] The first generation of Protestant leaders, such as Martin Luther and Ulrich Zwingli, did not set about to split from the Catholic Church, much less to create a series of separate religious traditions. They and their followers saw themselves as true Christians in line with the New Testament church and the earliest Christian teachers. It was during the earliest decades of the movement that the hallmarks of classic Protestantism would emerge, namely an emphasis on the centrality of the Bible in matters of faith and morals, the belief that one's salvation was brought about through faith in Christ alone and the priesthood of all believers. Though Protestantism evolved, developed, and even suffered multiple splits into various denominations,

---

7. The term *Protestant* refers to the letter of protestation by the Lutheran princes against the decision of the Diet of Speyer in 1529, which reaffirmed the edict of the Diet of Worms in 1521 that banned Martin Luther's 95 Theses of protest against the beliefs and practices surrounding the sale of indulgences. Eventually, the term was used to refer to all groups that disagreed with or split from Roman Catholicism.

these traits have remained central across the many differences between the many Protestant traditions.

Despite the multiplicity of Protestant traditions in Latin America, the Argentine scholar, José Míguez Bonino, has divided them into four categories:[8]

- *The Liberal Tradition:* The churches and movements that began to enter Latin Americain the 1840s that, while attempting to stay above the often harsh politics of the era, worked with Liberal leaders in common causes such as education and religious freedom in addition to ministering to the spiritual needs of both native Latin Americans and expatriate Europeans and North Americans.[9]

- *The Evangelical Tradition:* Fueled by the revivals of the late-nineteenth and early-twentieth centuries (led by D. L. Moody and Billy Sunday, for example, and leading to the Student Volunteer Movement in missions and the birth of American fundamentalism), this tradition emphasizes the individual's personal conversion experience and responsibility to live morally. With the dominance of Positivism and some antireligious strains in the late nineteenth century, evangelical Christians retreated from the cooperation an earlier generation had sustained with government leaders and focused on individual conversions and the growth and sustenance of their churches.[10]

8. Bonino, *Faces*, 8ff. Significantly, in this work, Bonino refrains from a more traditional categorization of Protestantism according to their historical origins (Reformation, revivalist, Pentecostal, etc.) but rather, divides them according to their relationship to the histories and cultures of Latin America.

9. According to Bonino, the methods of the Protestant missions such as Bible distribution and education coincided with the agendas of the Liberals who sought to lead their respective nations into the modern world through changes in economics (mercantilism to production-based capitalism), education and religion (religious tolerance to stimulate foreign trade and immigration). Though they did not reject Catholicism, Liberal anticlericalism, in response to a variety of factors (the Vatican's support of Spain during the Wars of Independence, the perception of the Catholic hierarchy as exploitative or fostering ignorance among the masses, etc.) responded favorably to the Protestant approach of mission as an agent of cultural transformation. Bonino, *Faces*, 8ff.

10. Even as more mainline or progressively liberal traditions sought dialogue with the Roman Catholic Church in the wake of Vatican II, evangelical churches perceived this as theological compromise and further isolated themselves from those Protestant churches. Premillennial dispensationalism, popular in North American evangelical circles, became influential in Latin America through media such as the *Scofield Reference Bible*, Moody Press and Radio, international evangelical crusades and the missions movement. Its emphasis on biblical end-times prophecy and anti-Communism helped

- *The Ethnic Tradition:* During the latter half of the nineteenth century and into the twentieth, as various Latin American nations sought to extend hegemony into the interior and encourage development (often at the price of indigenous life and culture), immigrant groups were encouraged to settle and colonize, resulting in the establishment of Protestant churches that were tied closely to their original cultures and languages (German Lutherans, Russian Mennonites, etc.). With the passage of time and the passage of generations, the ethnic church traditions changed and adapted, sometimes creating links with similar bodies (German Lutherans and American Lutheran missionaries, for example) or coming closer to the Latin American evangelical or Pentecostal traditions.[11]

- *The Pentecostal/Charismatic tradition:* Growing out of the Holiness movement at the turn of the twentieth century, Pentecostalism (and later the Charismatic movement in the 1960s) focused on the ongoing work of the Holy Spirit among Christians as manifested in speaking in tongues, miracles and faith healing. Observers have offered different reasons as to the success of Pentecostal and Charismatic churches throughout the continent but it is obvious that their growth coincides with the rapid industrialization and urbanization of large sectors of Latin America, particularly in the latter half of the twentieth century.

Though there were minor incursions into Latin America during the colonial era, a significant Protestant presence was not established until after the Spanish colonies won their independence in the first third of the nineteenth century.[12] After the overthrow of the Spanish crown, the new republics faced the challenge of religious liberty—namely, the desire to maintain Catholic identity and hegemony while seeking to establish diplomatic and financial ties with the United States, Germany, and Great Britain, all traditionally Protestant nations. Religious toleration did not come about in one fell swoop for the entire continent. Debates occurred and battles flared that centered on the Catholic identity of the

---

develop and strengthen the dichotomy in evangelical thinking and spirituality between the gospel and the surrounding culture. Cf. Bonino, *Faces*, 40ff.

11. Bonino, *Faces*, 79–106.

12. Bastian, *Historia del Protestantismo*, 42–94; González and González, *Christianity in Latin America*, 186–88.

new republics and their relationship to the industrialized world. These debates were settled as early as 1824 in Brazil and as late as the 1850s for Mexico with the triumph of Benito Juarez's presidency. As religious toleration became the law of the land, we begin to see the establishment of Protestant churches and denominations in Latin America (particularly the Methodists, Presbyterians, and Baptists), first to minister to those doing business from abroad and later, to spread their particular message to the population. Since then, mission agencies have continued to send their agents to evangelize and establish churches that have, with varying degrees of success, become self-governing and self-propagating.[13] Missionary activity to Latin America from abroad, particularly from conservative, evangelical bodies, increased after mainland China closed its borders to foreigners in the late 1950s as a result of the Cultural Revolution. However, the role of the missionary has changed in the last sixty years. While they may continue in a prime role in some areas, with the awareness that church bodies should be of the prevailing culture and self-governing, missionaries have taken on more secondary roles such as helping maintain ties to sister churches abroad or assisting with educational or logistical resources.

A second means of Protestant incursion occurred as the result of immigration. In the nineteenth century, particularly in its latter half, Argentina, Brazil, and Paraguay, seeking to penetrate the interior, introduce modern farming techniques and displace the indigenous population, invited religious minorities from Russia and Europe to establish communities. As a result, groups such as the Mennonites, Waldensians, and Lutherans became a part of the religious landscape in some parts of South America. Additionally, African-Americans migrated to Haiti and the Dominican Republic to flee the racist policies of that United States. While initially isolated and maintaining the language and traditions of their former homelands, with the passing of the generations, these various traditions have become more fully integrated into the cultures of their host nations.[14]

13. The changing role of missions in Latin America, be they Catholic or Protestant, have changed and adapted over the years, sometimes with the goal of conversion to another faith, as participants in social action or advocates and assistants to local churches. See, for example, Bosch, *Transforming Mission* for a survey of the changing faces of mission.

14. González & González, *Christianity in Latin America*, 190–205. Bastian, *Historia del Protestantismo*, 102–16.

Whereas immigration to Latin America accounted for some forms of Protestantism in Latin America, other traditions were introduced as a result not of individuals crossing the border, but rather of the border crossing them. With the victory of the United States after the Mexican-American War of 1848, large populations of Mexicans found themselves U.S. citizens on newly acquired U.S. soil (Texas, Arizona, New Mexico, California, etc.). Similarly, after the Spanish-American War of 1898, the United States found itself in charge of Spain's last colonial holdings, namely Cuba and Puerto Rico in the Caribbean and the Philippines in the Pacific. Protestantism came to these areas by way of missionaries as the United States sought to win the hearts and souls of the people, particularly in the American Southwest and Puerto Rico, which remained a possession of the United States even after Cuba and the Philippines became independent.[15]

Pentecostalism, a phenomenon that has since become truly global in its reach and acculturation, took root in Latin America through a variety of entry points. As a result of the Azusa Street Revivals of 1905–6, some Hispanic adherents of the movement began to spread the word of the Holy Spirit's continuing power among the Mexican-American communities of the Southwest and in northern Mexico. Participants from the Azusa Street Revival were also instrumental in converting people to the Pentecostal cause who would later found churches in the Caribbean and among Latino communities in the United States. In Valparaiso, Chile, the pastor of a Methodist Church, Willis Collins Hoover (1858–1936), began corresponding with participants from the various Pentecostal revivals going on around the world. The Chilean congregation began to experience manifestations of the Spirit in 1909 and upon being forced to leave the Methodist Church, founded the Methodist Pentecostal Church. At about the same time, two Swedish Pentecostals from the United States, convinced that God called them to Brazil, traveled to the region of Pará and established a congregation there that has since become the Assembléias de Deus, the largest Protestant church in Latin America.[16]

Whereas Pentecostalism became its own tradition, the Charismatic movement, dating from the 1960s in the United States, featured the emphasis on the Spirit's movement and power within the historic Protestant and even Roman Catholic traditions. Both of these strands stress the

15. Sandoval, *On the Move*, 37–74.
16. Anderson, *Pentecostalism*, 64–82.

individual's relationship with God and the Holy Spirit's power within as the legitimating factor in leadership. Ministers and leaders do not necessarily attend any formal training but are called, either by the community or by one's interior promptings, to propagate the faith (indeed all members are called to moral Christian living and evangelization). Consequently, Pentecostal and Charismatic churches multiply more rapidly than those traditions that require formal training for its leaders. These churches represent Spirit-led, Bible-centered movement(s) from below, and because of this, seem more apt at acculturating themselves than the more historic denominations that carry with them longer traditions of believing and doing certain things. These newer communities feel freer to adapt and borrow elements from the greater culture (for example, music and religious worldviews) and perhaps are more reflective, for good or for ill, of the communities they represent.

Scholars have pointed to a variety of factors in the growth of evangelical and Pentecostal/charismatic churches (the reproduction of rural forms of community as migration to cities increase, the appeal of divine power and healing to those who are marginalized and subject to economic and health challenges, access to middle-class stability when smoking, drinking and extra-marital affairs are abandoned in the interests of family and work, etc.) but the fact remains that these traditions represent some of the fastest-growing populations and portend a demographic shift in Latin America, particularly in its megacities.[17]

A History of Histories

As important as Protestantism in Latin America is when contemplating both the current state of the region and the trajectory of Christianity, relatively little attention has been given to its history. Up until the latter decades of the twentieth century, most histories of Latin American Protestantism were made up of denominational or missionary histories, designed not as critical works of scholarship but as vehicles to garner the support of church bodies in the United States or elsewhere towards the evangelistic enterprise. Similarly, some histories of Protestant churches or traditions were composed by missionaries in order to explain the significance of the enterprise in the Latin American context, usually as a challenge to Roman Catholic dominance and as a sign of modern progress

---

17. See, for example, Stoll, *Is Latin America Turning Protestant?*; Martin, *Tongues of Fire*; and Chestnut, *Born Again*.

vis-à-vis traditional religions or Catholicism. In short, these early histories tended to be partial and uncritical, apologetic and aimed at proselytism (either to gain converts to the faith or to the cause). Meanwhile, a polemical side of this kind of history was produced by Roman Catholic authors who sought to demonstrate that Protestantism was part of the imperialistic designs of the United States.[18]

This historiographical situation began to change in the 1940s as social-historical methods began to be applied to Protestant movements in several Latin American countries by the International Missionary Conference of New York with the aim of promoting the Protestantism. Despite this effort, the works are based upon a superficial and uncritical use of historical sources and documents.[19]

Sociological analysis of Protestant religion in Latin America did not really come into its own until the 1960s when scholars who were wedded to the dependency theory applied it to the Protestant phenomenon. For them, Protestantism was a religious ideology, imported from the United States, which strengthened and legitimized economic and cultural dependency. This kind of analysis was used by some advocates of liberation theology who saw the growing influence of evangelical churches as a danger to their own efforts at addressing socio-economic problems and consciousness-raising amongst the poor. Jean-Pierre Bastian has noted that within this analysis, various kinds of religious groups are grouped together uncritically that, while considered dissident forms of religion, are nevertheless not considered part of the Protestant landscape—the Jehovah's Witnesses and Latter Day Saints for example. These kinds of studies, according to Bastian, rarely asked about the role(s) that dissident religion played in the believer's life.[20]

From the late 1960s and particularly into the 1980s, historians, sociologists, and anthropologists have begun seeing Protestantism as a complex and pluralistic phenomenon within Latin American culture. These have included some of the first academic research on Pentecostalism as well as case studies focusing on particular areas. The results produced during this time generally looked at how Protestantism has inserted itself into the dominant culture as well as the role it plays in the lives of its adherents. Some studies have noted how marginalized groups

18. Bastian, *Historia del Protestantismo*, 12–13.
19. Ibid., 13.
20. Ibid., 14.

have used Protestant beliefs and symbols to create religious and sociopolitical alternatives to the surrounding culture. Others have described how Pentecostal and charismatic expressions have allowed indigenous groups to create a religious expression that stands in continuity with traditional worldviews and maintain their own cultural identities vis-à-vis the modern world.[21] Tellingly, however, these studies continue the narrative thread that describes Protestantism as an endogenous movement, brought to Latin America from the outside that has nonetheless put down roots in foreign soil.

New ground was broken and the perspective on Latin American religion was altered through Guieros Vieira's *O Protestantismo, a maconaria e a questão religiosa no Brasil* (Protestantism, Freemasonry and the Religious Question in Brazil). In this study, Vieria broke with the Protestant-Catholic axis that had dominated Latin American religious historiography and placed the emergence of Brazilian Protestantism within the greater context of ideological and religious issues in nineteenth-century Brazil, thus exploring the concept of Protestantism as a form of liberal religious renewal. This perspective was continued in the work of Jean-Pierre Bastian, particularly in his 1989 monograph *Los Disidentes, sociedades Protestantes y revolución en México, 1872–1911* (The Dissidents: Protestant Societies and Revolution in Mexico, 1872–1911). Here, Bastian explores dissident religion in late nineteenth-century Mexico as an expression of liberal reform and places the beginnings of Mexican Protestantism within the greater context of Liberal-Conservative tensions earlier in that century. This effort to place Protestantism within its socio-political roles characterizes Bastian's *Historia del Protestantismo en América Latina* (History of Protestantism in Latin America) and its revision, *Protestantismos y Modernidad Latinoamericana* (Protestantisms and Latin American Modernity). Other scholars have followed these precedents, linking Protestant faith with social change during the Mexican Revolution and in Cuban history.[22] Despite this contextual perspective, observers continue to see Protestantism as an exogenous religious phenomenon.

Protestantism in relation to Roman Catholicism continues to occupy some studies of Latin American religion and major works still reflect the religious convictions or preferences of their authors. John Mackay's classic 1932 work, *The Other Spanish Christ*, anticipated this trend when

21. Ibid., 15f.
22. Ibid., 17–18.

he sought to interpret Christian Latin America from a Christological perspective, positing that the crucified and dead Christ arrived from militant Spanish shores in the sixteenth century, whereas the powerful, resurrected Christ was preached by the Protestants.[23] Hans Jürgen Prien's *Die Geschichte des Christentums in Latein Amerika* (The History of Christianity in Latin America) sees the development of Protestantism from a decidedly European perspective, as an agent of secularization, despite the fact that most Protestant religion In Lain America takes on Pentecostal and charismatic forms.[24] Meanwhile, Prudencio Damboriena's *Protestantismo en América Latina* (Protestantism in Latin America), takes on a polemic edge, seeing Protestantism as a danger to Catholic culture and faith. What these two studies have in common however, is the lack of insight into what factors within Latin American culture and religion have contributed to the growth of Pentecostal and charismatic faith.[25]

A leading figure in the promotion of the study of Christianity in Latin America in the last several decades has been the Argentine philosopher and writer Enrique Dussell (b.1934). Dussell, a founding figure in the establishment of CEHILA, (the Commission for the Study of the History of the Church in Latin America and composed of both Roman Catholic and Protestant scholars) believes that given the impossibility of a truly objective history, the starting point of research and writing should be ideological commitment. For the Christian historian, this means writing from the perspective of God's preferential option for the poor and their struggles for liberation. The 1980s saw the publication of the multivolume *Historia General de la Iglesia en Latinoamérica* (General History of the Church in Latin America) produced by CEHILA under Dussell's general direction to explore the how the Christian Church has

---

23. While John Mackay's contributions to ecumenism and missions are truly notable, and his years of service in mission and education in Peru laudable, there is something naïve at best, and paternalistic and Manichean at worst about his analysis of Latin American Christology, at least from a modern perspective. He fails to notice that the dead Jesus of Latin American devotion is, at the same time, the Crucified God that preaches its own *teologica crucis*; a God who identifies with the poor and suffering of Latin America, who is known by His scars and reigns victorious from the cross. Triumphant North American Protestantism of the nineteenth and early twentieth centuries, raised on revivalist calls, postmillennial hopes, and spiritual, economic and political Manifest Destiny, seems to have little time for Good Friday on the way to Easter Sunday.

24. Spanish translation: Prien, *Historia del Cristianismo*.

25. Bastian, *Historia del Protestantismo*, 18–19.

(or has not) contributed to the social, political, and spiritual liberation of the people. Each volume details a geographic region and includes a chapter on Protestantism written by a Protestant. In 1992, to commemorate the quincentennial of Columbus's voyages, *The Church in Latin America 1492–1992* was published in the United States. This introductory work distills and summarizes much of the larger, more cumbersome series and while focusing on the many aspects of Roman Catholic Church history and life, includes a separate chapter on Protestantism written by Jean-Pierre Bastian.

Two other general histories are of note here, the *Historia del Cristianismo en América Latina* (History of Christianity in Latin America) written by the Argentine evangelical scholar and pastor, Pablo Deiros, and *Christianity in Latin America: A History*, co-written by Ondina E. and Justo L. González. Both of these works provide accessible overviews of the five hundred years of Christianity in Iberian America. Given their Protestant credentials, the authors provide a detailed introduction to the growth and spread of Protestantism in the region. These kinds of works, valuable and informative as they are, treat the Catholic and Protestant traditions separately—in separate chapters or sections. While this may be warranted given the often different and divergent nature of their histories, it lends to the assumption that the traditions are unrelated, that their stories carry on independently of one another rather than being intertwined and inter-related to one another.

In the last several decades, academic interest in Latin American Christianity has widened. Particularly since the eruption of civil wars in Central America, studies in the growth of evangelicalism and Pentecostalism have proliferated. David Martin's *Tongues of Fire: The Explosion of Protestantism in Latin America* sees the spread of Pentecostalism in the region as part of a cultural struggle between Iberian and Anglo-Saxon notions of empire, Catholic authoritarianism versus Protestant voluntarism. David Stoll takes on a different approach in *Is Latin America Turning Protestant?* He attempts to trace the history of Protestant growth and place the popularity of evangelicalism within its social and political contexts such as the Vatican's increasing conservatism under John Paul II and the openness of Protestant churches to social action (whereas once it concentrated on spiritual matters almost exclusively). Regional studies on the role and enculturation of Pentecostalism continued to be published seeking more local answers to the question of Protestant growth.

The 1990s seemed to take on the roles of Protestant tradition within the greater Latin American culture(s) with greater curiosity as scholars delved into the relationship between the evangelicals/Pentecostals and religious liberty, social action, and political activism. In these kinds of studies, the issue of Protestantism's foreignness is sidestepped, if not altogether ignored. Taking as their assumption the established place of Protestant religion in Latin America, these scholars have gone the extra step to address questions of acculturation as they explored the faith's Latin American identity and identification with the problems and struggles of their fellow citizens.

The work of William A. Christian in studying the popular devotions of Renaissance and modern Spain opened up a field of inquiry into the religious practices and beliefs of the people, as opposed to the official decrees, beliefs and actions of the religious institutions.[26] Historians and sociologists have, in the last twenty years or so, sought to further explore popular religious expression throughout any given time and branch of Christian faith. In Latin American religious studies this has often focused on modern popular Catholicism, on studies of practices and beliefs in the colonial era or on "outsider" expressions such as messianic movements or Afro-Christian traditions.[27] The exploration of Protestant popular religion (one can indeed make the argument that some forms of Protestantism are by their nature, strictly popular religion) is not as prevalent and tends to focus on sociological observation of modern faith (particularly among native indigenous) rather than historical inquiry. Despite this, the research into Latin American Protestantism does not appear to be abating anytime soon. Interest continues, due not only to the growing statistics on evangelical/Pentecostal growth on the continent and the acknowledgement of the region's religious diversity but also thanks to the more recognizable presence of Latino/Hispanic Protestants in the United States, whether in urban storefront churches, mainline denominations, business or academia.

Regarding the Church of Jesus, very little attention has been given to either the movement or to the Constitutionalist Fathers in scholarship.

---

26. Christian, Jr., *Local Religion*; Christian, Jr., *Apparitions*; Christian, Jr., *Person and God*; Christian, Jr., *Visionaries*.

27. For example, Nesvig and Johnson, *Local Religion*; Nesvig, *Religious* Culture; Graziano, *Cultures of Devotion*; Pessar, *From Fanatics to Folk*; Samson, *Re-Enchanting the World*.

Works from the nineteenth and early twentieth century that describe the Church of Jesus do not go into great depth on their origins and makeup but comprise mainly of contemporary accounts from Episcopalian observers and surround the challenges of incorporating the Church of Jesus into the Episcopal Church's foreign mission effort. They maintain a propagandist tone to them in their desire to drum up financial support for the Mexican cause.[28]

In 1958, Fay Sharon Greenland wrote "Religious Reform in Mexico: The Role of the Mexican Episcopal Church" as an MA Thesis for the University of Florida (Gainesville) that attempts to analyze the origins and decline of the independent Church of Jesus. Another MA thesis, by Alpha Gillet Bechtel, "The Mexican Episcopal Church: A Century of Reform and Revolution" (1966) describes the broader history of Anglicanism in Mexico from the Constitutional Fathers to the 1960s. In 2000, John Steven Rice wrote, "Evangelical Episcopalians and the Church of Jesus in Mexico 1857–1906" as an MA thesis for the Graduate School of the University of Texas. Here, Rice focuses on the interaction between it and the Episcopal Church and finds the reasons for the failure of the Church of Jesus in the struggles within the PECUSA in the last half of the nineteenth century between its Evangelical component and Anglo-Catholicism. None of these works seek to look at the broader context for the emergence of the Church of Jesus itself.

Primary among secondary sources is Jean-Pierre Bastian's *Los Disidentes; Sociedades Protestantes y Revolución en México, 1872–1911* (1989) that takes a socio-political perspective on dissident religious societies from the Juarez era to the eve of the Mexican Revolution. Bastian's analysis of the motivations of the Constitutionalist Fathers and the role of American Protestant missionary societies and dissident socio-political groups, such as the Masons, has been unmatched but the emphasis of the book's emphasis lies upon the foreign Protestant societies that evangelized during the Diaz regime. It is essential, nonetheless, in gaining an understanding of the tangled political and religious strands of post-Independence and Liberal Mexico.

Deborah Baldwin, in *Protestants and the Mexican Revolution* (1990) focuses on the Revolution but includes some analysis and bibliographic information on the early Mexican Anglican Church as does Kurt

---

28. These include Hooker, "Mexican Leaflets" and "Letters from a Lady"; Lee, et al., "Origin and Outline" and Creighton, "The Church in Mexico"

Derek Bowen in *Evangelism and Apostasy: The Evolution and Impact of Evangelicals in Modern Mexico* (1996). Additionally, in the 1990s the Anglican Church of Mexico has published several tracts that describe the history of the denomination directed primarily at church members desirous to know more about their history.

Pamela Voekel, who detailed the role of Enlightened Catholicism in eighteenth-century Mexico in *Alone Before God*, authored a chapter in Martin Austin Nesvig's edited work on *Religious Culture in Modern Mexico*. Her article, "Liberal Religion: The Schism of 1861" does seek to tie the Constitutionalist Clergy movement with the Enlightened Catholics of the eighteenth century but her focus is more on establishing the religious credentials of the Liberals rather than the Liberal credentials of the clerics.

METHODOLOGY

As we noted briefly above, some historiographies of Latin American religion take an institutional approach. They focus on the church or denomination as an institution and often differ little from political histories; missionary X from Y tradition arrives and plants the church. This approach is visible particularly in the early histories of Latin American Christianity written by Motolinía and others that emphasized the extirpation of native religions and the establishment of Catholicism. Such histories reinforce the notion of the Church as vehicle of salvation and custodian of grace and even equate the progress of the Church with salvation history. It is a perspective that is also seen in some of the writings of the Episcopal Church in their dealings with the Mexican Church when they equate the gospel with the diffusion of Protestant missions in order to rescue the people from "papal idolatry." Such denominationalism tends to focus on the role of foreign missions in the land. By neglecting the role of indigenous religion (whether Nahuatl or Catholic), they impose the image of the faith as foreigner, a stranger that is imported rather than native to the people. It easily leads to a triumphalist notion of the religion as conqueror over other competitors, defining the church or denomination as a civilizing power in a "pagan" land.

Another approach that is seen in the writing of Latin American Christian histories is the missionary history. A popular genre, they are usually written by missionaries or their protégés and are designed to tell how the missionary and missionary societies have crossed cultural barriers to communicate the gospel to such-and-such a people. Many of these are uncritical hagiographies that do not include cultural context or historiographical methods. Their histories are not related to secular history and the recipients of the message are seen as objects to undergo conversion rather than agents in their own right. The role of the missionary history is often propagandistic and is intended to drum up support for the mission in the home country or to provide an edifying tale of faith and heroism in the name of Christ for its readers. In this respect the popularization of the story of Nate Saint and Jim Elliot among the Waodani people of Ecuador is not too different from the hagiographies of the Middle Ages or the missionary biographies of the nineteenth century. Further, while the role of missionaries is undeniable, the idealization of missionary agents and structures distorts the history of the Church and ignores a wider understanding of evangelistic strategies as well as the inner life of the Church.

In the last several decades, the sociological approach to writing about Christianity in Latin America has gained prominence. Jean-Pierre Bastian's works on Latin American Protestantism and dissident religion and those edited by Martin Nesvig focusing on popular religion in colonial and modern Mexico, for example, have proven useful, perhaps indispensable in bringing forth the stories of the subaltern or those groups usually marginalized in more institutional histories. However, these histories often fail to explain or deal with the inward, purely religious dimension of the historical actors. There must be a balance between the inward and outward factors; explanation of religious change must address purely religious factors and motivations as well as outward (ecological, political, cultural) factors.

One of the priorities in the writing of Christian history from a liberationist perspective is to draw out the stories of the poor and marginalized. Theologians on both sides of the border have, in the last few decades, plunged into the world of popular religion in order to rediscover the ways in which the gospel is present in the devotions and rituals of these poor, such as Virgilio Elizondo's work on the Virgin of Guadalupe. The underlying thesis or assumption is that the religion of the marginalized not only expresses the gospel in some manner different from that of official or elite religion but that it can be a more authentic expression of such as the Good News received by the poor. The study of popular religion has been aided in a great way by sociological studies into the area with the caveat that sociologists, following anthropological studies into tribal religions, seek to study the religious expressions of the subaltern whereas liberationists seek the Church of the poor in its theological definition as those who are excluded from the bases of power and towards whom God expresses a "preferential option."

One of the difficulties and challenges of this kind of methodology is that it sets up an artificial dichotomy between the poor/elite, uneducated/educated, powerless/powerful. Carlos Eire, the Cuban historian, has noted that during late antiquity and the Middle Ages the relation between what was Christian and non-Christian could be "fluid and uncertain and somewhat variegated according to time, place, and social class . . . Syncretism and antagonism were as intertwined as were the clergy and the laity, the elites and the non-elites, the towns and the countryside, zeal and indifference, the sacred and profane."[29]

An ecumenical historiography would stress that the organizational structure of any given Church tradition does not constitute the total character of the Church. It must give regard to the continuities and discontinuities between the native (indigenous, Catholic, African, etc.) and the adopted religion. In the Latin American context this means taking into account the complexities of the continent—the cultural stew composed of indigenous, Africans, and Europeans (primarily Spanish and Portuguese). It should also look at the complexity of religious faith and pluralism in Latin America from the official pronouncements of hierarchy and church leaders to popular religious expressions to syncretistic religions such as *santería* and *candomblé*.

In the United States it has appeared popular of late to focus on the role of popular religion in Latin America, usually sociological glimpses into the faith expressions and experiences of the subaltern. Historians of a liberation theology persuasion have emphasized the theological side of this—the study of the religion of the poor and marginalized to whom

29. Nesvig, *Local,* 9–10. Eire describes the confused state of defining popular religion when he observes that the concept of popular religion in itself has various polar opposites—official/unofficial, clerical/lay, and so on. And whereas liberationists may accentuate the category of the poor one must question as to whether that genre has been unduly defined by Marxism and whether the biblical concept usually translated "poor" encompasses a greater definition than deprivation and powerlessness. In the Hebrew Bible there are no less than nine words that are rendered as "poor" in modern translations, each with different connotations. Cf. Hoppe, *There Shall Be.* Ogbu Kalu has suggested that the concept of the poor must encompass a given culture's definition of poverty, such as the lack of familial connections. Kalu, *African Christianity,* 15.

Christ proclaimed the gospel as authentic expressions of religious faith rather than as syncretic aberrations of a barely-Christianized people.

Hence, for example, in our Latin American context we must note that aspects or devotions attributed to popular religion are not exclusively held by the poor or subaltern. The devotion to the Virgin of Guadalupe, to take an example, crosses across social, political, and economic lines. Further, it is a testimony to the often confused state of Latin American Church historiography when works such as those of CEHILA and Lutterworth, while maintaining their intention to write a history of the Church from the perspective of the poor, nonetheless spend the majority of ink and paper describing the actions of the institutional Church, not only because primary documents by and about the subaltern or poor may be scarce but also because the Church as institution intersects the Church of the poor and in some ways defines it through its liturgy, charities and devotions. In other words, the dividing line between official religion and popular religion (or whatever way that dichotomy is expressed) is blurred.

Castizaje

A conceptual framework that has been used to approach various social disciplines is that is *mestizaje*. In 1925, the Mexican philosopher, José Vasconcelos, wrote *La raza cósmica* (The Cosmic Race) as a refutation of Western, Anglo-Saxon affirmations of racial superiority and social Darwinism. For Vasconcelos, *mestizaje* (from *mestizo*, the colonial name for the product of European and Native American parents) describes the future of humanity as concepts of race are superseded through the proliferation of the *mestizo*, the intermingling of the world's races to create a new humanity. During the 1960s, the emerging Chicago/a movement latched on to the idea of *mestizaje* as a positive concept, affirming the worth and liberation of Mexican-American (and Latin American) peoples. Rather than being the source of pathological neuroses as Octavio Paz argued in his *Laberinto de la Soledad* (Labyrinth of Solitude) in 1950, for the Chicano/a movement, the heritage of mixture became a source of pride and creativity. Since the 1960s, the idea of *mestizaje* has been used in social and anthropological circles, in aesthetics and theological studies.[30]

30. See for example, Pérez-Torres, *Mestiaje*; Miller, *Rise and Fall*; and Elizondo, *Galilean Journey*.

The concept and language of *mestizaje* is not without its critics, however. The vision of the "cosmic race," the emergence of racial and cultural mixture, is sometimes expressed in terms of progress, as if the forces of history conspired to create the *mestizo*—*mestizaje* as the fulfillment or outbreak of cultural eschatology. In this perspective, where the Spanish and the Indian (or the African in the case of *mulatez*) come together in Hegelian choreography to create the *mestizo*, the identities of the former are threatened with oblivion. If *mestizo* culture is the goal of history, then the Spaniard and the indigenous are but stepping stones toward that goal, relegated to the past with little bearing or importance in contemporary life and thus ignoring the social and political struggles of modern native peoples. Similarly, *mestizaje* tends to take an essentialist and static concept of culture that ignores the differences and inequalities within said cultures.

Even the description of the admixture in Latin America as *mestizaje* has its problems. *Mestizaje* implies a bipolar process of interaction and hybridity between two axes, such as the Iberian and the indigenous. The cultural, racial, social, and religious realities of Latin American history are not limited in this way. The process of colonization across the continent created diverse new mixed cultures—alongside Spanish, Portuguese, African, and Native American ones. The combined horizontal and vertical aspects of the society (race and social status or gender for example) made multiple cultural expressions that in turn served as loci where Christianity incarnated new and sundry expressions of faith. It is a process that is not bipolar but multipolar, emphasizing not the end result but the course of interaction and relationship. To describe this ongoing process I prefer to tweak the idea of *mestizaje* with that of what I call *castizaje*, evoking the popular *casta* (caste) paintings of the colonial era.

The *casta* paintings, fashionable in the seventeenth century both to describe and delimit the social scale in colonial society sought to represent the most common blood mixtures possible (Spanish + Indian = Mestizo, Mestizo + Indian = Coyote; Mestizo + Spanish = Castizo, etc.) as well as their perceived social strata and cultural levels.[31] They served several purposes, not the least being souvenirs for European visitors. For

---

31. It should be recalled that the caste system in Latin America was in no way as stringent as the one we associate with India. The use of the colonial caste distinctions in no way implies a social hierarchy based on value but is simply a descriptor for the plural social locations in Latin American society throughout history.

one, they presented the supremacy of the Spanish. Scenes in which whiteness or Spanish-ness dominated tended to be more genteel, presenting the civilizing nature of European lineage to the extent that continued intermixing with Spanish blood could revert a mixed race individual to an earlier, purer ancestry (Castizo + Spanish = Spanish). On the other hand, they also served as a warning to the decivilizing results of miscegenation, particularly the mixing of European and African blood. These illustrations painted a chaotic picture of such domestic lives, sometimes depicting the overturning of the natural order of things (the wife beating the husband, etc.). The confusion of supposedly degenerative racial mixtures can be seen in the array of names given to them: nonsensical terms such as *torno atrás* (turn back) and *no te entiendo* (I don't understand you) or animal names like *lobo* (wolf) or *mulato* (mule). The following table represents an example of popular *casta* categories from the mid-1700s, understanding that there existed no authoritative list of race mixtures during the colonial period and that description and terminology could differ from region to region.[32]

Spanish + Indian = Mestizo	Mestizo + Spanish = Castizo	Castizo + Spanish = Spanish	Spanish + African = Mulatto
Mulatto + Spanish = Morisco	Morisco + Spanish = Albino	Spanish + Albino = Turn back	Spanish + Turn back = up in the air
African + Indian = China cambuja	China cambuja + Indian = Lobo	Lobo + Indian = Albarazado	Albarazado + Mestizo = Barcino
Indian + Barcino = Zambuigua	Castizo + Mestizo = Chamizo	Mestizo + Indian = Coyote	Heathen Indians

TABLE 1: Examples of *Castas*

Castizaje overturns the dichotomy inherent in traditional descriptions of *mestizaje* and moves the formation of identity from the Hegelian synthesis or the Judeo-Christian linear movement to the in-between spaces between states-of-being. It emphasizes the formation of identity as states-of-becoming, the constantly moving, flowing interaction between

32. Katzew, *Casta Painting*, 101–6.

cultures, languages, religions, gender, and sexual identities, etc. In our Latin American (and indeed modern U.S. and even European contexts), *castizaje* does not emphasize the static European/Native relationship resulting in the *mestizo* but rather, recognizes the continual interplay between identities: Native/Iberian/African/*mestizo*/*mulatto*/ and so on, along with the many facets that create individual and cultural identity: Spanish/Nahua/English/male/female/gay/straight/rich/poor/urban/rural, *ad infinitum*. It is, to summarize the concept, an identity of the borderlands.

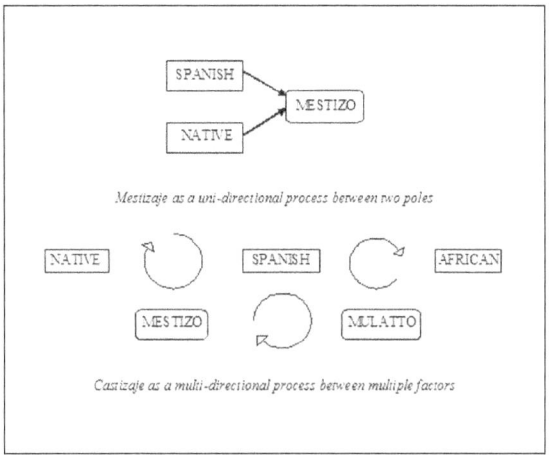

Figure 2: *Mestizaje* and *Castizaje* Compared

This concept of *castizaje* carries with it some characteristics of postcolonial criticism, namely hybridity and ambivalence: "One of the most widely employed and most disputed terms in post-colonial theory, hybridity, commonly refers to the creation of new transcultural forms within the contact zone produced by colonization. As used in horticulture, the term refers to the cross-breeding of two species by grafting or cross-pollination to form a third 'hybrid' species. Hybridization takes many forms: linguistic, cultural, political, racial, etc."[33] Latin American Christianity takes into account the cultural mixture that occurred between Spanish, Indian, and African and also that of their multicultural descendents.

Another postcolonial concept visible in *castizaje* is that of ambivalence: "[Ambivalence] describes the complex mix of attraction and repulsion that characterizes the relationship between colonizer and

---

33. Quoted in Sánchez, *From Patmos*, 9.

colonized. The relationship is ambivalent because the colonized subject is never simply and completely opposed to the colonizer. Rather than assuming that some colonized subjects are 'complicit' and some 'resistant,' ambivalence suggests that complicity and resistance exists in a fluctuating relation with the colonial subject."[34]

Ambivalence expresses the complexity and multi-facetedness of cultural interactions, including religious interactions. The casta paintings, for example, despite their function as an instrument to delineate and categorize the various racial and ethnic mixes in colonial society, demonstrated the very ambivalence of those categories. As one studies the facial features of their subjects, one notices the actual ambiguity of the racial categories as one caste resembles another. The lines between ethnic/racial categories are blurred as one individual melts into another. Even the original painters of these works sensed some of the ambiguity, if not ridiculousness, of such categorizing. If Spanish and Indian/black blood is intermixed enough the resulting product is sometimes called a *"torno-atras"*—a turn back (to Indian or black). Another mixture is named *"no te entiendo"*—I don't understand you.

This kind of process and ambiguity removes the dichotomy present in ideas of popular/official, lay/clerical, etc. religion as it blurs the lines between religious expressions. Additionally, *castizaje* subverts and disrupts the notion of a center (in this case, religious) and its attendant periphery created by colonization (and continued even after the independence movements). While expressions of religion among the people differed according to their social location—it is stating the obvious that the wealthy and educated exhibited different religious practices than the poor—there were and are interplay and commonalities, continuities and discontinuities between the various social groups and their religious expressions in Latin American Christianity. Witness the religious processions that included all kinds of people groups in colonial Mexico or the mixes of people at Pentecostal services in some modern megacities. It is becoming apparent to historians that gender, ethnicity, and geographical location have as much to do with the exercise of faith as do access to power, resources, and education. This idea of *castizaje* not only reflects these various social locations but it subverts the dichotomy inherent in the classifications of popular/elite, lay/clerical religion, etc. Instead of a set of polar opposites that the idea of popular religion undertakes and

34. Quoted in ibid., 9.

implies, the idea of *castizaje* takes and describes the many dots across the Latin American social and cultural spectrum. *Castizaje* and the critique it provides of the dichotomy between official (central) and popular (peripheral) religion emphasizes the in-between spaces where power is brokered, negotiated, and subverted, creating, interplaying, and transferring religious expressions from one or more groups to others. It recognizes that the elements of Christianity in Latin America, the members of the hierarchy, the religious orders, the mass of laypersons, interact with one another in their faith expressions. For example, works of charity and aid, which impact positively upon the poor, have traditionally been established by the institutional hierarchy and religious orders. In turn, the faith of the poor or marginalized affects the expression, piety, and priorities of the larger Church (*lex orandi, lex credendi*). *Castizaje* expresses the protean and yes, ecumenical, quality of Latin American religion and culture (Catholic, multiple indigenous, African, *mestizo*, creole, Protestant, etc.).

In describing the context out of which the Church of Jesus arose, this writer has sought to look at the character and nature of the Mexican Church (both in its Baroque and Enlightened manifestations), rooting it in the multicultural milieu of colonial society. Toward this endeavor I have especially depended on secondary sources from authors in the United States, Latin America and Spain.

In the aforementioned process I have sought to follow a comparative approach in historical method. Originally used by philologists to determine the common ancestry of human languages, the comparative method in history seeks to compare social groups or societies in order to clarify their differences or similarities. In the context of this work I have sought to compare the Church of Jesus and its ideology from 1859–72 to previous religious movements in Mexican history with the hopes that by describing the similarities and dissimilarities between them I could establish the genealogical links between the Church of Jesus and the overall course of Mexican religious history, thus establishing not only the immediate context for the movement but also its pedigree. To that end I have made an eclectic use of historical sources (mainly secondary sources—Jean-Pierre Bastian's social history, Martin Austin Nesvig's cultural history, Enrique Dussel's theologically guided history, etc.) to provide a holistic view of the overall context of the Church of Jesus—its political, ideological, religious antecedents that influenced its establishment and development. This eclectic methodology reflects the desire to describe the movements in question from various points of view, understanding that peoples and movements are not merely the results of politics or religious worldviews but that these and more are in constant interplay in the formation of historical events—the patronage debates, the Baroque worldview, the social classes behind the Catholic Enlightenment, and so on. My models for this kind of comparative history have included D. A. Brading in his studies on the Catholic Church in Bourbon Mexico and Pamela Voekel in her research on Enlightenment Catholicism to establish the religious roots of modernity in Mexico.[35] These authors have chosen to laboriously establish the worldviews and socio-political contexts of the movements they describe by comparing them to other movements, be they Creole nationalism, Baroque Catholicism, or Enlightenment religion and reinforcing the maxim that "the text without a context is pretext." That is, the attempt to describe any movement, personage, or text without establishing its context gives rise to the temptation or opportunity to mold or manipulate it not only to one's agenda (or to use Martin Luther's term for the malleability of the Bible—a "wax nose") but to distort it completely.

For the chapter on the Church of Jesus itself I have chosen 1859 as the *terminus a quo* as that is accepted as the year that the Constitutionalist Fathers assembled in support of the 1857 Constitution. For the *terminus ad quem* I have chosen 1872, the year that Manuel Aguas, the Church of Jesus' leader who helped organize the movement into an ecclesial organization, died. Coincidentally it is also the year of Benito Juarez's death—fitting in a way as his Laws of Reform were the impetus for the Constitutionalist Clerics' gathering and it was Juarez who on-again, off-again sought to be their patron.

Having established beginning and end dates for this research I took advantage of the materials at the Archives of the Episcopal Church in Austin, Texas, which holds most of the relevant primary documents. Using the letters and pamphlets written by participants, observers, and advocates, I scoured the materials for a commonality of themes present in both the Church of Jesus and Enlightened religion, prejudiced in favor of earlier materials and testimonies before the Church of Jesus became more influenced by North American evangelicalism.

35. Brading, *Church and State* and Voekel, *Alone Before God*. Voekel also emphasizes the use of cultural artifacts such as cemeteries and wills in establishing her argument.

3

Church and State I

The Royal Patronage

Down the *Avenida de la Reforma*, a few miles away from the green expanse of Chapultepec Park and its memorials to Mexican history, the great *zócalo*, or city square, sits astride the center of Mexico City.[1] This plaza was built upon the temples and buildings of the destroyed Aztec capital's own centre and like most municipal squares in the Spanish-speaking world, is home to the seats of Church and government—in this case the Presidential Palace and the Metropolitan Cathedral. In the Presidential Palace, along the stairway leading to the second floor, the artist Diego Rivera painted a series of murals depicting the history of Mexico from the indigenous past to the Mexican Revolution of 1910. For our purposes, it is important to note the paintings dedicated to the coming of the Spanish and the Conquest of Mexico. In these vibrant pictures, the Spanish, led by a disfigured, ogre-like and hunchbacked Hernán Cortez (the conqueror has not been remembered affectionately in modern Mexico), subjugate the Aztecs by two means, the force of arms and religion. Rivera, admittedly an atheist Marxist and no friend to Catholicism, does not depict the Catholic friars in a positive light. Distinctive in their robes, they collect tribute and force the natives to receive baptism. Only one friar, meant to

---

1. Chapultepec Park, once the summer residence of the Aztec emperors is now home to the world-renowned Museum of Anthropology, dedicated to the nation's indigenous past and present and to the Mexican History Museum now housed in a former military school and imperial palace.

represent the activist Bartolomé de Las Casas, is depicted positively as he defends a huddled mass of natives from the Spanish as the violence of the Conquest erupts around them.

Figure 4: Diego Rivera, *México en la Historia, Perspectiva: El Campesino Oprimido* (Mexico in History, Perspective: The Peasant Oppressed), National Palace, Mexico City, 1935. Author's photo.

Rivera's mural illustrates the relationship of Church and State in Mexican history, one characterized by both collusion (as in the friars abetting the conquerors) and collision (as in Las Casas's resistance to Spanish atrocities). If, as Robert Ricard stated in his *Spiritual Conquest of Mexico*, the sixteenth century contained the embryo of the subsequent evolution of the country, then it is imperative that we look with some detail at the early history of the Catholic Church in this country.[2] This chapter will focus upon the Church's relationship with the Crown, establishing a politico-religious framework that sets the context for the following chapters.

THE CROSS AND THE CROWN IN SPAIN: THE PATRONATO REAL

The evangelization of Mesoamerica in the sixteenth century did not take place in a vacuum. Precedents in the spiritual and temporal administration of the colonies had been rehearsed and established earlier in Spanish history as the kingdoms of the Iberian Peninsula sought to regain territory lost to Muslim forces in the eighth century. These events and determinants, we shall see, are the roots of the intertwined religious and political histories of Mexico.

In 722 combined Arab and Berber forces overtook the Visigothic kingdom of the peninsula, isolating the Christian rulers across its far northern stretch and establishing Muslim hegemony across what they would rename Al-Andalus. From the eleventh to the fifteenth centuries, the rulers of the nascent kingdoms of Spain and Portugal would take advantage of Muslim division and weakness to expand southward in what is often termed the Reconquest.[3] This process was all but completed in the thirteenth century with the victories of Fernando III of Castile when he conquered the southern stretch of Al-Andalus, including the important cities of Seville and Cordoba. The process was finally brought to an end in January 1492 when the last remaining Muslim kingdom, Granada, ceded to the combined forces of Isabel of Castile and Fernando of Aragon.[4]

---

2. Ricard, *Spiritual Conquest*, 3.

3. For detailed histories of Spain's medieval period see O'Callaghan, *History of Medieval Spain*; Collins, *Early Medieval Spain*; Reilly, *Contest*; Reilly, *Medieval Spains*; Ángel and Palenzuela, *Historia de España*. For recent histories focusing on the relationship of Muslims, Jews, and Christians see also Menocal, *Ornament of the World* and Lowney, *Vanished World*. A recent work that focuses on the cultural hybridity of medieval Castile between the three religions is Dodds et al., *Arts of Intimacy*.

4. The Reconquest itself carries within its own debated history. Though some romantic and nationalistic concepts date the Reconquest to the Battle of Covadonga in 722, these and subsequent battles appear to be no more than skirmishes along the borders of al-Andalus and the nascent Christian kingdoms. The idea of reconquest—an effort to drive back the Muslims and retake the former Visigothic kingdom with all the

This Reconquest brought with it a religious aspect. Though in itself it is not considered a Crusade by most scholars, as it lacks certain aspects of Crusading to the Middle East, nonetheless, the wars in Spain did carry with them some aspects in common with the simultaneous endeavors to recapture the Holy Land. Joseph O'Callaghan notes in his *Reconquest and Crusade in Medieval Spain* that popes granted indulgences to soldiers fighting on the Iberian front, endowing them with the same spiritual benefits as those going on Crusade to Jerusalem. Sermons, special prayers, and other liturgical accoutrements accompanied the Spanish as they sought to "regain" the peninsula from the Muslims and "liberate" the churches and individuals from the Muslim enemy.[5] It is no coincidence that with the overthrow of the last Muslim kingdom of Granada in 1492, Christopher Columbus was granted royal permission to embark upon his expedition to "discover and subdue" whatever territories he encountered.

The conquistadors who were driven to the Americas by God, gold, and glory saw these battles through the inherited lens of Crusade and Reconquest—of a battle fought against the unbelievers and idolaters who stood under the power of the devil and had to be subjugated by the children of the true God. For the Spanish, the conquest of Tenochtitlán was run through and through with the supernatural. Apparitions and miracles accompanied the conquerors on their mission according to the Bernal Diáz de Castillo, who accompanied Cortez.[6] Artwork and even a perusal of place names throughout Spanish America testify to the importance of Santiago Matamoros, Saint James the Moor-Killer in Iberian ideology. The subsequent colonization cemented the Christian victory over the pagan gods as the victors constructed churches over the temples and sacred sites of the vanquished to further trumpet the supplanting of the old religions.

The Aztecs no less perceived the world through a religious lens. Aztec life and governance was built upon religious ritual. It was ritual bloodletting that guaranteed the survival of the gods and Aztec expansion and conquest was designed not only to bring wealth to the central

---

political, religious and expansive notions it carried, does not seem to have come into vogue until the eleventh century almost coterminous with the beginnings of Crusade ideology elsewhere in Europe. O'Callaghan, *Reconquest*, 7ff.

5. O'Callaghan, *Reconquest*, 21, 177ff.

6. Also note Gruzinski, *Images at War*, 33.

city but also captives for sacrifice.[7] From birth to death Aztec life of all classes was marked by ceremony and ritual towards a multitude of deities. Like the Christians who observed their own ceremonial (liturgical) calendar that noted God's own dealings with humanity (for example, Christmas, Easter, saint days), Aztecs also followed a ritual calendar that defined the cosmos, guided its adherents, and regulated the past, present, and future.[8] It was through their religious worldview that the Mexica reacted to the news of bearded, white-skinned newcomers and Mocteuzoma's deliberate yet cautious actions may have stemmed from the fear that the Spaniards might have been gods returning at the end of the fifty-two-year Aztec calendar cycle.[9]

In 1521, the great city of Tenochtitlán, besieged by Spanish brigantines from without and smallpox from within, fell. In 1524, while the ruins of the old city were being plundered to construct the new colonial capital, a group of twelve friars of the Franciscan order, specifically requested by Cortéz, made their way to the city on foot to commence the work of evangelism. To this end, they and the missionaries who followed in the coming years and decades, sought to extirpate the remains of the old gods—destroying temples, statues, and codices—and to teach the native peoples the beliefs, practices, and rituals of the Christian faith. The apparatus, both theoretical and practical, towards the official establishment of the Church had been instituted long before in the *patronato real* (*padroado real* in Portugal) or royal patronage.

The backbone of Church polity and organization in the Western Church from late antiquity on has been the power and presence of the bishops, the heirs of the apostles whose relationship with one another and the Bishop of Rome assures continuity with Jesus and the apostles. Royal patronage consists, in its essence, of the power of the secular arm to name or present individuals to ecclesial office.[10] Eugene Shiels notes, "Civil and sacred interests were intertwined in a system so thorough and complex as scarcely to be separated, so permanent and pervasive that the organic union escapes any but a careful observer."[11] However, this

---

7. See for example Townsend, *Aztecs*, 109ff.
8. Townsend, *Aztecs*, 122–28, 192ff.
9. Thomas, *Conquest*, 184–87.
10. Shiels, *King and Church*, 22.
11. Ibid., 9. Though patronage may incur with it other rights and privileges the right of the layperson (in this case the secular power) to present a cleric to the bishop for installation is its central concept.

was not a State Church in the sense that the State controlled faith and dogma—Spanish monarchs made no doctrinal decisions. It was however, a State Church in the sense that the Crown exercised tremendous power in administrating the Church. Whereas this might set the stage for a subservient Church, a rubber stamp for royal desires, this issue did not rear its head in any significant way until the Bourbons sought to control the Church in the eighteenth century.[12]

Basically there are two schools of thought as to the origins of royal patronage. One sees its origins in the concessions of the papacy to local rulers, thus finding the seat ecclesiastical authority in Rome. The other vantage point sees the power of naming bishops as residing locally. These two opinions would clash, not only throughout the history of the Church, but for our purposes, in the debates over patronage that arose after the independence of Mexico.

Those who see ecclesiastical patronage as residing in the pope note that with the fall of the Western Roman Empire, the Bishop of Rome filled the power vacuum left by the barbarian invasions. In short, the pope was a legitimate authority who represented Roman rule and who gave unity to the dismembered continent and to whom local rulers could appeal. Papal authority was founded, then, both on the *realpolitik* of the time and upon a soteriological (salvific) idea. Following St. Paul, Christian theology asserted that all human beings were called to salvation in Christ and that all legitimate power proceeded from God. It stood to reason then that temporal powers would gain legitimacy by ruling in agreement with the salvific goals of God and the Church. Non-Christian rulers or those who did not rule with their subjects' salvation in mind were thus illegitimate.

With this in mind, the pope, as the Vicar of Christ and successor of Peter who assured the means of salvation, held complimentary powers as regards the temporal powers. He could deprive rulers of their sovereignty when they did not exercise their authority towards just rule and he could concede power to rulers to expand or conquer in order to spread the Christian message.[13] Since the expansion of a ruler's realm

---

12. Ibid., 13.

13. Borges, *Historia de la Iglesia*, 63–64. Another aspect of the rise of the papacy's power is geographical. Rome was the only one of the five prominent sees (along with Constantinople, Alexandria, Antioch and Jerusalem) to lie in the West. The Eastern sees were thus better equipped to maintain a collegiality of bishoprics in a region where the Roman Empire never fell.

was conditional upon the spread of Christianity in a particular region, the papacy conceded the power of ecclesiastical patronage to local leaders in light of the financial needs of establishing new missions.

In Spain, Shiels notes that the councils of Toledo, the seat of the Spanish Church, state that the election of bishops continued in the Roman fashion, in the hands of the bishops. This continued until the late Visigothic era (late seventh to eighth centuries) when these rulers usurped that power, perhaps following the example of the Merovingians of France.[14]

During the Reconquest, as Spanish Christian kings took over Muslim lands, it fell to them to found and staff new churches and bishoprics and to aid the Church in its missions. The right of presenting candidates for vacant or recently created sees was complimentary to this task. Later the right to collect tithes would fall upon the kings as this concession was seen as necessary in light of the rulers' financial support and maintenance of the churches and monasteries. In short, the power of the rulers over the election of the bishops and consequently, over the affairs of the Church, expanded greatly during the Middle Ages. This evolution provides the backdrop for the role of the Crown within the Church in the New World as well as the Alexandrine Donations of 1493 that endowed the recently discovered lands to either Spain or Portugal.

The theological legitimacy of the Iberian expansion of the late fifteenth/sixteenth century rested upon their participation in the spread of the Christian message. Medieval precedent had already granted them the power to name bishops and this power was extended into the New World enterprise. Further, because the Crown invested heavily in the establishment of the Church in the New World, they were able to collect tithes and thus do more than reimburse themselves for their efforts. The papal bull, *Inter caetera*, issued by Alexander VI in 1493 not only divided the new discoveries between Portugal and Spain but carried the seeds of legitimacy for the kingdoms' already existing responsibilities and powers into the New World.[15] "The decrees of Pope Alexander VI—*Inter caetera* (May 3–4, 1493) and *Dudum siquidem* (Sept. 23, 1493)—'donate,' 'grant,' and 'assign' for life, to the Catholic Monarchs and their royal descendents, the newly discovered and yet to be discovered lands, and grant

---

14. Shiels, *King and Church*, 27. Shiels, a Jesuit, clearly falls on the side of episcopal prerogative in the debate over the power to name clerics.

15. Ibid., 66; Pope Innocent VIII, in 1486, had already granted the Catholic Kings the rights of royal patronage over the Canary Islands and the Kingdom of Granada; ibid., 66–67.

them the exclusive responsibility for converting their native inhabitants to the Christian faith."[16]

Shortly before his death Alexander VI had granted Ferdinand and Isabela the right to collect the tithe in the bull *Eximiae devotionis* of 1501.[17] Alberto de la Hera states that this privilege was given reluctantly in light of the overwhelming financial burden of establishing missions, dioceses, monasteries, etc. in the Indies. As noted, the founding and funding of new churches goes hand in hand with royal patronage. Within a few short years the mission in the Indies would have matured to the point of developing the first dioceses and with that, the inevitable naming of bishops. It would only be a matter of time before the right to present and name bishops would be conceded to the monarchs. In 1504 Julius II authorized the creation of the first three dioceses in the New World but neither confirmed the collection of the tithe by the Crown nor the grant of royal patronage. Ferdinand rejected this authorization as it would mean the investment of the Crown in the creation of the dioceses with neither the financial reward nor the power to name his own candidates to the bishop's chair. Ferdinand immediately dispatched his ambassador to Rome to negotiate the desired privileges.[18] Royal patronage was finally conceded in 1508 in the papal bull *Universalis ecclesiae*. This represents the foundational document for the Church in the Americas given as it would be cited as precedent for the Crown's entire ecclesiastical endeavor in the Americas.[19]

Those who see patronage as originating in the Crown or the lay power rather than the papacy point to another set of historical circumstances. In the early Christian church, including in Spain, it was the practice for the clergy and the people to appoint their bishops. As the prestige of the bishop of Rome increased this custom was continued, though there is record of some bishops being designated directly by the pontiff.[20] This process, however, sometimes degenerated into infighting and violence when disagreements over appointments arose. In these cases, the secular authorities stepped in to restore order and protect canonical elections.

16. Rivera, *Violent Evangelism*, 25; cf. 23–41.

17. Ibid., 46.

18. The right to name bishops, collect the tithe and the added right to determine the limits of dioceses.

19. Borges, *Historia de la Iglesia*, 70–74; Padden, "Ordenanza del Patronazgo," 29.

20. Mecham, *Church and State*, 6.

With the decline of the Western Roman Empire, the regional temporal powers began to take on a more dominant role in the naming of bishops; as regards to Spain, with the rise of a unified Visigoth kingdom after the fifth century. With the conversion of the Visigoths from Arian to Catholic Christianity in 587, the rulers, though recognizing the primacy of the Roman pontiff, established the practice of ecclesiastical patronage, reserving the right to convene and participate in church councils, to create new dioceses and episcopates and to appoint bishops.[21]

During the Middle Ages the concept of ecclesiastical patronage continued to develop. The monarchs of the Iberian kingdoms continued to elect bishops, found or restore dioceses, convened councils, and generally followed the Visigothic tradition as regards Church/State relations. The pendulum began to swing away from royal control as the Spanish Church began to look towards Rome as the basis of its identity and practice.[22] Under Pope Gregory VII (ca. 1015/28–1085) and the Cluniac reformers of the eleventh and twelfth centuries, a conscious effort was exerted to bring the Iberian Church into more conformity with Rome. An important result of this, and perhaps most visible to the people, was the substitution of the native Spanish liturgy of the Mass (the Mozarabic rite) with the Roman one. However, under the influence of the Cluniac reform, efforts were made to place matters of discipline and the election of bishops into the hands of the pope. The kings of Castile cooperated with these efforts as they shifted their axis away from the Muslim/Eastern world to their south and towards Catholic Europe to the north though they did insist that the decisions of the pope be approved by the monarch. By the fourteenth century, universal patronage—the right to elect all bishops—was lodged firmly in the papacy with respect to the most powerful Iberian kingdoms of Aragon and Castile. From this time forward the pope would maintain legates in the Court who represented him in disciplinary hearings and church councils. Thus by the fourteenth century universal patronage in Spain belonged to the pope.[23]

21. Ibid., 7; Shiels, *King and Church*, 27.

22. Whereas the Christians under Muslim rule began to culturally identify with Arab culture while maintaining Christian identity (the Mozarabs, a term that means "Arab-like"), the Christians of the north shifted their cultural axis towards Europe (particularly as the various taifas of Muslim Spain began to weaken), identifying and establishing cultural and political links with their coreligionists there, including at the center of Western Christendom, Rome.

23. Mecham, *Church and State*, 7–8.

Particular patronage, on the other hand, was the right of a patron, be it ecclesial or lay, to present or elect the clergy of a particular church they themselves founded or sponsored. In Spain this was especially pertinent during the period of the Reconquest when new districts were established or ancient churches came under Christian control once again. Popes Alexander II and Gregory VII conceded the rights of patronage over these churches in recognition of the effort and zeal that was exercised by the conquerors during this endeavor. This gave the Spanish rulers a foothold by which to continue the exercise of their power in ecclesiastical elections. Alfonso X of Castile (d. 1284) defined patronage in his *Siete Partidas*:

> The Latin patronus means "father of his trust." And just as one's father is charged with the care of his son, with his raising and protection and doing all the good for him that he can, so he who will build a church must meet its costs, be interested in all its needs, and protect it after he has built it. And patronage is the right or power that they gain over a church, the benefit that those who are its patrons obtain. And a man wins that right in a threefold manner. First is the land that he gives on which the church is built. Second is the building of the church. Third is the landed property that one gives when he leaves an endowment from which the clergy who serve it find their living, and with which they can fulfill their other duties, according to the title, "How they should build their churches."

Similarly three things belong to the patron by reason of the patronage. The first is honor. The next is the support that he deserves when in trouble. The third is the care that he should have to watch over the (spiritual) work. And when the church is vacant, he is entitled to present the priest for it.[24]

He additionally declared that the Castilian kings reserved the right to give consent in the appointment of bishops due to a) their efforts in the Reconquest that extended Christianity and reopened churches that had been converted into mosques, b) their founding of new churches, and c) their generous endowment of other churches.[25]

Additionally, various papal documents of the fifteenth century ceded rights of patronage to the kings of Castile over a number of benefices in Castile-Leon. In 1455 Pope Calixtus III stated that he would appoint only

---

24. Quoted in Shiels, *King and Church*, 22.
25. Mecham, *Church and State*, 10.

persons suitable to the monarch as archbishops, bishops and prelates in Castile and Aragon, a declaration that the kings of these regions interpreted as implying that candidates to these offices had to be approved by them before their formal election by the pope.[26]

By the end of the fifteenth century Ferdinand and Isabella exercised particular patronage over a number of sees based on medieval tradition and a number of papal concessions. The Catholic Monarchs sought, throughout their reigns, to consolidate their power over the Church in the form of royal patronage. Thus there were occasional tugs-of-war between them and the pontiff over individual appointments to vacant sees. At one point, in 1482, the monarchs threatened to convene a council to reform the Church if Pope Sixtus IV did not capitulate on his decision to name his nephew as bishop of Cuenca.[27] The next year, as Isabella and Ferdinand continued to build the apparatus of an absolute monarchy, they were granted control over the Inquisition in Spain.[28] Eventually Pope Innocent VIII conceded to Isabella and Ferdinand the rights of universal patronage and the tithe over all the sees in the Kingdom of Granada.[29]

During the reign of Philip II (1527–98) a challenge arose to the *patronato* in the form of unhappy missionaries in the New World. Franciscan friars were displeased with the administration of the colonies, accusing the *audiencias* of seeking gold instead of service to God and the salvation of souls. Word of this tumult reached the pope who began to issue indulgences to get friars to volunteer in the Americas. While Philip and the Council of the Indies sought to resolve matters, Pius V instigated an investigation of the Church in the New World and appointed a papal nuncio to oversee the situation and belay papal orders to the bishops overseas. One of his men suggested that the pope retract the royal patronage but he thought better of it, instead relaying to the king his own suggestions for the amelioration of the problems plaguing the American Church.[30] By the end of Philip II's reign in 1598 the Crown controlled the Church in the matter of appointing clerics.

Whereas papal bulls issued throughout the colonial period may have strengthened or expanded the royal powers, they did not really add

---

26. Ibid., 8.
27. Padden, "Ordenanza del Patronazgo," 28.
28. Ibid.
29. Mecham, *Church and State*, 10–11.
30. Shiels, *King and Church*, 222–25.

anything to its nature. Of importance in the history of the *patronato* and the papalist-regalist debates are the bulls of Benedict XIV of 1753 the first of which confirmed the rights of the Spanish king in the New World and throughout the Spanish Empire.[31] The second bull, issued in June, is of particular importance to those who claim the power of patronage as originating in the civil power. It "declared that the royal patronage was acquired 'by foundation and endowment, by privilege and apostolic concession, and by other legitimate title.'"[32]

PATRONATO REAL IN COLONIAL MEXICO

Through the *Patronato*, the Church in Mexico, and indeed in all of Spanish America, was tied to the civil power. In the words of Agustín Churruca Peláez, "the 'render to Caesar what belongs to Caesar and to God what belongs to God' became, in our Colony, give to Caesar the temporal and the divine."[33] As the Conquests of the Americas were consolidated in the early sixteenth century, the Crown and the Council of the Indies, appointed to administer the New World affairs, appropriated to themselves remarkable powers over the Church under the aegis of the royal patronage. The monarchs and their representatives (the Council of the Indies, viceroys, governors, *audiencias*, and so on) would determine Church finances, building projects, evangelistic endeavors, call and lead councils, enact discipline and ecclesial jurisdictions among other things. This was beyond the rights enumerated in the papal concessions. Rome tolerated some of these liberties taken but never sanctioned them. Books that advocated a royal and absolutist interpretation of the *patronato* were forbidden by the papacy.[34] To illustrate the emphasis the Crown placed upon its administration of royal patronage it is enough to note that even before any bulls could arrive from Rome confirming the king's choice, the newly appointed bishop, upon being given his mitre and symbols of his office received a copy of the *Patronato* and a collection of fifty-six laws that applied to his relationship to the Crown and further served to drive home the point of his submission to the king.[35]

---

31. Discussed at length in Shiels, *King and Church*, 229–42.
32. Ibid., 20.
33. Peláez, *Historia*, 40.
34. Dussel, *Tomo V*, 57.
35. Ibid., 66.

During Philip II's reign the Crown expanded its control over the Church in the Americas. Disputes over the jurisdiction of the secular priests and religious orders had arisen, particularly on the mission fields, which were monopolized by the Franciscans, Dominicans, and Augustinians.[36] Whereas the secular clergy and the episcopal administration were subordinate to the Crown, the regular orders perceived themselves as apostolic representatives who were commissioned by the Vicar of Christ himself, the pope in Rome. As a result, while the friars and monks in general were pleased to obey the law in secular matters, they did not agree with its ecclesiastical pretensions.[37] In short order, the Crown sought to bring the mendicant orders under its control and limit their financial independence. Philip had planned to reorganize the ecclesiastical structure to his ends, but had to do it in a manner that would limit the resistance of the various religious orders and, ideally, have the pope on his side.

Juan de Ovando, whom Philip had appointed as president of the Council of the Indies in 1571, sought to revive the idea of a Patriarchate of the Indies composed of two Patriarchs, one over Mexico and one for Peru. These men, who would be appointed by the king, of course, would represent the highest ecclesiastical authority for the Americas. This idea ultimately failed when Pope Gregory XIII sought to refer the question to a committee of cardinals.[38] Instead, Ovando would prepare a revision to the royal patronage that would restructure the Church in New Spain. The *Ordenanza del Patronazgo* issued in 1574 declared that the mission fields were to be opened to secular clergymen and qualified laypeople who would be presented by the viceroy. Prelates of the religious orders were to maintain lists of monasteries and their functions including a census of inhabitants and the roles and qualifications of working friars. The removal or replacement of individual friars was placed in the hands of the local governor and secular prelate, thus enabling the government to limit the power of the orders. Though reaction to the *Ordenanza* varied according to region, as a long-term result, the power of the mendicant orders was greatly diminished in New Spain, though they maintained some autonomy on the frontier regions. The effect on the secular clergy was just as impressive. The improved pay and job security

36. Padden, "Ordenanza del Patronazgo," 30–35.
37. Ibid., 33–34.
38. Ibid., 38–41.

that came with the implementation of the *Ordenanza* encouraged more young men to enter the clergy. Competition for posts was enhanced by improvements in education, partly brought about by the introduction of the Society of Jesus into New Spain in 1571.[39] By 1600 the secular clergy and its episcopal power was ascendant.[40]

Given that both the king and the Council of the Indies lay across the Atlantic, the viceroy of New Spain maintained significant powers to exercise the rights of the *patronato*. He would, as the king's representative, establish churches, hospitals, schools and centers of charity as well as convene church councils and control the clergy, both secular and religious.[41] The viceroy could also legislate some of the powers of the *patronato* to local governors in order to facilitate administration. This, at times, caused friction between the Church and the civil power as the former could not administer its own affairs as it saw fit. This was especially visible in the administration of the tithe as governors could retain church monies if they were in disagreement with bishops or prelates, thus reducing the Church to virtual servitude.[42]

The innumerable laws decreed from Spain along with vice regal decrees and local interpretations could usurp church power in favor of the state. Some viceroys governed the Church in a despotic, or as we might say, micro-managerial manner, naming not only bishops but parish priests and chaplains. It became apparent, even to some parishioners that ecclesial power resided in the governor or viceroy and not in the bishop.[43] To the leaders of the Church, the problem with royal patronage as the Spanish Crown exercised it in the Americas lay with its inflexible legislations without realizing the distinct needs and contexts of the New World.

The royal patronage in the Americas was, in the words of Mecham, an "extraordinary patronage." In essence, the Spanish monarch controlled

---

39. Schwaller, "Ordenanza del Patronazgo," 67, cf. 49–69; for a more detailed description of the enforcement of the Ordenanza in colonial Mexico. Cf. Mecham, *Church and State*, 32–34.

40. Padden, "Ordenanza del Patronazgo," 42–43.

41. Mecham, *Church and State*, 23. Though the religious orders were dependent upon a provincial or custodian general who was appointed by the pope, the members of the orders were expected to live in accordance with the religious and secular laws administered by the viceroy, Peláez, *Historia*, 41; Mecham, *Church and State*, 33–34.

42. Dussel, *Tomo V*, 65.

43. Ibid.

the Church over a region extending from the today's Southwestern United States to the Tierra de Fuego in South America to a degree unprecedented in history. The king was not only a patron but, because of his authority that reached into matters of polity and enforcement, such as church councils, he was a "quasi-pontiff." In addition to exercising the privileges and responsibilities of the *patronato* in establishing churches, religious orders, schools, and hospitals and furthering the Catholic message to the natives, the Spanish monarch also commanded the allegiance of his people. The Crown in Spanish America was intertwined with the Church to the extent that the Church became as much an instrument of Conquest and Colonization as was the force of arms. Bishops and clerics owed their positions to him and consequently, this devotion to God's anointed king filtered down to the populace who lived daily with the physical evidences of the triumphs of the Church and the Crown.[44]

The issue of patronage is complicated and at times, murky. Both sides, the pontifical and the royal, perceived the privilege as rooted within their own sphere of authority, and, indeed, the historical argument lends weight to both parties under different historical contexts. It is probably no coincidence that forms of Bourbon Jansenism would become popular in some educated circles in eighteenth-century Spain and Mexico. This form of Jansenism, as we shall note in a following chapter, is Gallican in conviction. That is, its proponents believed that the authority of the Church and the responsibility for Church reform lay with the king and his representatives, rather than the pope.

The question as to whether the right to appoint bishops (and thus friendly representatives and powerful influence *in situ*) resided in the lay or in the papal power would come to occupy the heirs of the tradition in the newly created Mexican republic. The leaders of the emergent nation would debate the right and consequently, the nature of the Mexican Church. It is pertinent in our discussion of the Church of Jesus in that the movement, supported in its early years by the administration of Benito Juarez, can be seen as an extension of those very debates over royal, and now civil, patronage privilege and responsibility.

---

44. Mecham, *Church and State*, 36–37.

4

The Character of Mexican Catholicism in the Colonial Era

TWO EPISODES

THEN THE PLAGUE CAME. The silent attacker targeted Mexico City, located on an island surrounded by stagnant waters and ripe for disease, in 1736. Subject to frequent floods and rains because of the deforestation of the surrounding hills, crops would rot, leading to famine and pestilence. The poor, particularly Indians, were often left to die alone despite the best efforts of many priests who ministered to the sick, the dying, and the dead. By January 1737 the church sepulchers were full and the smell of death hung in the air. The funeral pyres that burned the bodies of the unfortunate poor at San Lazaro's cemetery cast smoke and soot into the sky for over seven months. An early account states that over 192,000 people died in central Mexico during that outbreak. Seeing the ongoing plague as a sign of God's displeasure, the faithful and not-so-faithful filled the city's churches to seek divine aid. They looked to the city's collection of divine images for help and in December 1736, an image of Our Lady of Loreto was paraded through the streets. When the plague did not abate, the city council turned to Our Lady of Remedios, Mexico City's patron from the time of the Conquest and since 1597 a frequent object of supplication in times of trouble. As many times before she was removed from her site on the outskirts of the city and paraded amidst pomp and petition until she was installed on the high altar in the cathedral. But the pestilence continued. Other images, statues, and relics of the saints were brought out in hopes that the unmoved God would at last react to this conspicuous display of piety and abate his wrath. St. Joseph, St. Bernard, bloody Christs accompanied by bloody penitents and seemingly innumerable Virgins of this-or-that would form the repentant processions. Finally, in early 1737, the members of the city council went to Tepeyac hill and there held a novena of sermons, masses, and prayers in honor of the Virgin of Guadalupe. An eloquent preacher, Bartolomé de Ita y Parra, called upon the city council to declare her the patron of the city and of New Spain. A silver image of the Virgin made its way through the festooned streets that May accompanied by civil and religious officials, members of all the orders and numbers of ordinary people, Spanish and Indian, in honor of her official adoption. Within weeks, neighboring cities and towns joined in the popular acclaim. By the fall of 1737, the plague that had precipitated the occasion waned. In 1756, Pope Benedict XIV approved the election of the Virgin of Guadalupe as principal patron of New Spain.[1]

Holy Week observances, or rather, celebrations, in late eighteenth-century Mexico City lasted from Monday until Saturday. Important confraternities carried floats through the city streets displaying their particular patron saint. Others highlighted scenes from the Passion of Jesus. Members of the confraternities followed dressed as Roman soldiers or as penitents. The relative economic boom of the era had drawn immigrants from the countryside, many of whom had set up shop along the streets to sell tamales, fruit drinks, and ice cream to the throngs of visitors who had converged upon the capital for the spring event. Yet, despite outward appearances, not all were in a celebratory mood. The viceroy, Juan Vicente Güemes Pacheco, Conde de Revillagigedo (1740–99), was one of the ablest men to hold that post and responsible for transforming Mexico City into a modern metropolis. He had ordered the city streets paved and lighted, thus reducing crime at night. He cleared the central plaza of street vendors and established markets in other parts of the city. Additionally, he founded the Museum of National History and the General Archives to preserve the history of the colony. The viceroy noticed that people wasted their money in renting costumes and arms for the spectacle—so much so that some fell into serious debt. Others, including several bishops, complained that such celebrations invited drunkenness, prostitution, rape, and theft not only during Holy Week, but during other public religious

1. Brading, *Mexican Phoenix*, 120–32.

celebrations. Both the over-the-top religious displays and their dishonorable effects invited the ridicule of religion, according to the critics. In 1793 Viceroy Revillagigedo issued an edict banning religious festivals except for Christmas, Corpus Christi, and a handful of others. Such ostentation, according to some, not only opened the door to the Devil and his temptations but they also distracted the faithful from the true piety and virtue that the saints were meant to inspire.[2]

These two episodes, though separated from one another by only six decades, illustrate a seismic shift in religious perception and worldview. This chapter will lay the foundation for the changes in religious worldview that occurred in the eighteenth century among some members of society, including some bishops and rulers. In short, whereas colonial Mexican spirituality for most of the epoch was characterized by what can be termed a Baroque worldview, during the eighteenth century different modes of thought began to take root in the colony, particularly among the educated. Influences from the European Enlightenment as well as from the Jansenist revivals in the Netherlands and France made their way into Spain where they flourished in regalist circles and from there to Mexico. It is important to note this development in Spanish Catholic ideology as it will form the seedbed for later developments in the colony. Not only were some of the leaders of the Independence insurrection Enlightened Catholics but the Mexican Enlightened emphases on nationalism, interior piety, reason, and church reform find their echo in the reform movement of the mid-nineteenth century that created the Church of Jesus. This chapter will thus explore the nature of Tridentine Mexican Catholicism in the colonial era, whereas the next one will describe the rise of the Catholic Enlightenment in Spain and Mexico.

Mexican Catholicism during the greater part of the colonial era was characterized by two aspects. One the one hand, there was the cultural diversity brought about by the intermixture of the various Native American, Iberian, and African peoples that created a variety of religious expression. Secondly, post-Tridentine, Baroque spirituality and epistemology and theology served as a unifying umbrella by which many religious forms could be deemed legitimate.

---

2. Brading, "Tridentine Catholicism," 16–17; cf. Brading, *Church and State*, 165–68. Voekel, *Alone Before God*, 52–54; Beezley and Curcio-Nagy, *Latin American*, 127; cf. Dussel, *Tomo V*, 142.

A MULTICULTURAL NATION

To take into account the variety that made up Mexican (and Latin American) Colonial Catholicism we must be cognizant, first of all, of the multiverse of different people-groups that made up the continent. Roberto Levillier eloquently described the First Nations of Latin America:

> The Tekestas and Tahinos of Cuba were Indians, tame and hospitable; the cannibal Carib was Indian; the primitive Otomi living in caves was Indian; the wild Jibaro was Indian; the Uro, more fish than man, living in the waters of the Titicaca was Indian. Indian were the artisan stonecutter Mayan; the Chibchan goldsmith; the wise Inka legislator, and the delicate Yungan ceramist. The Coya weaver was Indian. The heroic Aztec, the cannibalistic Chiriguayo, and the untamable Diaguitas and Araucans were Indians. The shy Juri, the Lule nomad, the sedentary Comechigón, and the fierce Guarani were Indians. They were different in intelligence, cruelty, and mildness. Their skin colors, languages, rituals, and theogonies were different. The *veri domini* could be confused with the usurping Indians who subjected them to obedience. They were not the same in their juridical standing, their physical aspects, their language, their tastes, their mannerisms, nor in their creative abilities.[3]

This reality was further amplified through the introduction of African slavery in the sixteenth century, particularly throughout the Caribbean and coastal regions.

Slavery had long been a fact throughout the world on all its populated continents. It was an established part of Muslim civilization and was practiced by Christians and Muslims on the Iberian Peninsula. The Arab slave trade, begun in the ninth century, involved people regardless of race, color, or religion and in its early period most slaves were taken from Central and Eastern Europe. As the interior of Africa became more accessible through land routes, the trade in slaves from the continent increased.[4] With the onset of the European Age of Discovery in the late fifteenth century through the excursions of the Portuguese along the coast of Africa the Atlantic Slave Trade was born. As the Indian popu-

---

3. Quoted in Rivera, *Violent Evangelism*, 15. *Veri domini* is a scholastic term referring to the true owners of the land, used during the disputes as to whether it was legal to have dominion over the territories of pagans and non-Christians. cf. n.24.

4. For a discussion of the Muslim/Arab context of the slave trade see Lovejoy, "Context of Enslavement."

lation of the Americas dwindled, African slaves were imported by the Spanish and Portuguese (often with the collusion of friendly African nations) to work the mines and plantations that maintained their far-flung empires. These forced immigrants came from West Africa from Senegal to Angola and even Mozambique and Madagascar, and represented over forty different ethnic groups from the Wolof of Senegal to the Igbo and Yoruba of Nigeria to the Makua of Mozambique.[5] These peoples, faced with an uncertain and alien new world, brought with them their own languages, worldviews, cultures, and religions that they used to survive and that inevitably interacted and intermingled with the Iberian and Amerindian parts of society.[6]

The dominant powers in the Americas during the first century or so after European contact were, of course, the Iberian. Spain and Portugal were heirs to 800 years of cultural diversity that has often been described as *convivencia*, where Jews, Christians, and Muslims lived side-by-side, kingdom-by-kingdom, sometimes in a state of war or persecution. This period can be painted as one of uneasy peace where one culture invariably absorbed aspects of another or created new aspects to define themselves vis-à-vis the other. This was a period where architectural styles could meld Jewish and Arabic elements as in some of the remaining medieval synagogues of Spain, where science and philosophy could be enriched through the common effort of translation and where the thirteenth-century Christian king, Alfonso X (d.1264) sought to establish a university where Latin and Arabic would be used side-by-side to enrich the enterprise of learning. Throughout this period, we see curious societies one might refer to as multicultural (though hierarchical based on race and religion). While not readily admitting to rough tolerance if one reads their political and religious edicts, laws and treatises, on that more abstract concept we call culture, revealed through poetry, song, art, and architecture, there was a give-and-take, a more active interplay between the cultures and peoples to which official documents may not admit.[7]

Yet, as noted in the previous chapter, this period is also recognized as one where the Christian kingdoms to the north sought to extend their rule throughout the peninsula over against the Muslim states to the south.

---

5. See for example Hall, *Slavery*; Lovejoy, *Transformations*; Rout, *African Experience*.

6. An introduction to the African influence in Latin American literature, music and religion can be found in Fraginalis, *Africa in Latin America*.

7. An excellent recent study of this is Dodds et al. *The Arts of Intimacy*.

Religion did play a part in these struggles and the Church would emerge as a strong, central institution that gave a sense of identity and purpose to the Christian states, but *realpolitik* had as much a role during this era as anything else. Muslim rulers could ally with Christian leaders against a common foe, whatever his religion. Subjugated kingdoms were a source of additional income through levies, taxes and tributes and this was one reason why the enemy was not simply wiped off the map.[8] In other words, religion mattered except when it did not matter and did not matter except in those times when it did. The final push of the *Reconquista*, headed by Isabella of Castile and Fernando of Aragon in the fifteenth century, reflects the gradual change in Spanish society that undermined the *convivencia*, emphasized religious uniformity and resulted in the forced conversion or exile of Spain's Jewish and Muslim populations.

With the final triumph of the united Spanish crowns over the last Muslim state of Granada in 1492, a new nation-state had emerged that saw itself as the protector of Catholic faith and imbued with a sense of destiny that accompanied the surrender of the city. Christianity, long preserved by the Iberian kingdoms since the days when Don Pelayo rebelled against the Arab governor in the eighth century, had emerged victorious over the Muslim crescent. In the process of Reconquista, Spanish identity had been forged. The Crown, as patron of the Church perceived itself as responsible for spreading and defending the Christian faith not only across the Iberian Peninsula, but also across the Atlantic.

As Isabella and Fernando established themselves in the Alhambra, Christopher Columbus was recalled to the court to further discuss the enterprise he had long been trying to sell the monarchs of Portugal and Spain. When the Reformation won peoples and kingdoms for what would be called Protestantism, Spain would see itself as especially chosen by God to preserve the Catholic faith in Europe and to spread it to the millions of peoples recently "discovered" across the Atlantic. The lessons learned through centuries of warfare would be used to establish Christendom at the point of the sword in these Americas to fulfill Spain's own particular brand of Manifest Destiny.

These paragraphs serve to paint, in very broad strokes, the variety of peoples, colors, and cultures that made up the Columbian Moment—

---

8. See for example, O'Callaghan, *History of Medieval Spain*; Ángel and Palenzuela, *Historia de España*; Chejne, *España Musulmana*; Thomas Mann et al., *Convivencia*; Menocal, *Ornament of the World*; Lowney, *Vanished World*; Cardaillac, *Toledo*.

that series of encounters, battles, conquests, enslavements, and relations that would make up the peoples of Latin America. The cultural and political dominance of the Europeans in America created a variety of socio-economic levels whose multiethnic yet stratified character was written into the very structure of colonial society.

Upon their initial encounters, the Spanish were at odds as to what to make of the peoples of the New World, especially after the Spanish came into contact with advanced societies such as the Aztec and the Inka who enjoyed large urban centers, hierarchical leadership, expansive military and economic structures and complex religious traditions. Were they fully human? What rights, if any, did they enjoy? What was their status under the ideology of Christendom? Influenced by the Spanish jurist, philosopher, and theologian, Francisco de Vitoria (1492–1546), leaders of the School of Salamanca taught that the indigenous peoples were indeed human but that, because of sin and isolation from Christendom, they had degraded in their intellectual and moral capacities. Consequently, it was the task and mission of the Spanish Christians to tutor these child-like people so that they could mature and eventually enjoy the benefits of civilization. In order to facilitate this pedagogy, colonial society was decided into two main categories. To protect them from the negative moral examples of the Spanish, the native peoples were segregated into the Indian Republic. Here, they enjoyed a certain degree of economic and legal autonomy under local leaders. They were ministered to by members of the regular orders who were to learn native languages and create catechisms, literature, music, and drama to aid in the evangelization and civilization of the Indians. The Spanish, meanwhile, composed their own Republic whose religious needs were met by the secular clergy under the local bishop. In theory these two groups were to be maintained apart—restrictions were made upon the presence of Indians among the Spanish and vice-versa, even in densely packed urban areas like Mexico City. Of course, the reality proved far different from the moment the first Spanish soldier came across a native woman. The inevitable results of such unions created a legal and social situation that officially did not exist—the *castas*, the hybrid peoples who resulted from the mixture of Indian, European, and African blood. The presence of the *castas* was embarrassing for a Spanish society that was preoccupied and prided itself upon *pureza de sangre*, purity of (Spanish) blood, a concept that rose as the kingdoms of Spain dealt with its identity crisis in the midst of its shared history among the Muslims and Jews. The *castas* formed a nebulous middle space between the Spanish and Indian Republics (and the mass of slaves at the bottom of the social pyramid). The various *casta* identities were not necessarily fixed but exhibited a certain flexibility that depended upon a variety of factors such as skin color, financial status, paternal recognition, etc. The caste paintings of the seventeenth and eighteenth centuries bear witness to the different strata of society and their resultant cultures based on perceived racial intermingling and preoccupations with *pureza de sangre*.[9] Below this were the free and enslaved Africans. Above was the viceroy, who reigned in the crown's stead and who received his orders from the Council of the Indies in Seville and the distant and benevolent king who himself reigned in the name of God.

Thus to what I refer to as the horizontal aspects of society—the multiple peoples and cultures of the region—was added a vertical dimension through the imposition of Iberian structures (as well as adaptation of similar native ones) that placed persons on a social ladder based upon their perceived race, economic status, social power, and privilege.[10] Upon these two axes would hang the many forms of Catholic piety and expression that would develop in colonial Latin America.

DIVERSE CATHOLICISMS

Up until very recently studies of the history of Christianity have painted Mexican Catholicism, and indeed most of Latin American Christianity, with the same broad brush. If the story of the Christian Church deviated at all from Europe and North America, there could be some discussion of the Spanish Conquests and the establishment of Catholicism on the continent.[11] This perception, however, is changing. Historians of religion

---

9. Cf. Katzew, *Casta Painting*.

10. Ever circular, this structure also determined one's social status or economic or political power. Thus American-born Spaniards were unable to hold the highest positions of power during the colonial era. Exemptions to the rule existed but were relatively few. Mixed-race children recognized by their Spanish fathers could attain wealth or status, as could the children of Indian nobility or freed blacks. But while wealth, education, or recognition could provide one with greater latitude within the social structure, there was little chance of completely trespassing it.

11. Cairns, *Christianity Through Centuries* and Walker, *History Christian Church* devote only a few paragraphs to Latin America and that only in the context of European expansion in the sixteenth century. Developments in Africa and Asia are given the same

have taken advantage of the social sciences in their studies and no longer are they satisfied with the decrees of Church Councils and records of bishops and rulers to paint a portrait of Latin American Christianity. This in turn has changed the perception of Catholicism and religion in the region. In *Local Religion in Colonial Mexico* Martin Nesvig writes that historians have begun to shy away from the concept of a unilateral Spiritual Conquest popularized by Robert Picard's 1933 book. Picard had posited a triumphant and monolithic orthodox Catholicism imposing itself upon the Mexican people like a juggernaut. As a result, many might be inclined to believe that there is not much to tell about religion in Latin America.[12] The study of local or popular religion, animated in part by William Christian Jr.'s studies of local religion in Spain, as well as insights on the role of power in human relationships, has changed that perception.

Likewise the recent focus on power as multidirectional and contested has begun to influence scholars of religion in Mexico. The irony is immense. The political historians of Latin America, born of the Old Left and the Old New Left, "discovered" cultural history in the late 1990s. With their epiphany these political historians fused an older model of political economy and material neo-Marxist inquiry, with a study of the culture of politics, the methods of the underdogs (subalterns), and the complicated and ever-contested nature of power. In other words, while older models emphasized the top-down or high-level politics of formal parties, revolutions, and policies, the newer cultural history of politics emphasized the role of the peasant, the under-represented, and the "popular." In similar fashion, studies of religion moved towards more prosaic and popular manifestations of religious sensibility. Thus while political historians were discovering the multiplicity and complexity of power among social actors, historians of religion began to see the

---

treatment unless part of the story of Protestant missions of the nineteenth century. Ray Petry's two-volume collections of primary sources in Christian history (*History of Christianity*) never once touches on Latin America, modern Africa, or Asia. The only significant exceptions to the rule are the works of Kenneth Scott Latourette, who, perhaps because of his interest in missions and the effects of Christianity, delved in detail into the traditions and histories of non-European/North American churches. This tendency is being corrected gradually. Beginning in the last two decades of the twentieth century works by David Edwards, Justo Gonzalez, Adrian Hastings, Philip Jenkins, Dale Irvin, and Scott Sunquist have broadened the geographical and confessional stage on which Christian history is viewed.

12. Nesvig, *Local Religion*, xviii–xxi; cf. Picard, *Spiritual Conquest*.

same potential fruits of a cultural history approach. The result is that North American historians of religion in Mexico are challenging the assumptions of a vast undifferentiated Iberian Catholicism in colonial Mexico.[13]

Having stated this we cannot go further without mentioning the effects of liberation theology in Latin America upon the study of history. Liberation theology takes as one of its central premises God's "preferential option for the poor"; the initiative of God, as stated in the stories and admonitions of the Old Testament (the exodus story, the election of Israel, the Psalms and Prophets) and the Gospels (the *Magnificat*, the life and teachings of Jesus, and witness of the early Church) that God is ultimately on the side of the poor and oppressed—those who have neither the access to power nor the stuff of life's necessities.[14] The philosopher-theologian-historian Enrique Dussel brings this out in his introduction to *The Church in Latin America 1492–1992*, published in recognition of the 500th anniversary of the American/European encounter: "If 'bringing the good news to the poor' was his [i.e., Jesus'] specific historical purpose and that of his church, this must also be the absolute and primary criterion of a *Christian* interpretation of the history of that church—a scientific interpretation, certainly, but also Christian (based on faith). The 'meaning' of an event, then, is deduced from the effect (positive or negative) it has on the poor, the oppressed, the ordinary people."[15]

The introduction to the multivolume and interdenominational history of the Church in Latin America published by CEHILA (Commission for the Study of the History of the Church in Latin America) elaborates:

> The history of the Church reconstitutes the life of the Church in accordance with historical methodology. It is a scientific endeavor. But at the same time, the history of the Church includes the interpretation in the light of the faith as a constituent moment in the reconstruction of historical fact. It is a theological endeavor. The history of the Church in Latin America is understood theologically as the history of that sacramental institution of communion, of mission, of conversion as a prophetic word that judges and saves,

---

13. Nesvig, *Local Religion*, xx, italics mine.

14. This can mean not only to refer to the lack of life's necessities such as food, water and safety but also the things that enrich one emotionally and spiritually. In some African cultures, for example, one may be monetarily well off but considered poor if lacking in family connections or children.

15. Dussel, *Church in Latin America*, 1.

as the Church of the poor. Even though all of these aspects are living expressions of one Body, it appears to us as most convenient to pay special attention in our historical focus to the poor out of evangelical and historical reasons as well as present necessities. For in Latin America the Church has always found itself before the task of evangelizing the poor (the indigenous, the African, the creole, the workers, the peasant, the people).[16]

As a result of these theological as well as methodological criteria, Christian historians in Latin America have begun to uncover the voices and experiences of the subaltern. For this reason, the term "popular religion" has come to have a slightly different shade of meaning among Latin American historians and theologians. Not only does it refer to the religion of the people, the *populus*, but to the faith expressions of the poor and marginalized.[17]

Thus, in recent years, the picture of Christianity in Latin America has changed drastically. One of the characteristics of Christianity in Mexico (and Latin America) that scholars have come to recognize is the reality of hybridity. Obsessed with "purity of blood" (*limpieza de sangre*) the Spanish rulers of the Americas began a detailed and, from our perspective, somewhat laughable attempt to catalogue the mixtures of peoples and colors that came as a result of the inevitable and intimate encounters between Spaniards, natives, and Africans (as well as their

---

16. Dussel, *Tomo I*, 11.

17. As stated above this may be expanded to include those who are lacking in family connections or relationships that make life worth living beyond physical sustenance. Liberation theology asserts that not only are those ravaged by hunger and war caught up in institutional sin and poverty but those who victimize them or who take advantage of their situation are victims of a greater system of evil and exploitation. This reminds me of an assertion of the Jewish scholar Ellis Rivkin when confronted by the question of whether the Jewish leaders or the Romans killed Jesus. It was not a matter of *who* killed Jesus but *what*. The Roman Imperial system devoted to conquest through violence made victims of the actors in the Passion and dehumanized both the Roman governor, the soldiers and the Jewish leaders to the extent that they participated in the execution of an innocent man. Cf. Goss, "John," 558. This perspective means that the faith expressions of the powerful or elite are also worth studying from the liberation theology perspective to see how the Gospel is articulated in their lives when subjected to systems of institutional sin that in turn may make them victimizers of others. This recognizes of course that physical poverty and hunger do not automatically exempt one from becoming a victimizer. Witness the use of abused and traumatized boys as soldiers by some militia groups in modern Africa.

progeny).[18] In the eighteenth century artists began to represent these categories in *casta* paintings. Not only were these paintings produced as souvenirs for Europeans visiting the "exotic" New World but they also fed the Enlightenment desire to classify and catalogue aspects of natural history. Fortunately these paintings provide modern historians and anthropologists a window into daily life, customs, and surroundings of the time.[19] The most common in New Spain was the *mestizo* or child of a Spaniard and an Indian.

The modern term *mestizaje* represents the cultural and physical mixture between cultures. Historians often use this term to describe the combination or mixing of cultural, including religious characteristics into a new entity. To take an example, the Virgin of Guadalupe and the *Nican Mopohua* that describes her apparition are sometimes described in mestizo terms. Both the image and the narrative take on elements from the Spanish (the structure of the apparition story, the Christian imagery) and Indian (the Virgin is brown-skinned and appears on an Aztec sacred site, the story, written in Nahua, interweaves native language and imagery for the divine).[20]

This cultural and cross-cultural pluralism extended to the establishment and spread of Christianity in Latin America. Iberian Catholic belief and varied forms of devotion intermingled with native and African ones, resulting in a vast array of inculturated and synchronous expressions of faith. This is evident especially in New Spain/Mexico and throughout South America, where, unlike the Caribbean, large numbers of indigenous peoples survived the Conquest and became a part of colonial society along with African slaves and both immigrant and

---

18. *Limpieza de Sangre* was a tool conceived of to regulate Spain's hierarchical society. The absence of Jewish or Muslim forbears defined one as an honorable Old Christian, whereas having the Jewish or Muslim blood of a *converso*, relegated one, a New Christian, to second-class status or even suspicion of infidelity of faith. Ironically, two of Spain's most famous and diametric figures, the Grand Inquisitor Torquemada and the mystic and reformer, St. Teresa of Avila, were of New Christian families.

19. Cf. Katzew, *Casta Painting* and Olson, "Casta Paintings." It should be noted that though *casta* is translated into caste in English, the actual social structure did not have the rigidity that comes to mind with the Indian (Asian) caste system. Social mobility was possible, not only through intermarriage (to someone with more Spanish blood or whiter skin) but through the recognition of darker-skinned children by their Spanish fathers, for example.

20. See for example Nebel, *Santa María Tonantizin* and Leon-Portilla, *Tonantzin Guadalupe* as well as Brading, *Mexican Phoenix*.

American-born Spaniards. Stafford Poole and Susan Schroeder recognize these multiform expressions of religion when they say that

> religion is immediate, and it is cultural. It can be personal or shared, and it can be based on an attempt to reconcile the mysterious and unmanageable forces of nature such as storms, droughts, floods, infestations of pests, epidemic diseases, and sicknesses. In popular form, it is an attempt to control the uncontrollable. Religion can also be an institution that is as all-pervasive as today's media yet, in spite of itself and because of itself, is manifested in a multitude of forms. These protean qualities of religion are a classic paradigm for the situation in colonial Mexico, where there was a convergence of the institutional church, Spanish popular Catholicism, and indigenous spiritual practices. As an imperial religion, Catholicism was a political-ecclesiastical ideal. Every one of New Spain's inhabitants was expected to conform to the church's precepts. The reality of Mexican Catholicism, however, was a convergence of beliefs and practices and seemed to reflect degrees of actual spirituality, the product, doubtless, of the colony's many cultures; and some people were never fully co-opted by Catholic dogma and its ministers.[21]

In many cases these various expressions of Mexican Catholicism were tolerated and even encouraged by the ecclesial authorities and missionaries. Some of this diversity—such as the use of indigenous languages, the multiplicity and variety of devotion, and so on, was tolerated in realization of the variety of peoples in the land (as well as the differing approaches of the secular Church, and the evangelization efforts of the religious orders). A classic example of this might be the differences between the two major religious orders in post-Conquest Mexico. The Franciscan approach, influenced by the theology arising out of Joachim of Fiore's (d.1202) millennial thought that posited the discovery of the Americas as a sign of the return of Christ and as God's recompense for the millions lost to Protestantism in Europe. Thus the Franciscans sought out the conversion of the local leader and from there baptized the people with little or no catechesis in anticipation of the Age of the Spirit to be brought about in the New World. The Dominicans, on the other hand, sought an extended period of education for the people before administering baptism.[22] Many other examples abound throughout

---

21. Schroeder and Poole, *Religion in New Spain*, 1.
22. Cf. Pardo, *Origins Mexican Catholicism*, 3–4; Blank, *Teología y Misión*, 21–34.

Latin American Christianity of this hybridity that, by their very nature and expression, carried with them the seeds of further interpretation and adaptation by subaltern (the poor, natives, slaves, Africans, women, etc.) that may have been unintended by those (missionaries, clergy, theologians) who created or approved them.[23] On the most basic missiological basis, they represent an adaptation of the Christian message to the cultural milieu of its recipients. Since Spanish did not become the predominant language of New Spain until the next century, missionaries had to translate the Christian message into that of the peoples, including into pictograms as written alphabets were nonexistent in the Americas. As anyone who has attempted a translation knows, every translation is also an interpretation since languages and forms of speech or writing do not mesh with one another equally but are laden with cultural baggage. Spain itself, as we have noted, had a long history of variant religious expressions living side-by-side and even after the suppression of Judaism and Islam, local varieties of Christianity flourished.[24]

Other reasons for the emergence of plural expressions of Catholicism would include the demographic, the simple lack of priests (particularly in rural areas, thus allowing more popular and hybrid varieties to arise, or the resistant), the appropriation and interpretation of the Christian message in a manner that would allow the marginalized to resist or find succor in the midst of dehumanizing circumstances.[25] On the other end

23. Two examples: the use of native pictographs to express Christian themes such as the Virgin Birth or the Resurrection in itself lends dignity to the native language and consequently the culture, as it is employed to carry forth divine ideas. Cf. Hall, *Mary, Mother and Warrior*, 90–94; Alberro, *El águila y la cruz*, 53–54. Further, the Virgin of Remedies is often considered the quintessential Spanish icon of Mary used in Mexico—after all, according to tradition she was carried forth by the conquistadors during the wars against the Aztecs and was later the standard for the royalist forces against the insurgents in 1810. Nonetheless she was a popular devotion among the natives of the region and the stories of the statue's discovery associated her with the maguey (from which pulque, used for indigenous religious ceremonies, was made) and with a temple dedicated to Ehecatl (a form of the god Quetzalcoatl associated with the wind, which in turn, according to Christian thought, is associated with the Holy Spirit (Gen. 1:2)). Additionally, a mural in the chapel to Remedios shows the Virgin giving a staff denoting authority to a native while saying "Peace be with you. You are no longer guests or strangers but citizens in the Household of God." Hall, *Mary, Mother and Warrior*, 69f., 126–27.

24. See Christian Jr., *Local Religion* and *Apparitions*.

25. As an example it can be argued that the various bloody Christs popular in Latin America are a form of resistance—the reinterpretation of a traditional imagery in a manner that while orthodox, would be imbued with meaning to their adherents, mainly the identification of the Son of God with the suffering of His people.

of the scale of religious pluralism and mixture there was the continued exercise of traditional religions behind the guise of Christian saints—the "idols-behind-the-altars" feared by early missionaries.[26] It is beyond the scope of this work to detail the picture of religious hybridity and pluralism in any detail but two examples may suffice.[27]

Holy Wednesday

One of the methods used by early missionaries to evangelize the native populations was drama. Louise Burkhart has scrutinized one of the earliest of these works in her book Holy Wednesday. Originally written in Spain this play was translated by a Nahua author who had most likely been educated by the Franciscans in the College of Santa Cruz. Burkhart has noted the differences between the two plays, which focus on Christ taking leave of his Mother before the events of the Passion. In the Spanish version he leaves her matter-of-factly, focusing on his coming mission of suffering. In the Nahua version there is much more attention given to the relationship between Mother and Son. Here, Christ seems torn between his Father's will and his Mother's anguish. This Nahua Christ and Mary, like their intended audience, submit to a violent destiny over which they have no control. Burkhart notes that the play would have resonated with the Nahua's subjection to the Spanish and with their bloodletting rituals, comparable to Christ's own sufferings.[28] "If the play's 'great city of Jerusalem' stands for the great city of Mexico, when Christ falls into the hands of abusive strangers these are Spanish hands."[29] This in itself lent a subversive streak to the work as the listeners would identify Christ's sufferings with their own oppression.

Additionally, the author adds or elaborates on things left simpler in the Spanish version, such as Mary's description of her heart being broken. Burkhart reminds us of the role of the heart as the seat of the soul in Aztec symbolism as well as the tearing of the heart from the sacrificial

---

26. Some Franciscans suspected the Virgin of Guadalupe to be just that kind of religious observance—the continued worship of the Mother Goddess of Tepeyac Hill under the name of Mary. Other examples would include the Afro-Caribbean religions of *santería*, *vodún*, and *candomblé* that preserved African religions by substituting the names of Christian saints for the traditional spirits.

27. The recent works edited by Nesvig and Schroeder and Poole can serve as windows into this multiform world for the reader.

28. Burkhart, *Holy Wednesday*, 97–98.

29. Ibid.

victim in Aztec rituals. Thus the text takes on several layers—not only an allusion to Simon's prophecy to Mary about a sword piercing her heart (Luke 2:35) but also allusions to Nahua cosmogony and symbolism.[30] The Nahua Jesus is less abrupt in his parting than his Spanish counterpart. Whereas the original version has Christ rejecting Mary's embrace, telling Mary Magdalene to hold her back, in the Nahua play Jesus shows concern for his Mother, asking Magdalene to support her to prevent her falling. As if to highlight this tenderness between Mother and Son and consequently, between Christ and the audience, the Nahua author has inserted four speeches at the end of the play that elaborate on the painful parting and Jesus' warm benediction of his Mother.[31]

Sor Juana Inés de la Cruz

Sor Juana Inés de la Cruz (1648–95) was one of the most prolific writers of the colonial era. This cloistered Hieronymite nun had taught herself to read at the age of three and as a child desired to dress as a boy so she could go to school. After a few years as a lady-in-waiting in the viceregal court, Juana decided to enter a convent, partly out of a desire to have the freedom to pursue her learning without the hindrance of husband and children (as was expected of a woman at the time). Settling into the more relaxed convent of St. Jerome she flourished through her writings of plays, poems, and religious and secular music. Coming to the attention and under the protection of the new viceroy and vicereine Sor Juana was hailed as the "Tenth Muse." Later, when one of her theological works was publicly attacked in 1691, bringing her close to the dangerous attention of the misogynistic archbishop of Mexico and the Inquisition, she wrote the "Reply to Sor Filotea," an autobiographical essay that among other things defends a woman's right to study and learn, including theology and sacred subjects.[32]

The theme of hybridity is present in Sor Juana's poetry and songs. Though a cloistered nun for most of her adult life she had a great awareness of the mixed populace of Mexico City and was able to reproduce the languages, accents and dialects she encountered in one way or another.[33]

---

30. Ibid., 118–19, 180–81.

31. Ibid., 159–63.

32. The definitive account of Sor Juana's life in English is Paz, *Sor Juana*. See also Rappaport, *Sor Juana* and López-Portillo, *Sor Juana y su Mundo*.

33. Cf. Michelle Gonzalez conjectures that she perhaps encountered indigenous

By giving voice to the indigenous and African peoples outside her walls Sor Juana, through her poetry, was able to criticize the Conquest and exploitation of others in a way that she never could through a straightforward criticism.

In the introductory poem (*loa*) to her play, *The Divine Narcissus*, which was meant to be performed in the Spanish court, Juana inscribes a conversation between Occident, America (both Indians) and Religion and Zeal, representing Roman Catholicism and the Spanish military, respectively. America and the Occident celebrate the feast of the god of the harvest, using language analogous to Christianity.

> Moreover, his protection
> is not restricted to nurture
> of material food,
> but later by eating
> his very own flesh
> (purified in advance
> of bodily dross),
> we may be cleansed of the
> stains on our souls.[34]

Upon entering, Religion attempts to convert them to Christianity but upon their refusal, Zeal threatens them. The Conquest (Zeal) is presented as brash and irrational while Religion seeks to persuade America and the Occident to convert through reason, convincing them that their religions were anticipations of Christianity, celebrated through the Eucharist.[35] At the end of the *loa* Juana pushes the envelope further, seemingly equating the Christian God with the Indian "God of the Seeds." America, Occident, and Zeal sing:

> As we say, already
> the Indies know
> who is the true
> God of the Seeds!

---

and African peoples growing up on her grandfather's hacienda and come to sympathize with native concerns through her friendship with the scholar Carlos Sigüenza y Góngora who devoted himself to the study of Mexico's Indian cultures. Another source of her familiarity with the accents of the people might be her forays into the city as lady-in-waiting to the vicereine. González, *Sor Juana*, 120.

34. Rappaport, *Sor Juana*, 71.

35. Ibid., 79ff.

> And with tender tears
> that pleasure distills,
> let us joyfully repeat
> with festive voice;
> ALL
> Blessed be the day
> I came to know the great God of the Seeds!³⁶

By noting the complexity of indigenous religion in this play meant for the Royal Court in Madrid, Sor Juana gives voice to the indigenous people and, in effect, seeks to evangelize the Spanish on the dignity of the native religion, placing it on par with Greco-Roman religion as a prefigurement of Christianity.³⁷

Gonzalez notes that, though black accents had been used in colonial poetry prior to Sor Juana, in her we find a defense and privileging of African voices to give them a public forum by which their concerns and experiences could be expressed.³⁸ Additionally, in at least two *villancicos* (carols) Juana describes the Virgin Mary as *Morenica*—black, perhaps an allusion to the dark-skinned Virgin of Guadalupe as well as to the Song of Songs (1:5–6).³⁹

> Black is the bride
> The sun shines on her face
> Ebony against a red sky
> she calls herself black
> not for being in the shade,
> rather constantly
> her purity is fired
> in the furnace of the sun . . .

---

36. Ibid., 88.

37. González, *Sor Juana*, 116–18; since the time of Justin Martyr (second century) Greek and Roman religion and philosophy were considered, by some Christians, as anticipations of Christianity—the Old Testament of the Gentiles—and some combed classical imagery for such prefigurations (e.g., Orpheus's descent into Hades, Ulysses tied to the ship's mast, etc.).

38. González, *Sor Juana*, 119.

39. Though some commentators emphasize the dark-skinned Mexican Virgin as an anomaly amidst pale-skinned, blonde ones found in many traditional representations, the Black Virgin has a very long tradition in Catholic piety and is found all over Europe. The original Virgin of Guadalupe in Spain, that most conquistadors would have been aware of, was a dark-hued statue. For more on the tradition of Black Madonnas see Begg, *Cult Black Virgin* and Oleszkiewicz-Peralba, *Black Madonna*.

> Black she is, she confesses
> But this blackness, she says,
> brings even greater beauty.
> For in the first day's first light
> Grace was morning star
> to her first step.[40]

According to Gonzalez the majority of the times that Sor Juana used indigenous and African accents were in her poems dedicated to the Virgin Mary, thus raising the possibility that Sor Juana's own spirituality connected Mary with social justice and the Divine identification with the marginalized.[41] Coupled with the *villancicos* she wrote in Nahautl and in African voices, these poems portray not only Sor Juana's positive opinion of non-Spanish cultures and languages but it reveals some of the hybridity that was present in Mexican colonial religion, not only among the ordinary people or what is referred to as "popular religion" but among the educated as well.

BAROQUE EXTRAVAGANCE

These multiple expressions of colonial Catholicism in literature, art, music, and devotion were able to flourish in New Spain under the umbrella of the Baroque. Far more than just a description of a certain period in art or music history, the Baroque, which extended into the eighteenth century, denotes a particular ethos, or spirit that pervaded the greater culture that emerged out of the Council of Trent (1545–63). Convened as both an effort to clean the Church of abuses and to provide a positive elaboration of belief and practice in the light of Protestantism, the effects of the Council of Trent were felt far beyond Europe. In the Americas, where there was neither pre-existing Church to reform nor Protestants to extirpate, the decrees of the Council served as a blueprint for the nascent Church.[42]

As a reaction to Protestantism's emphasis upon the early Church and their rejection of the medieval devotions, sacraments, and elaborate liturgy, the Council of Trent reformed and emphasized them. If the doorway to the spirit for the children of the Protestant Reformation was the *ear*—through the unmediated Word—for Tridentine Catholicism it was

---

40. Rappaport, *Sor Juana*, 47–48.
41. Gonzalez, *Sor Juana*, 119–20.
42. Stevens-Arroyo, "Marriage Made," 39.

through the *eye*. Trent had affirmed that because of humanity's weakness, material reminders of God's greatness were necessary.[43] "The Tridentine reformers and their successors seized on the emotions and the senses, and encouraged clerics to utilize feelings to promote devotion, to cultivate piety with works of art, myriad images, and specialized devotions, like that of the rosary."[44] Baroque Catholicism engendered a distinct theology, an interpretation and commentary on, in the words of Brian Larkin, the "very nature of God."[45] For Baroque Catholicism, God was not the ineffable Wholly Other, separated from humanity. God and the saints were immediate, as close as the nearest pilgrimage site, as sumptuous as the liturgy with its candles, vestments, and processions and as tactile as a piece of cloth touched to a relic or the body-made-bread Eucharistic host touched to the lips.[46] As if to emphasize this, ceremonies and structures virtually exaggerated the dramatic potential of the Christian message and sacraments. "The combined effects of lighting and decoration seemed to highlight the theatricality of the Catholic sacraments: what was the Catholic Church if not the theater of salvation, as suggested by numerous devotional and theological treatises of Catholic reform bearing titles such as 'Theatrum vitae humanae' or 'Theatrum sacrum'?"[47] In short, the spectacle of the liturgy—the swirling trompe l'oeil leading the eye upwards, the clouds of incense, the fine vestments, soaring choirs, and so on became the epistemological apparatus of the Baroque, meant to evoke the very kingdom of heaven and bring it into present reality.[48]

While successive popes employed artisans to create churches whose gilded columns and swirling statues led the eyes of the faithful towards ecstatic depictions of the saints in triumphant glory, in the Americas builders took pleasure in the continent's rich humanity and included symbols and images from the indigenous past and native art styles to impress the viewer in silver and gold enriched churches that eventually developed into what historians have termed churrigueresque or ultrabaroque, a style that seems to have had the intention of dizzying and disori-

---

43. Schroeder, *Canons and Decrees*, 147.

44. Bradley and Van Kley, *Religion and Politics*, 124.

45. Larkin, *Very Nature*.

46. Voekel, *Alone before God*, 17–18; cf. Hsia, *World Catholic Renewal*, 160ff. For a brief introduction to the concept of sacred immanence see Larkin, *Very Nature*, 28–38.

47. Hsia, *World Catholic Renewal*, 161.

48. Taylor, *Magistrates of the Sacred*, 266ff.

enting the viewer as he moved his eye across the narrative ornamentation towards the soaring heights of the church.[49] Stevens-Arroyo makes the point that while Trent in Europe sought to reform medieval devotions of superstition or commercialism, in the Americas, where there was no long-lasting ecclesiastical past, the Church "reformed" or "baptized" the indigenous past, asserting that pre-Christian religions predisposed the natives to accept Catholicism through similar points-of-contact. As a consequence of this (and of the actual potential of perceiving the divine in so many areas) religion in the Baroque leaned towards pluralism and enculturation.[50]

A PUBLIC FAITH

The public performance of liturgical piety has a long history in Christian history dating as far back as the fourth century or earlier when the local bishop would process from church to church in his city to distribute a common Eucharistic meal, thus binding that city's Christian community in a common identity and mission. Celebrations of martyrs, saints, and holy days were increasingly celebrated publically as the Church became coextensive with society and its needs. The apex of these public liturgies in the Middle Ages was the summer celebration of Corpus Christi, first developed in the thirteenth century as a communal reinforcement of the Fourth Lateran Council's (1213) proclamation of the doctrine of Transubstantiation.[51] The Council of Trent regulated the performance of the Mass and encouraged the visual and emotional impact of the liturgy which included the public celebration of the Eucharist in processions and Corpus Christi festivals.

These public liturgical celebrations served not only to reinforce community cohesion or the role of the Church in society but also the symbolic identification of the individual and the community with Christ and the saints. The decrees of the Fourth Lateran Council and Trent identified the priest as the only legitimate celebrant of the Mass, emphasizing his symbolic identification with Jesus as the consecrator and celebrant of

---

49. Larkin, *Very Nature*, 78ff.
50. Stevens-Arroyo, "Marriage Made," 47.
51. Larkin, *Very Nature*, 54ff. The doctrine of transubstantiation follows Thomas Aquinas in his description of the Real Presence of Christ in the Eucharist, namely that while the accidents of bread and wine (taste, touch, smell, etc.) remain the same, the substance of bread and wine were transformed into the Body and Blood of Christ.

the Eucharist. Similarly, liturgical processions connected the community with the Eucharist or patron saints. Paraliturgical gestures such as the making of the cross, the flagellation of the penitents, or the dedication of money or gifts in honor of some event in the life of Christ served to identify and link the believer with the Passion of Christ, for example, and bring her closer to the Son of God.[52]

New Spain was no stranger to the manifestation of the Baroque. Elaborate public festivals were a visible and great part of Baroque Catholicism. The experience of Baroque spirituality and faith was not confined to the churrigueresque altarpieces of the churches. Because the presence of the Catholic Church was an integral part of colonial society, the splendor and movement of church ornamentation virtually spilled out into the streets through the public celebrations of liturgical and para-liturgical festivals. Antonio Rubial García describes, for example, the Feast of All Saints in 1578 when the Jesuits brought 214 relics of European saints to Mexico under the pope's orders. García describes the reliquaries of precious metals and stones constructed to protect the relics as well as the sumptuous processional to the cathedral, replete with banners, triumphal arches, dances, and theatrical representations, converting Mexico City into a sacred space.[53]

Not only were celebrations for holy days or patron saints opportunities for the Church to affirm its religious role or for the community's businesses to make money, but they were also opportunities for society to assert its common identity such as the episode described at the beginning of this chapter that resulted in the naming of the Virgin of Guadalupe as patron saint of New Spain. Additionally, such celebrations, including funerary ones as described by Pamela Voekel, affirmed the social order. Processionals, particularly those in large cities such as Mexico City, often included the government and ecclesiastical dignitaries in their order of rank. Remembering that Corpus Christi celebrated the presence of the body of Christ in the Eucharist and consequently, in the people we note:

> Among the processions of New Spain none reached such influence and solemnity as the day of Corpus Christi . . . The bells pealed, the cathedral filled (with people), the brotherhoods with colorful standards and lanterns; the confraternities with their badges and standards carried candles in silver holders; the people and the

52. Larkin, *Very Nature*, 55–56.
53. Nesvig, *Local Religion*, 48.

guards dressed in their best—Spanish and creole ladies in their shawls and brocaded dresses held flowers and lighted tapers, the university officers in velvet robes of purple, college students in dress uniforms, seminarians in their robes and blue sashes; the third orders carried crosses, the regulars in their habits, the minor orders in surplices, the processional cross and torches, the children of the choir, the secretary of the town council and the priests and upper clergy with chasubles or dalmatics; the council dressed in copes were preceded by six acolytes in copes and silver scepters, the viceroy and the court ceremonially attired and finally, under a canopy and a shower of flowers was the sacrament carried aloft by the archbishop, accompanied by one of the dignitaries of the council and a canon. The guard lowered their flags which were blessed and presented arms between clouds of incense and canticles accompanied by musical instruments.[54]

Similarly, funeral processions were ostentatious and announced the family's social status and wealth through material displays of vestments and candles as well as the employment of confraternities, religious and ordinary folk to accompany the body to the church.[55]

THE CULT OF SAINTS

The use of the printing press, first established in Mexico as early as 1539, churned out devotional materials in the form of books and images for the literate and illiterate faithful. Through these, as well as religious drama and art, the cult of the saints spread throughout New Spain. The saints hereafter took the place of the traditional deities of the Indians, at times filling the occupational niches of these deities. Thus St. John the Baptist became associated with the rain god Tlaloc and took his place as lord of the east. St. Francis, because of his association with animals, was connected to Mixcoatl, lord of the hunt.[56] It was a process of assimilation long familiar in the history of Christianity, differing little from the experience of European peasants isolated from more rigorous catechetical education.[57]

---

54. Dussel, *Tomo V*, 145–46.

55. Cf. Curcio Nagy, *Great Festivals*; and Voekel, *Alone before God*, 24–31, 39–42. Regarding funerals Voekel says, "The comforting side of baroque corporate identity was its numbers; the underbelly was its rigid hierarchy," 31.

56. Nesvig, *Local Religion*, 43.

57. Ibid., 45, cf. Christian Jr., *Local Religion*.

The saints were a familiar and integral part of Baroque spirituality. The theological cosmology of the medieval and early modern world consisted of projected reflections of earthly hierarchies. Just as the lord or emperor sat remotely from the people so God the Father and Jesus Christ appeared as nebulous, far-away figures. Far more accessible were the members of the Heavenly Court, the Mother of God herself and the saints who, like lesser members of the earthly court, could be called upon to intercede for the needy. Mary and the saints thus served as patrons and intercessors for individuals, families, and communities. Their statues and images were often cherished possessions. Individuals or groups would devote time, money, and ornamentation towards the cult of a patron saint and in the process both identify themselves with that saint's devotion and hope to incur divine support against time spent in purgatory come the afterlife.

The cult of the saints was affirmed over and again through the apparatus of churchly splendor and liturgical performance. Elaborate altarpieces and statues celebrated their lives and sufferings even as paintings and murals depicted their celestial triumph to the faithful. The saints were celebrated through triumphant processionals, dances, incense, candles, floats and floral displays was affirmed in the Third Mexican Provincial Council of 1585, affirming the decrees of the Council of Trent. They were present in relics and sacred sites, physically immediate and accessible to anyone, rich or poor, with the means of reaching them. During this period the secular clergy sought to integrate the natives into the greater socio-religious realm as opposed to segregating them from external forces as the missionary friars had desired. The use of papal and episcopal saints such as St. Gregory the Great was integral in this as it connected the cult of the saints to figures in the secular (as opposed to regular) realm.[58]

Private devotion was expressed in the erection of altars and sacred niches in the homes of the rich and the poor, adorned with the printed image of the saint and perhaps accompanied by printed prayers of indulgence. Images were worn to protect against illness or accident or to aid in harvest or difficulties of life, such as childbirth. They were proliferated throughout New Spain through books and hagiographies, prayer guides, novenas, and even in non-religious documents such as contracts and gossip sheets.[59] The saints served as important lynchpin in colonial

---

58. Nesvig, *Local Religion*, 49.
59. Ibid., 54. Taylor, *Magistrates of the Sacred*, 266–91.

Baroque society, bringing the divine to earthly realms, reaffirming the power of the Church to determine the guide and determine the lives and afterlives of its members, and cementing individuals, families and groups in communal identity.

CONFRATERNITIES

The corporate spirit was bolstered in New Spain as guild corporations placed themselves under the protection of the particular saint entrusted to their craft (such as carpenters under St. Joseph). Meanwhile, founding saints were celebrated in the monasteries as secular priests put forth the notion, through art and word, that they were the successors of the apostles.[60] Confraternities, universities, members of the third orders (laypeople attached to the rule of a particular order but not attached to a monastery and rarely taking vows), and other groups found cohesion around the veneration of a saint whose function was to attend to the needs of the particular group in this life and the next (through their intercessions for those in purgatory). It was, in effect, the concept of a city's patron saint writ small. In return, the faithful would display their gratitude through ex-votos, festivals (complete with relics), or other vows. If the saint proved ineffective, devotion could be transferred to another saint, as we saw in the proclamation of the Virgin of Guadalupe as New Spain's patron thanks to her aid in a time of plague.[61]

Confraternities had been a part of the religious landscape of Europe since the twelfth and thirteenth centuries, and had been introduced into New Spain shortly after the Conquest. An important religious institution, analogous perhaps to being part-union, part-welfare, and part-funeral insurance, they performed a number of important functions for their members. Through the fees incurred on members they distributed charity, and sponsored religious festivals, particularly for a patron saint.

Brian Larkin emphasizes the role of confraternities in the performing of charitable works throughout local communities. Through the fees and contributions of its members confraternities were able to fulfill an important responsibility of Baroque faith, namely the dispensing of charity to the poor. Through this function confraternities were able to assist their members in the quest for salvation. The giving of alms enabled the

---

60. Nesvig, *Local Religion*, 50.
61. Ibid., 51.

individual to obtain grace and gain merits that would help them shorten their time in purgatory. Additionally, the recipients of charity, the poor, were traditionally identified with Jesus Christ. They would devote their prayers and intercessions towards their benefactors.[62]

Most of all, confraternities assisted in and ensured the rites of the dead through masses, perpetual prayer, and funeral arrangements.[63] "In and through all of their activities confraternities cultivated a sense of Christian unity and fellowship among their diverse memberships."[64] Voekel adds, "In funerals and church burials, then, those lucky enough to command respect for their final wishes united the dominant themes of baroque spirituality. On the one hand they paid homage to external nodes of sacred power by demanding access to saints' images and earthly relics; on the other, they summoned the collective efforts of the visible and invisible Church to speed them on their way and intercede on their behalf."[65]

Through public ceremony and the proliferation of devotional materials as well as through art, architecture, and music, the Baroque expressed an opulent Christianity that made the supernal accessible and immanent. Whether through the feasts of the Church or the cult of the saints, expressed through relics, images, and other means, human beings were able to touch the holy. The Baroque enabled the variety of devotions and religious expressions already fermenting in the hybrid cultures of New Spain across the race and color spectrum and up and down the social order, producing a diversity of pieties. Religious orders and secular priests popularized devotions, including those to recently canonized saints, thus multiplying the pantheon of holy intercessors in the colony.[66] While this wealth of religious observance could have induced a rapid individualization of religion, quite the opposite was true. The public celebrations in honor of Christ, the Virgin, or the saints, including the Mass, served as a vehicle of cohesion and affirmed the social order while at the same time suspending social divisions by bringing all of the faithful together under one act or liturgy.[67] Further, guilds and confraternities were especially

62. Larkin, *Very Nature*, 97–98, 109–12.
63. Nesvig, *Local Religion*, 190, Voekel, 27–31.
64. Nesvig, *Local Religion*, 190.
65. Voekel, *Alone before God*, 38.
66. Nesvig, *Local Religion*, 52–53.
67. Ibid., 192; Catholic orthodoxy and practice maintained that salvation was not a matter of individualism, though individual faith was important but an act of the

important in uniting people under the auspices of a particular saint or devotion much as members of a religious order might be united under St. Francis or St. Dominic. This communal bond continued long after one shuffled off this mortal coil as members of the confraternities took charge of funeral rites for deceased members and sought to aid their brother out of the fires of purgatory through their intercessions in the Mass.

This mentality of a Christian corpus began to deteriorate in the eighteenth century. Clergy and statesmen, particularly in Spain, imbued of Enlightenment thought, began to rethink the Tridentine emphasis on the immanency of the sacred and, consequently, its communal character as exercised in Baroque Christianity. As a result, a new variety of Catholicism would arise that would reexamine the rites and devotions that accompanied this faith, along with the exuberance for which it called. Enlightened Catholics, while adhering to Tridentine orthodoxy, would nonetheless call into question its Baroque interpretation and give a stronger emphasis on reason, history, and interior piety. The protagonists of this Enlightened Catholicism would also come to question the role of the papacy in the administration of the national churches in matters unrelated to doctrine. This new emphasis, springing from the multiplicity of Baroque Catholicism would affect not only the exercise of religion in Spain and the New World, but lead some in Mexico to call into question the very foundations of the Iberian colonial enterprise with lasting results.

---

communion of saints both living and dead. Through acts of charity unto others, through participation in the Mass and other devotions and through the prayers of the faithful and the intercession of the saints in glory the individual could achieve salvation.

5
The Catholic Enlightenment in New Spain

At the stroke of four on the twenty-fifth of June, a loud shout was heard at the door of the great college. When the porter asked through a little window who was there and what was wanted, he got the reply that he should open immediately, that on superior orders certain evildoers who were in the college were to be sought out . . . Amid much noise three hundred men entered the college with fixed bayonets and heavily-loaded muskets, each man being provided with twenty-five cartridges. They took control of the belfry and, for fear that the alarm would be rung, immediately cut the bell ropes. Two hundred men remained in the court and at the portal, the others occupied large halls and staircases of the extensive college . . . The Señor Visitor came to the room of the Father Rector with the command that he assemble all Jesuits without exception to hear a royal decree . . .

When we were all assembled they were ordered to surrender their keys, which was immediately done. Next, a briefly worded royal decree was read by a quivering and weeping secretary. "Because of weighty considerations which His Majesty keeps hidden in his heart, the entire Society of Jesus and all Jesuits must leave the country, and these establishments and properties must be turned over to the Royal Treasurer."

What manner of emotional manifestations now occurred can more easily be imagined than described. Some stood there quite dumbfounded and immobile; tears streamed from the eyes of others. Some lifted their hands and eyes passively to heaven while others sobbed. One became insane on the spot, and another had a fit of apoplexy. Most, however, stood there with well-controlled feelings and expressions.

—Joseph Och, SJ[1]

THE EXPULSION OF THE Jesuits from the Portuguese and Spanish territories in 1759 and 1767, respectively, along with their suppression by Pope Clement XIV in 1773, is a landmark in the history of the Church in Latin America. In a way, it represents an apogee in a tidal change in the way in which religion was apprehended by some and particularly in the relationships between the Church and the State and between faith and reason. Whereas the Enlightenment is often regarded as a product of French intellectuals like Voltaire and Rousseau that resulted in anti-religious feeling and outbursts such as those that accompanied the French Revolution, historians are coming to see that the Age of Reason encompassed a larger part of the European intelligentsia. A number of religious intellectuals, including clerics on Protestant and Catholic sides, perceived of the new thinking as tools by which they could greater accommodate the faith with reason and communicate it to their members, particularly in light of atheist attacks.[2] What is less well known is that the Enlightenment reverberated throughout Latin America.[3] The most obvious result would be seen in the Independence movements of the early nineteenth century whose leaders had imbibed of French, British, and North American (U.S.) Enlightenment thought. However, the Enlightenment in its decidedly Catholic incarnations would affect the Church and Christian thought as it touched on both religious and secular spheres long before Miguel Hidalgo, a priest whose own ideas and perspectives on the Church and political reform echoed the Catholic Enlightenment, climbed up the stairs of the bell tower in Dolores to proclaim Mexican Independence in 1810.

This chapter will explore the Catholic Enlightenment, particularly in Spain and Mexico. To begin with we will briefly describe the political

1. Reprinted in Penyak & Petry, *Religion in Latin America*, 113–14.

2. Cf. Ward, *Christianity Ancien-Régime*, 147–201, Aston, *Christianity and Revolutionary Europe*, 93; also see Sorkin, *Religious Enlightenment*.

3. And indeed in the United States as well. Not only did theologian Jonathan Edwards (d.1758) avail himself of Locke in forming his revivalist theology, but his heirs, the leaders of the Princeton School, used Thomas Reid and Scottish Common Sense Realism to defend Christian orthodoxy. Indeed it can be argued that evangelical epistemology, hermeneutics, and theology are derived from Common Sense Realism.

and religious setting of Spain in the eighteenth century with the rise of the Bourbon kings. The rise of the Jansenist movement, born of doctrinal and pious concerns but eventually upsetting the foundations of Church/State relations will be described. Having established a foundation and context we will explore the two streams of the Enlightenment in Spain—the relationship between the Church and the Crown and the perception of religion among some of the leaders of religion and society, focusing upon the reign of Charles III, perhaps the ablest of Spain's kings in this period. The movement itself was highly complex and religious and political concerns are often difficult to detach from one another. Eventually we will make our way to New Spain to see how the Catholic Enlightenment, in those religious and secular concerns, was expressed in the New World. Further, we will note how the Enlightenment was transmuted in New Spain, particularly in the growth of Mexican nationalism. To do so we will focus on the controversial Dominican friar Servando Teresa de Mier (d.1827) who straddles the era between the colony and the early Mexican republic and whose concerns would touch both religious and temporal affairs.

EPISTEMOLOGY OF THE CATHOLIC ENLIGHTENMENT

As mentioned above, the Catholic Enlightenment of the eighteenth century was both a continuation and a break from Barqoue Catholicism. The latter, teeming with variety through its multiple ways of apprehending the divine, provided the fertile ground through which a new expression of orthodox Catholicism could emerge that in turn would criticize and rebel against the baroque.

The Catholic Enlightenment differed from the baroque in its fundamental assumptions about the nature of the world, the individual, and their relationship with God.

	BAROQUE CATHOLICISM	CATHOLIC ENLIGHTENMENT
Adherents	The general public; the masses	A literate minority
Sources of knowledge/ authority	Tradition, the miraculous, emotion/experience/ mysticism	The Bible, early Church, reason

	BAROQUE CATHOLICISM	CATHOLIC ENLIGHTENMENT
God as...	Immanent; manifest in physical world throgh relics, liturgy, holy people, etc.	Known in inward piety of prayer and the Bible; through the Eucharist
Piety	Externally manifest in ritual, processions, the miraculous; holy people, places, and things	Internal relationship with God manifest in works of charity
Communal/ Individual	Communal: processions, confraternities, the body politic and the body spiritual	Individual emphasis on one's own apprehension of God
Social structure	Reinforced social hierarchies	Emphasized equality of all people before God

TABLE 2: Baroque Catholicism and the Catholic Enlightenment

- Whereas the baroque characterized the faith expression of the general public during most of the colonial era, the Catholic Enlightenment—in Spain and the Americas—was spearheaded by a literate and powerful minority. This movement was led by rulers, bishops, theologians, and clerics who supported changes in the religious topography, a reform of education and religious practice that sought to rid the Church of "superstition" and encourage literacy and interior piety.

- The supporters of this reform re-aligned the sources of authority for matters of faith and practice. They emphasized the Bible, the writings of the early Church, and the use of reason over and against contemporary claims of the miraculous and against the baroque emphasis upon emotional experience.

- Whereas the baroque posited a God who was as immediate as a holy relic or saintly person—the divine made palpable through the material world, the Catholic Enlightenment held to a God known primarily through the Bible and through the Mass (the one true and consistent miracle promised by the words of Christ). The experience of the divine was therefore not external to an individual—in the next church, the next town, or the next miracle—but was accessible to the human heart through the Scripture, the Eucharist, and the works of charity that such piety inspired.

- Through art, music, elaborate liturgies, and public spectacle the baroque sought to move emotion towards the pursuit of God. Endeavoring to show the Catholic faith superior to Protestant heterodoxy, Tridentine Catholicism encouraged the staging of elaborate ritual to dazzle the spectator into faith. The Catholic Enlightenment took a different route. Seeking to encourage interior piety based on Scripture and reason, individuals were encouraged to demonstrate their piety through good works and charity towards the poor rather than spend money on candles, vestments, and other physical trappings of ritual.

- The adherents of the Catholic Enlightenment emphasized the light and grace of God as it transformed the individual's heart. This is in stark contrast with the baroque that emphasized the communion of saints (both the heavenly and earthly ones) through public, religious celebrations and confraternities that celebrated and maintained the religious and political community.

- In the baroque, these traditions maintained the hierarchical status quo. The present social structure was reinforced whether in processionals celebrating a community's patron saint or the burial of the dead in proximity to the church's altar. Alternately, if God dispenses his grace feely upon the human soul through the Mass, through charity and the Bible, then wealth and class have no bearing upon one's relationship to God. The advocates of the Catholic Enlightenment emphasized this equality before God even while maintaining the social structure of the body politic.

The growth and promotion of the Catholic Enlightenment in Spain and its colonies did not take place in a vacuum but rather, grew partially out of the concerns of the Crown vis-à-vis its relationship to Rome and its efforts to consolidate power around the king during the Bourbon era. The effects of French Jansenism in this effort cannot be discounted even as matters of theology, politics and polity took center stage in the effort to reform the Church in the interests of the Crown.

EIGHTEENTH-CENTURY SPAIN

Charles II (d. 1700) would reign as the last of the Hapsburgs in Spain. The result of generations of inbreeding, this monarch, known as *El Hechizado* (the Hexed) and seemingly always on the verge of death, baffled observers by reigning for thirty-five years. By this time, the European powers, led by France, sought to carve out Spain's extensive territories for themselves.

French designs were aided when Charles, unable to father a child, left the Spanish throne upon his death to Philip, the grandson of Louis XIV of France, with the stipulation that the empire remain intact. Castile accepted Philip, Duke of Anjou, but Aragon feared he would rule as despotically as the French king so they joined with Austria, Great Britain, and the Netherlands (and later Portugal) to deny him his throne. With the end of the War of Spanish Succession in 1713/1714, Spain lost some of its European holdings but kept the American empire intact.[4] By this time, many in Spain, particularly among the young intellectuals, welcomed the change in power, most notably because it meant a stronger connection with the rest of Europe, and with that, a link to the philosophical and scientific advances France, Germany, and Great Britain were undertaking.[5]

Philip V (d.1746) would consolidate government in Spain under the crown as it never had before. He abolished the *fueros* (charters) of the eastern kingdoms like Aragon that allowed them to resist Castilian rule. He was successful in bringing the Spanish kingdoms under the Castilian crown, abolishing the semi-independent regional councils, placing their viceroys (now captains-general) under his control and enforcing the use of Castilian in all levels of government. Additionally, Philip reformed the government of Castile itself, placing secretaries to act as executive officers in charge of the various departments of state to streamline the affairs of the cumbersome Council of Castile, the Council of State and Council of the Indies, which had previously handled affairs of the court, the state, and empire, respectively. Throughout the eighteenth century the secretaries, representing the king, would take on more responsibilities, leaving most of the councils as little more than high courts. Spanish

---

4. Carr, *Spain*, 170–71, 173–74.
5. Ibid., 142.

government, in this way, became more centralized and consequently, the king became more powerful.[6]

Along with the Crown the most powerful institution in Spain remained the Church. "Church and monarchy were different aspects of absolute power applied to the religious and secular worlds."[7] During the War of Spanish Succession it proved itself an able ally of the Crown by stirring up the people against the British. The king, showed his gratitude by placing large territories under the jurisdiction of the bishops and monasteries. As the collector of the tithe, the Church was also an integral part of the king's income as two-ninths of it went to the royal coffers as did the full tithes of the richest farmer in each parish.[8] The Church, as W. R. Ward ably describes, was an urban phenomenon. Towns and cities attracted disproportionate numbers of clergy who found it easier to climb the ecclesiastical ladder there than in the rural areas where they were underrepresented. Religious orders also tended to flock to the urban centers as they could acquire property and money with which to fund their missions. Further, as one of the two largest landowners and the collector of the tithe, the Church contributed to the poverty of the countryside. They rented lands to farmers and others but that money, along with the tithe, was generally invested in the cities and towns despite any efforts of the bishops towards social reform.[9]

It was under the reign of Fernando VI (d.1759) that the concordat of 1753 was reached with the pope, giving the Spanish monarch the right of universal patronage over the whole of the Spanish Empire, including Spain. Additionally, it declared ecclesiastical properties to be taxable. Under Charles III (d.1808) the king's power over the Church increased as he reserved the right to grant royal approval before any papal bulls could be published in the realm.[10] The Bourbon kings were abetted by a series of weak popes who reigned for the latter half of the eighteenth century.[11] Charles III, however, would use the power of royal patronage

---

6. Ibid., 176–77.
7. Callahan, *Church, Politics*, 3.
8. Carr, *Spain*, 178.
9. Ward, *Christianity Ancien-Régime*, 35.
10. Carr, *Spain*, 178.
11. Callaghan, *Church, Politics*, 3.

to build up a body of royalist clerics loyal to his vision of the reform of Church and State.¹²

JANSENISM

Though not as well known as the *philosophés* of the Enlightenment or the struggles of the Jesuits in Europe and abroad, the Jansenist movement is integral to the understanding of the history of the Catholic Enlightenment, including to that of the New World. The movement was, in a very real sense, the link that brought together royalist aspirations with Church reform and so it concerns us to devote some attention to them as their own emphases will be instrumental in both the relationship between the Crown and the Church as well as the spiritual redirection of the Church even long after their own power had waned.

As a religious sect, Jansenism is derived from the writings of Cornelius Otto Jansen (1585–1638), particularly his posthumously published writing *Augustinus* (1640). As can be inferred from the title, Jansen's work sought to make Saint Augustine's theology, particularly his anti-Pelagian writings, normative for faith and piety. Jansenism was, in part, a reaction to forms of Catholic scholasticism and thus runs parallel to contemporary movements within seventeenth-century Protestantism, namely continental Pietism and English Puritanism, which also reacted to what they perceived as religious ossification within their particular traditions. Jansen and his followers emphasized the priority of an irresistible grace from God, without which obedience to God was impossible. Since this grace was irresistible, the fate of human beings was determined by God's will in predestination.¹³ The corollaries to such ideas were obvious even to Jansenism's detractors: human endeavor towards the good was useless without the work of grace and further, if the grace of God was an interior work, the ceremonies, relics, processions, and other outwards means of directing the individual to God—so emphasized at the Council of Trent and in the growth of the Baroque—were all but useless as means of grace. Whereas the Church, its hierarchy and sacraments could nurture the soul, what truly mattered was the pious disposition of the person active in love which was an individual matter, not one mediated by the

---

12. Ward, *Christianity Ancien-Régime*, 37.
13. Cross and Livingston, "Jansen, Cornelius Otto" and Cross and Livingstone, "Jansenism," 862.

saints.[14] Jansensists saw themselves as a part of the reforms set forth by the Council of Trent and sought to revitalize the individual and the institutions of the Church such as the priesthood and monasticism. In short, Jansenism emerged as another link in the Christian discussion regarding sin and redemption, freedom and grace.[15]

Contemporary critics noted Jansenism's affinity with Protestantism in regards to sin, salvation, and grace. Like the Jansenists, the reformers Martin Luther (1483–1546) and John Calvin (1509–64) relied heavily on Augustine to put forth their respective theologies of human nature and God's grace. For Luther, Calvin, and their respective followers, human nature was severely damaged in the Fall. Affected by sin, human beings are unable to pursue the Good, to fulfill God's righteous requirements for salvation. The notion of free will was a sham, curable only through external intervention, namely God's grace that applied the righteousness or the benefits of Jesus Christ's life, death, and resurrection to the individual through Word and Sacrament.

Because Protestantism adhered closely to the ideas of Augustine on sin and grace, the Society of Jesus, seeking to counter Protestant theology, minimized the effects of humanity's sinfulness as a result of Adam's fall. The Jesuits, following Luis de Molina (1535–1600) asserted that humanity lost God's supernatural gifts in the Fall but that its capacity to choose good or evil—the individual's free will—remained intact. Instead of predestined, efficacious grace proclaimed by the Protestants, the Jesuits put forth the idea of a sufficient grace that came as a result of God's foreknowledge of the individual's virtuous choices.[16] Thus whereas this area of Jesuit theology arose in reaction to Protestantism, Jansenism came about in reaction to the dominant interpretation of the Council of Trent that to them, smacked of a "devout humanism." For the Jansenists this not only exalted human ability and nature, echoing the beliefs of the Renaissance, but it also watered down the rigorous moral demands of the Gospel. To them, a human nature that is not morally corrupt vis-à-vis God does not need a radical conversion. Molina's thought became more popular once Jansen's *Augustinus* was published and the followers of Jansen, influential

14. Cf. Voekel, *Alone before God*, 44–62.
15. Sedgwick, *Jansenism*, 194–95; Cf. Saranyana, *Teología*, 2/1: 31–34, 189–94.
16. Ibid., 48–49.

in the Netherlands and parts of France (especially in the abbey of Port-Royal), and the Jesuits, were to be locked in mortal battle.[17]

In 1653, in a move that was orchestrated in part by political interests and in part by religious ones, Pope Innocent X condemned several of the theological propositions put forth by some of the Jansenists, who by now had made inroads among some of the French aristocracy and bishops.[18] By 1656 the Jansenists, increasingly forced to recant their beliefs, were in danger of persecution. Unable to convince the theologians of the Sorbonne that their position was orthodox, they appealed to the public through the writings of the scientist Blaise Pascal (1623–62), a recent convert.[19]

Pascal and his allies counterattacked in a way that would point an accusatory finger at someone other than the Jansenists. They incited public horror by accusing the Jesuits of undermining the ethical demands of the gospel through probabilism, the practice that in ethical dilemmas one should follow what is probably right.[20] The Jesuits were already under public suspicion for supposedly condoning theft and murder for the greater good and it was during this time that the Chinese Rites controversy over how to best adapt the Christian message and liturgy to the Chinese missionary enterprise had just begun. To many this latter move had smacked of compromising with paganism.[21] By this point, Jansenism had gained some sympathizers from among the lower, secular clergy who resented the power of the Jesuits and questioned their ethics. They appre-

17. Van Kley, *Jansenists*, 7–8. Whereas Jansenism might share similar traits with Protestant, especially Calvinist thought, it differs in important respects. Jansenism did not hold to a notion of justification by faith but rather, that human beings are saved by the good works that divine grace enabled them to perform ("charity"). Jansenism, having no notion of secular vocation as did Protestantism, tended towards ascetic retreat from the pleasures of the world. Cf. Sedgwick, *Jansenism*, 196, 201. Another point in common that Jansenists had with the Protestants was their devotion to patristic studies. The Council of Trent sought to legitimize and reform the medieval worship practices that Protestants attacked and against which they appealed to the Church Fathers. Jansenists, maintaining the right and responsibility of the laity to educate themselves in spiritual matters advocated the study of church history and the translation of the Fathers into the vernacular. Sedgwick, *Jansenism*, 162; For more on the beginnings of Jansenism in France see Sedgwick, *Jansenism*, 14–46.

18. Van Kley, *Jansenists*, 12–13, Sedgwick, *Jansenism*, 68ff.

19. On the debate within the Sorbonne see Sedgwick, 110–11.

20. Saranyana, *Teología*, 2/1: 194–97.

21. Ibid., 16; For more on the Chinese Rites Controversy see Charbonnier, *Christians in China*, 246–70.

ciated the Jansenists' exaltation of the priesthood and their insistence on a greater role for the lower clergy in governing the Church.[22] However successful Pascal's ploy may have been, Van Kley notes that it also compromised the Jansenist message. However separated from the world they may have desired to remain, by stirring up the public and creating an enemy the Jansenists inexorably entered the public sphere and created allies who had to be mollified if they were to keep the anti-Jesuit momentum going.[23] As a result, Jansenism became a movement far larger than the spiritual and doctrinal reform movement originally intended. By the eighteenth century it would become synonymous with opposition to the Jesuits and along with that, to papal absolutism in the Church.[24]

The Jansenists won another victory when they convinced a number of bishops and a member of the French parliament that to allow a papal commission to move against the Jansenists would infringe upon the traditional rights of the Gallican Church. Gallicanism, which dates back to the fourteenth century, asserted that the French Church had the right to govern itself according to its own traditions, that papal bulls and briefs could only be disseminated with the unanimous consent of the episcopacy and that in secular matters, the king of France was subject to none but God.[25] Godefroi Hermant, a Jansenist professor of theology at the University of Paris, wrote:

> The most ardent of these flatterers of the Roman court have had the temerity to maintain in public that the bishops are only vicars and the viceroys of the Holy Father, owing to him alone all their power and jurisdiction. They even dared preach that there is only one vicar of Jesus Christ, the successor of Saint Peter, the visible head of the entire Church. He alone has the power to decide and enunciate matters pertaining to faith, and everything that he ordains must be received by all the faithful with complete submission as proceeding from an infallible authority. The Church of France, on the other hand, has always professed another doctrine. She

---

22. Sedgwick, *Jansenism*, 205.

23. Van Kley, *Jansenists*, 17.

24. Ibid., 18. These differences would further highlight the question of papal authority. Some would contend that the pope was infallible in matters of dogma but not necessarily in matters of fact. This came to the fore during the period when Jansenists were forced to recant their views and many affirmed the pope's dogmatic rejection of certain Jansenist tenets but would not concede that he had all his facts in order.

25. Ibid., 22.

has maintained that the bishops' office has no other founder than our Lord Jesus Christ and is not the work of men. Their authority comes from none other than God, who has given them the power to govern their churches and to watch over their flocks as His immediate vicars and apostolic successors. Until recently, it has always been upheld in the Gallican Church that, by virtue of this power, the bishops have the right to judge in all matters concerning the faith and the safety of their flock, and because of this right, they may assemble together when they deem it necessary for the good of their churches, in order to administer to their needs.[26]

Gallicanism's opposite, Ultramontanism ("beyond the mountains," as in the Alps, towards Rome) saw the rule of the Church as firmly in the hands of the pope. Some of its primary defenders were the Society of Jesus who owed their obedience to the See of Peter.

Pope Alexander VII, along with King Louis XIV, reaffirmed the condemnation of *Augustinus* in 1665. The death-knell for Jansenism was sounded with the papal bull *Unigenitus* in 1713. The abbey of Port-Royal had already been dissolved by the pope in 1708 and its nuns evicted.[27] In 1715 three theological faculties refused to accept *Unigenitus* without some modification and in 1717 several bishops, along with priests, nuns, and the parliament called for a general council to address the issue. Clement XI issued a bull excommunicating all who had called for the council, but the French continued to appeal to one. A short schism on the matter of the papal bull in the French Church resulted between those supporting Rome (constitutionaries) and those who did not (appellants) and it was not resolved until 1728.[28]

Though banned from the Church, Jansenism's influence would continue to be felt.[29] For one, though originally other-worldly, Jansenism became almost synonymous with Gallicanism as a result of their allies in parliament and the Church. This emphasis on a national church pre-

---

26. Quoted in Sedgwick, *Jansenism*, 157.

27. Hsia, *World Catholic Renewal*, 207.

28. Ibid., 22–26; Ward, *Christianity Ancien-Régime*, 30.

29. Some Jansenists fled to the Netherlands during persecution where it was tolerated and even accepted by some within the Catholic Church. In 1723 the Dutch Jansenists in Utrecht, acting independently of Rome, elected for themselves a schismatic bishop whose own consecration, though apostolic, was done irregularly. This began the formation of the Old Catholic Church in the Netherlands, Cross and Livingstone, "Jansenism" and "Old Catholic Church," 862, 1179.

serving its own rights over and against the centrality of the pope would be felt far beyond the French Church, as would their opposition to the Jesuits.[30] Secondly, though the tenets of Jansenism were condemned, the spiritual reverberations of the movement would become an integral part of the Catholic Enlightenment through their emphasis on an individual's conversion and a rejection of Baroque ostentation.

THE BOURBON REFORMS AND THE CATHOLIC ENLIGHTENMENT IN SPAIN

Throughout the seventeenth and eighteenth centuries, the Enlightenment made an indelible mark throughout Western Europe. The rule of law, religious toleration, freedom of the press, and governmental reforms had accompanied the new learning as did the emerging scientific theories and methodologies of people like Francis Bacon and Sir Isaac Newton.[31] The various Christian confessions had also been affected. Change came easier for Protestants who did not have the entrenched hierarchy of the Catholic Church and whose own Reformation traditions had emerged out of critical inquiry and humanist scholarship. In some regions, particularly in Revolutionary France, the Church and its doctrines were on the defensive from deists and anticlerical detractors.[32]

The Enlightenment, however, through its philosophical and scientific inquiries forced Christians to re-evaluate their message and the manner in which it had been traditionally articulated, particularly in the latter half of the seventeenth century. Clerics reassessed ecclesiastical practices and beliefs in light of the criticism coming from other parts of society. However, it would be a mistake to see Christianity's relationship with the Enlightenment as solely one of animosity or defensiveness. According to Nigel Aston, the Catholic Enlightenment can be seen as a continuation of the reforms begun by the Council of Trent in the sixteenth century—the ongoing education of the clergy as well as the abolition of practices and beliefs deemed superstitious that had no grounding in history or dogma—such as the veneration of certain saints deemed more myth than history. This was more of an elite and urban movement—appealing to the literate and educated who sought to reform the faith of the lay majority.[33]

30. Aston, *Christianity and Revolutionary*, 128–29.
31. Aston, *Christianity and Revolutionary*, 93.
32. Ibid., 94–111.
33. Ibid., 112.

As noted, with the accession of the Bourbon kings, Spain began to emerge from her isolation and come into greater contact with the rest of Europe, particularly in terms of science and philosophy. In previous decades, Spain had resisted reform due to an entrenched religious and aristocratic machinery for whom change threatened their vested interests and who, to maintain the status quo, exploited the financial weakness of the monarchy.[34] The Bourbons, following the example of their kin in France, sought to reverse that and put all institutions, including the Church, in the service of the Crown. To that end, Philip V and Fernando VI sought to streamline government and make it more answerable to the king through the use of ministers who represented the monarch at assorted councils.

For many, Europe became a point of contact for Enlightenment learning—for medicine, industry, technology, science, and art.[35] Greater trade between Spain and the rest of the continent meant greater interaction between peoples. Political and philosophical ideas made their way into the country, even if most of it was accessible to only a small minority of educated persons. At the same time, adherents of the Enlightenment would look to Spain's past and sought to revive the Golden Age associated with Philip II and writers such as Teresa of Ávila and Fray Luis de León.[36]

The Enlightenment in Spain took on various expressions. Benito Jerónimo Feijóo, (1674–1764) a Benedictine professor at Oviedo, described foreign scientific advances in a manner that resonated with the literate public. Noting that scientific curiosity was not incompatible with religious concerns, we point out that Feijóo, in his writings, also sought to root out superstitious practices and devotions. Gerónimo de Uztáriz and others sought the reform of industry in Philip V's court in a manner reminiscent of French mercantilist thought. Additionally, botanical research excelled in Spain partly because of Spain's vast American colonies and partly because of Fernando VI's famed botanical garden.

Since the Enlightenment was a movement of the educated elite who sought to disseminate knowledge and ideas and to uproot superstition and error, the most common means to do so was the printed word.

---

34. Elliott, *Spanish World*, 54.

35. For a more in depth study of the role of the Enlightenment in various areas see Alberola, and La Parra, *Ilustración Española*.

36. Estévez, *España de la Ilustración*, 86–87.

"The most adequate means by which the new 'ideology' was universalized was not the spoken word, the pulpit—a clerical monopoly and for illiterate societies—but the written word, the book, the newspaper. Therefore, books and the press are signs, realities and vehicles of relay 'from more secularized mentalities to sacralized ones.'"[37] By the middle of the century, European works translated into Castilian began to appear. Books banned by the Inquisition, such as those of Voltaire and others, were smuggled into the country.[38] Meanwhile, since 1762 Charles II began to limit the censoring of materials by the Inquisition.[39] Because the Inquisition's machinery was inconsistent and slipshod, Jansenist, Gallican, and other suspicious books circulated freely since the 1770s.[40] Meanwhile, to reach the illiterate, other means were used including sermons, theater, and public discourse.[41]

As Enlightened Monarchs, the Bourbon kings sought to create a Church that was both independent of Roman influence and submitted to the needs and desires of the Crown in temporal matters such as church finances. As a result, the Catholic Church, which remained undisputed in matters of faith and morals, saw itself using its resources more and more in support of the Crown, particularly over and against the papacy.

This effort began early on during the War of Spanish Succession when Pope Clement XI, pressured by the Holy Roman Emperor, shifted allegiances from Philip to Charles, the Hapsburg contender. Spain, in effect, had two kings and two papal nuncios. Philip blasted the pope in a document circulated among church officials whereby he accused the pope of being an Austrian puppet. Clement condemned the text, whereupon Philip expelled the papal nuncio. Tensions continued between Rome and Madrid, leading some regalists to move even further in affirming the right of the Crown to appoint bishops and to push more towards a universal patronage. In short, Madrid was taking on the Spanish version of Gallicanism.[42]

The War of Spanish Succession saw Spain's imperial power and territories greatly diminished in Europe. Philip V sought to reverse this

---

37. Estévez, *España de la Ilustración*, 100.
38. Ibid.; Carr, *Spain*, 180.
39. Martínez y Gómez, *Siglo de las Luces*, 117.
40. Bradley and Van Kley, *Religion and Politics*, 142–45.
41. Estévez, *España de la Ilustración*, 100–105, 112.
42. Martínez y Gómez, *Siglo de las Luces*, 237–38.

entropy by regaining its Italian holdings and by invading Scotland in 1719. It is in this context that the king sought greater control over the Church. The Crown already had considerable power through the *patronato*, but Philip wanted jurisdiction over all ecclesiastical institutions including the Inquisition. He continued a regalist policy, seeking a universal patronage (2/3 remained in the hands of the pope at this time) as well as the income generated through vacant sees. He also maintained that, since the King held jurisdiction over all institutions in the realm, the pope did not have the authority to collect tributes in Spain nor could clergy appeal to Rome except through the Crown. The pope, despite agreeing with the king that the Spanish Church was in need of reform, came into conflict with the monarch regarding his regalist notions.[43]

In 1737, the Spanish monarch and the pope signed a concordat whereby the king would have the right to collect fees on vacant sees and that, among other matters, the Church would hereafter not be exempt from taxation.[44] The matter of universal patronage remained unresolved despite the king's strong desires otherwise.[45]

These regalist policies were continued under Fernando VI who, in 1753, finally obtained the right of universal patronage from Benedict XIV. The discussions between the Spanish and papal officials had been conducted in secret, and in the end an accord was reached in exchange for two and a half million pesos in money and gifts to many curates, a cardinal and the pope himself.[46] This concordat is a landmark in Spanish history as it gave to the monarch virtual control over the entire Catholic Church (save for fifty-two offices that the pope reserved for himself). Commenting on the importance of this decision for regalist policies Martínez and Gómez quote, "The king wore the (papal) tiara and his ministers officiated as bishops."[47]

Though the patronage question had been settled, events in Spain continued to move the nation in a regalist direction. In 1754 Fernando VI's pro-Jesuit chief minister, the Marques of la Ensenada, fell from power. A year later his ally, the Jesuit Francisco Rávago was removed.

43. Estévez, *España de la Ilustración*, 72–73.

44. Ibid., 73.

45. Martínez y Gómez, *Siglo de las Luces*, 239.

46. Estévez, *España de la Ilustración*, 74; Martínez y Gómez, *Siglo de las Luces*, 250–51.

47. Martínez y Gómez, *Siglo de las Luces*, 252.

This latter, confessor to the king, had used his office to influence policy in a pro-Jesuit direction and dominate the Inquisition. With the removal of these two men policy continued to move against the Society of Jesus and in favor of Jansenist elements in government. Within a few years, Fernando VI was dead, and his successor, Charles III, who was suspicious of Jesuit power, would prove disastrous for the order.[48]

Charles III's reign is pivotal in the history of Church/State relations in Spain and to the implementation of Catholic reform. Lauded as the best of the Bourbon kings, he was personally pious, belonging to a number of religious associations including the Franciscan Third Order.[49] He attended Mass daily and took Communion during major festivals and even alighted from his carriage to allow a priest carrying the Eucharist to ride it down Madrid's streets as he ran alongside it.[50] However, his piety, and consequently the piety he sought to promote in Spain was not that of Baroque extravaganza, of ostentatious processions or grandiose public displays of collective faith.[51] He hoped to reform the Church from abuses and devotions he perceived as superstitious as well as improving the educational quality of the clergy to serve the people better pastorally.[52] Thus Charles and his ministers would continue to use the Church for their own ends, not only towards advancing the policies of the State in its reform efforts but also for the perceived spiritual wellbeing of the people.

Because of this, Charles sought to reform the Church from the top-down. Bishops consisted of an educated elite, who though diligent (for the most part), in their duties to support their congregations and help the poor, nonetheless were drawn from a small group of secular clergy with access to wealth and education. In contrast, the vast majority of parish priests received only a rudimentary education, less so if they attended a seminary instead of a university, and had little hope for advancement.[53]

To improve this situation Charles sought to reform the seminaries and place them under state control rather than under the authority of the cathedral-chapter whose canon often saw seminarians as sources of

---

48. Bradley and Van Kley, *Religion and Politics*, 120–21.

49. Callahan, *Church, Politics*, 10; Gilabert, *Carlos III*, 18ff.

50. Gilabert, *Carlos III*, 19.

51. For a portrait of the Spanish Church in this century see Callahan, *Church, Politics*, 52–67.

52. Callahan, *Church, Politics*, 5.

53. Ibid., 10–15.

cheap labor to assist with the logistical demands of the liturgy and church upkeep. The Crown also sought to implement a series of competitive exams, much like civil service exams, to find the best qualified priests for vacant parishes and to weed out unsuitable candidates. These, like the seminary reform project, varied in success from diocese to diocese though one can't help but see that the line between Church and State continued to blur.[54]

The reform of the religious orders, which the king viewed with greater suspicion, was attempted. Like the secular priesthood, the monastic orders were dominated by a small elite of educated men. Unlike the seculars, however, their members did little within the greater society, given that the traditional task of the monastics was to pray and worship. The Crown complained that they, as well as the mendicants, ignored works of piety and charity, but in the end, despite efforts to reduce the number of religious and redirect their energies outward in support of the State's reforms, little change occurred.[55]

As noted above, Charles III had no place for the Society of Jesus in his vision of the Spanish Church. Imbued with strong regal-centric notions, he had little patience for this powerful order that vowed obedience to the pope. Callahan lists several objections to the order in the years leading to their expulsion and suppression:

- the Jesuit's overseas power and influence, especially in the case of the Guaraní missions (which to many seemed like an effort to establish a republic free of royal control)
- their opposition to the canonization of an anti-Jesuit Mexican bishop
- their sympathy towards the return of Ensenada, the former chief minister
- the Society's refusal to pay the full ecclesiastical tax on the produce of their estates in the colonies
- their suspected opposition to the king's policies and his ministers.[56]

Callahan explains that many among Charles' ministers and in the church hierarchy suspected the order of having too much political influence.

54. Ibid., 17–19.
55. Ibid., 21–27.
56. Ibid., 29, Gilabert, *Carlos III*, 80–84; Brading, *Church and State*, 12.

Additionally, the Jesuits held a near monopoly in education and taught a classical curriculum among the noble elite that was supposedly better suited to their class. This was out of step with Charles' efforts to improve the secondary and university education towards mathematics, the natural sciences and economy and politics.[57] Further, the specter of probalism in moral theology still haunted the Jesuits since the days of the Jansenists. Charles and the hierarchy of the Church, who desired to improve the morals of the people and rid the Church of baroque excesses in religious devotion, saw the Jesuits as an impediment to their efforts.[58]

The riots in Madrid in March 1766 against the reforming minister, the Marqués de Esquilache, who was trying to promulgate a degree forbidding the wearing of long capes and broad hats, provided the convenient reason for the formal persecution of the order.[59] They had already been expelled from Portugal in 1759 and from France in 1762.[60] Despite a lack of evidence, the Jesuits were accused of having fomented the Riot of Esquilache with the goal of overthrowing or assassinating the king.[61] The members of the Society of Jesus were expelled from Spain and her colonies in 1767, and with them went the only force able to present any ideological resistance to the king's reforms.[62]

An integral part of the reforms of the Catholic Enlightenment that was present among some of the hierarchy as well as among the laity was Jansenism. This was a form of Jansenism that had been shorn of its Augustinian theology and instead was dedicated towards a regalist and episcopal type of Church governance and a reform of Catholic piety. These Spanish Jansenists (or "Philojansenists" as some historians refer to them) find their foundation in the Erasmian tradition of the sixteenth century with its emphasis on the interior, moral life and Bible reading as well as an aversion to scholasticism and religious formalism. Upon

57. Martínez y Gómez, *Siglo de las Luces*, 117, Gilabert, *Carlos III*, 82–84.

58. Callahan, *Church, Politics*, 30, Brading, *Church and State*, 11–12, Estévez, 75–76; on anti-Jesuit feeling elsewhere in Europe see Aston, *Christianity and Revolutionary*, 128–29.

59. Gilabert, *Carlos III*, 93–103, Brading, *Church and State*, 9ff; though brought about by this decree regulating fashion the crowds were already exasperated by a bad harvest and rising prices.

60. Estévez, *España de la Ilustración*, 76.

61. Gilabert, *Carlos III*, 103–7.

62. Estévez, *España de la Ilustración*, 76; Gilabert, *Carlos III*, 113–17; pressure from the Bourbon kings in Spain and across Europe upon the pope resulted in the suppression of the order in 1773.

this base were added certain episcopal and regalist influences including but not limited to the Gallican inclinations in traditional Jansenism with their suspicion of the papacy as well as impulses (ironically some of them Jesuit) that respected the new sciences and intellectual vigor.[63] The works of the regalist Belgian jurist Zeger van Espen and others are quoted by some of the Spanish Jansenist clerics. Martínez and Gómez sum up their characteristics: "The Spanish reformers can be described as: Thomist and Augustinian in doctrinal matters; rigorous in moral matters; close to regalism in the political; opposed to baroque manifestations of religiosity; episcopalian and anti-jesuit."[64]

By mid-century Spanish Jansenism was a multifaceted phenomenon —protean, reflecting the interests of those who formed and advocated for it. Politicians could focus on its regalist tendencies while churchmen could favor its episcopalism; priests and laypeople would emphasize its moral vigor and intellectuals its advocacy for enlightened ideas. As a result of so many faces it could be contradictory—gentle and pastoral but also fiercely political and morally strict.[65] This diversity, however, it attracted many, laypeople as well as clerics, to the movement. Among them were very influential political and intellectual figures. In the 1760s Jansenist clergy began to be promoted into the church hierarchy to promote reform (regalist and spiritual) and to oppose Jesuit and ultramontane forces.[66] "Those pressing for reform formed a minority of the clerical elite, but their education, intellectual gifts and religious commitment produced a vital ecclesiastical culture that the Spanish Church would never know again."[67]

Despite its varied and often incongruous threads, Spanish Jansenists could agree on their opposition to papal interference in the State and papal domination of the Church as well as a need to reform the Body of Christ.[68] To weaken papal authority they deemed it necessary to strengthen relations between the Crown and the Miter and, consequently, to strengthen the authority of the bishops against papal intrusion. They opposed the Jesuits and others whom they perceived as too morally

63. Martínez y Gómez, *Siglo de las Luces*, 118–19, Callahan, *Church, Politics*, 68.
64. Ibid., 118, Bradley & Van Kley, *Religion and Politics*, 125.
65. Bradley and Van Kley, *Religion and Politics*, 126.
66. Ibid., 127.
67. Callahan, *Church, Politics*, 69.
68. Cf. Appolis, *Les Jansénistes*, 1.

lax (probabilism once more) and too loyal to the Roman pope. When it came to the positive revitalization of the Church, the solution would be pastoral.[69] They sought to raise the educational standards of the parish priests in hopes that his education and example would help do away with baroque ostentation and the external props that that worldview imposed upon the faith, fostering superstition and immorality such as the veneration of relics and drunken processions. They instead aimed for a renewal of the individual's heart through Scripture, prayer, and contemplation of the Eucharist (Christ's tangible presence among His people). The renewed heart ought to be moved towards works of charity and service towards others, especially the poor, instead of focusing on outward rituals or spending money on candles, scapularies or images.[70]

The means to renewal and reform were varied. As stated, the key to this would be the parish priest, who had access to the people. If the people were to be reformed then the priests must be made partners in that effort.[71] The Jansenist hierarchy, along with the king, sought to improve the educational quality of the seminaries, so that priests would know more than just a rote recitation of the Latin Mass. Periodic spiritual conferences were encouraged as was an effort to make preaching simpler and more accessible to the people.[72] Popular devotions were either banned, such as the case with public flagellation and indecent songs in processionals, or brought under scrutiny as the case with the Jesuit-backed devotion to the Sacred Heart of Jesus. In short, they sought to remove anything that they thought impeded the individual from the central act of worship, the Mass.[73] In step with the Jansenist emphasis on Bible reading the Inquisition (which had already experienced reform-minded Inquisitor-Generals under Charles III) in 1783 lifted the ban on vernacular translations, thus opening the door to the first Catholic translation of the Bible into Castilian, published in the late 1790s.[74] This act, in the words of Pamela Voekel, "ultimately helped crack the clerical

69. Callahan, *Church, Politics*, 68–69.
70. Bradley and Van Kley, *Religion and Politics*, 127.
71. Ibid., 130.
72. Gilabert, *Carlos III*, 61.
73. Ibid., 62.
74. Callahan, *Church, Politics*, 69–70; Some readers will remember that the first translation of the complete Bible into Castilian was that done by the Protestant Casiodoro de Reina in 1569 two hundred and fifty years prior; for more on the reform of the Inquisition see Gilabert, *Carlos III*, 39–43, Bradley & Van Kley, *Religion and Politics*, 142–45.

monopoly on religious interpretation, opening the way to individual evaluation of dogma."[75]

The reform-minded goals of the Jansenist clergy and intellectuals dovetailed nicely with the aims of the monarchy, thus facilitating the close alliance between Church and State.[76] Charles III's desires to improve the education and morality of the clergy, his efforts to limit or eliminate papal intervention and even the expulsion of the Jesuits, were welcomed by the reformist churchmen.[77] In short, as Callahan notes, the Jansenist clergy knew that only the king had the power both to limit the reach of the pope and legislate against stubborn religious customs.[78]

In general, the initiative to reform the Catholic Church did not achieve the results desired by either king or clergy. Callahan notes that even the emergence of a reforming elite depended upon the imbalanced structure of the Church itself. Despite efforts to improve the education of the parish clergy, there was no overall restructuring of the Church that would have redistributed money and personnel to those areas that needed them the most. The powerful and intellectual minority of reformers may have held back the weaknesses of the Church during Charles' reign, but with his death it became apparent that the Spanish Church, its structures and devotions, remained much the same as it had been at the beginning of his rule.[79] By the end of the century and the reign of the incompetent and cuckolded Charles IV (1748–1819), the reformist enterprise, in its Jansenist and regalist expressions, had been all but obliterated by a resurgent ultramontane and a stronger papacy.[80] That is not to say that the reforms of the Catholic Enlightenment were a complete failure. Perhaps, like the proverbial yeast in the dough, the concerns and priorities of the Enlightened clergy may have had some effect through the books, pamphlets, and sermons that were propagated in Spain and abroad. For example, according to Charles Noel, by the end of the eighteenth century fewer people were invoking saints in their wills or providing for elaborate funerals, preferring to leave money to

75. Voekel, *Alone befoe God*, 48.

76. De la Hera, *Iglesia y Corona*, 462–68.

77. Gilabert, *Carlos III*, 117–20, cf. Appolis, *Jansénistes Espagnoles*, 39–46, Brading, *Church and State*, 23.

78. Callahan, *Church, Politics*, 70.

79. Callahan, *Church, Politics*, 71, Bradley & Van Kley, *Religion and Politics*, 128.

80. Bradley and Van Kley, *Religion and Politics*, 145–47, Callahan, *Church, Politics*, 76.

charity.[81] Whatever successes were enjoyed by the monarchs and leaders of Spain's Catholic Enlightenment it is incumbent to realize that did not just occupy the Spanish peninsula but also reached their vast colonies in the Americas, especially New Spain, where its different cultural, religious and political contexts formed the matrix for a particularly Mexican variety of Catholic Enlightenment.

ENLIGHTENED MEXICO

The plans for reform in Spain that began under Philip V at the onset of the eighteenth century took over fifty years to reach the American colonies. By the time of Charles III it became apparent that in order to create a more efficient and centralized empire, the Bourbon reforms had to be applied extensively overseas, partly as a result of the fall of Havana in 1762 and the results of the Seven Years War which lost Florida to Great Britain but brought Spain the Louisiana Territory from France (albeit temporarily).[82]

The Bourbon kings' goals not only included the renewal of Spanish society through economic, educational, and politico-religious change but also the restructuring of Spain's American colonies to better serve the Mother Country. Historians have focused on the economic effects of the Bourbon reforms and the financial boom that occurred, particularly during Charles III's reign.[83] However, equally important was the effort to reduce the autonomy of the colonies, meaning that the viceroyalty had to be brought closer in line to the authoritarian rule of the king. Additionally, as in Spain, the power and influence of local institutions, chief among them the Church, had to be curbed and controlled in service to the Crown. The old Spanish conception of corporate parenthood—the Crown as Father while the Church was Mother—gave way to an absolutist conception whereby the Church was practically another department of State.[84] One of the means to do so was to appoint Spaniards who were regalist in spirit to fill government and church positions.[85]

81. Bradley and Van Kley, *Religion and Politics*, 128.

82. Taylor, *Magistrates of the Sacred*, 13. The Seven Years War is known as the French & Indian War in the United States.

83. Meyer and Sherman, *Course*, 254–55; these improvements proved short-lived, however, thanks to the inept reign of Charles III's successor, Charles IV.

84. Taylor, *Magistrates of the Sacred*, 14.

85. Meyer, *Oxford*, 277–78.

To begin with, the Crown reasserted the royal patronage, secularizing parishes much to the infuriation of the regular clergy. Previously, the regular orders held extensive power and authority as evangelizers of the Indians, particularly in the frontier areas. Part of this initiative came from the early colonial separation of the Republic of the Indians, as it was called, from that of the Spanish, a concept founded on the idea that the native peoples, as a corporate entity, had already been ruled by their own laws and customs. One of the reasons for this division was to keep them away from the unchristian behavior of the Europeans to accommodate and facilitate catechesis and conversion.[86] Practically speaking, this created two separate churches in the Spanish colonies, that of the Indians under the administration of the religious orders and that of everyone else under the secular clergy. To gain control over such a situation and to integrate the two major sections of colonial society, Fernando VI, in 1749, brought the Indian parishes under episcopal control and greatly reduced the number of monasteries and those entering them.[87]

This effort to bring the Church under greater control of the Crown continued throughout the latter half of the century as priests were ordered to give a greater accounting of church finances and the traditional rights of the clergy in the larger society were curbed. Their jurisdiction over cases of idolatry, drunkenness and property disputes was limited, for example, so they could focus more on spiritual matters.[88]

In New Spain, the expulsion of the Society of Jesus in 1767 provoked outrage given that order's role in education and mission work. Six hundred seventy-eight Jesuits, almost two-thirds of whom were Mexican-born, were forced to leave the colony. About half of the missionary houses belonged to the Society as well as twenty-three colleges. Violent demonstrations followed in several communities, provoked mainly by Indians, among whom the Jesuits had lived and ministered.[89] The

---

86. Meyer, *Oxford*, 184–85.

87. Brading, *Church and State*, 62–81, 183–84, Taylor, *Magistrates of the Sacred*, 15, Meyer, *Oxford*, 280; this enactment included the stipulation that all subjects of the Crown learn Spanish, a law that struck at the practice of maintaining the Indians separate from the rest of the colonists and looked to their integration into colonial society (though at the cost of the continued existence of indigenous languages and cultures). Taylor, *Magistrates of the Sacred*, 13.

88. Taylor, *Magistrates of the Sacred*, 15.

89. Cf. Borges, *Historia de la Iglesia*, 254.

Crown duly confiscated the Order's properties, and in some cases, such as that of several schools, redistributed them to other orders.[90]

One of the ecclesiastical institutions radically affected by the Bourbon reforms was the Inquisition in New Spain. The Inquisition itself was, by its nature, a cumbersome and ineffectual entity. There was simply no way that the Holy Office could monitor beliefs and materials from the southwestern California to Costa Rica. Consequentially, Enlightenment pamphlets and books ranging from science to philosophy to politics continued to enter the colony despite all of the Holy Office's efforts. During the eighteenth century the Crown sought to bring the much-feared institution to heel and limited its power, making it less a power to itself than an arm of the State.[91] However, it would not be until 1790 that the Inquisition banned numerous French Enlightenment authors such as Diderot, Rousseau and Voltaire. Some figures, including Hobbes, Descartes and Hume were never placed on the Index of Prohibited Books. This discrepancy may owe itself to the revolutionary, rather than religious, nature of the banned authors who called into question the authoritarian nature of the State.[92]

Some have attributed the reforms in the Spanish and Spanish-American Church as coming from an irreligious or anticlerical impulse, but, as we have seen above, many of the reformers, including Charles III, were personally pious and held to later Jansenist principles on morality, interior piety, and Eucharistic devotion while maintaining a regalist attitude towards papal and ecclesial authority. According to Jaime González Rodríguez, the Enlightenment in Spanish America was a Catholic Enlightenment that, despite its foreign influence, nonetheless had roots in the Church's experience of the previous two centuries, including the humanist tendencies of the Jesuits.[93] Like in Spain, this movement would be advocated and undertaken by a minority of church officials and laypeople. Most of the priests and bishops accepted the absolute rights of the Enlightened Monarchs and, like Francisco Lorenzana, Archbishop of Mexico (d.1804), supported the expulsion of the Jesuits.[94] Pamela Voekel

90. Meyer and Sherman, *Course*, 277–78.

91. Meyer, *Oxford*, 179.

92. While making the distinction, it should not be forgotten that in an empire based upon the divine right of the monarch, treason is heresy and heresy is treason. Jürgen-Prien, *Historia*, 331–33.

93. Borges, *Historia de la Igleisa*, 799.

94. Borges, *Historia de la Iglesia*, 801, Taylor, *Magistrates of the Sacred*, 14–15.

concurs in her own study of the Catholic Enlightenment in New Spain. The reformers, many of them in the church hierarchy, came at the reforms from the mindset of the Catholic Enlightenment. These Mexican reformers were not only influenced by some Jansenist strands but were heirs to renewal impulses in Spanish humanism.[95] She has noted that the advocates of religious reform in Mexico shared qualities with their counterparts in Spain—

- a rejection of exterior displays of piety in favor of interior spirituality
- an emphasis on the unmediated grace of God operating in the human heart versus the baroque mediation of the saints
- a rethinking of the individual's role in the Church
- a questioning of papal power
- an emphasis on the individual rather than the corporate body[96]

In *Alone Before God*, Voekel illustrated the efforts of the Catholic Enlightenment by focusing on the issue of funeral processions and ceremonies of death. She noted that in the latter half of the eighteenth century, baroque funerals complete with hired mourners, elaborate coffins and decorative fabrics, candles, and floats, came under scrutiny and legislation as counter to the moderation that a Christian should display in life and in death.[97] The Archbishop of Puebla, for example, in 1769 banned all ostentatious funeral displays as vanity and profanity against the house of God.[98] She notes the change in religious demeanor among some parts of the population by the change in funeral fashion from baroque displays of piety to more humble funerals with money given more to charity than to provide for candles for a saint's image.[99]

---

95. Voekel, *Alone before God*, 63.

96. Ibid., 47–58.

97. Voekel, *Alone before God*, 62–66; In her book Voekel argues that the reforms of the Catholic Enlightenment paved the way for the modernization of Mexico. In her example of funeral rites the legislation against extravagance and in favor of secular cemeteries rather than church burials illustrates a shift in society whereby the civil realm takes over functions that were traditionally left to the religious sphere such as birth/marriage/death registries.

98. Ibid., 63.

99. Ibid., 66–76.

The reform of liturgy and piety in the Catholic Enlightenment should not be separated from the larger scope of the Bourbon Reforms and their effects on the colonies. In 1778, the Crown established free trade between Mexico and any Spanish port. Larkin rightly notes that this and other fiscal decrees destabilized and decreased the wealth of Mexico City's elite by ending their mercantile dominance. Additionally, free trade had the effect of flooding the Mexican market with European goods, thus causing prices to drop, and with them, profits.[100] In light of this, not only was income for candles, Masses, and endowments limited, but it was in the Crown's own economic favor to enact a program of reforming the piety of the people to get more money dropped into the imperial coffers rather than the Church's collection plates. This policy was continued and formalized under Charles IV under the Consolidation of Royal Bonds in 1804. Under this law, the Church was to transfer all endowments for perpetual Masses and the principal funds for chaplaincies and chantries to the royal treasury. This affected the many priests who earned their living mainly from serving at a chapel or by saying Masses for the dead. It forced the Church, as the colony's largest lending institution, to call in loans made through the principal for these foundations and endowments. This placed a burden not only on the Church but also upon those wealthy and merchants who took advantage of the Church's low interest rates to invest and prosper.[101]

For churchmen who supported the religious reforms, their concerns were not so much rooted in economics as they were in theology. The Archbishop of Mexico, Francisco Antonio Lorenzana, along with his successor, Alonso Nuñez de Haro y Peralta, and the Bishop of Puebla, Francisco Fabián y Fuero, sought to regulate religious practice through Episcopal edicts and instructions to priests. They visited parishes and schools and communicated their ideas to believers directly through regular sermons. Additionally, Archbishop Lorenzana convoked the Fourth Mexican Provincial Council in 1771 to update polity and enact reform of pastoral care.[102]

According to Larkin, these three prelates based their vision of reform in their conception of God as Spirit, warning their parishioners to not attribute corporality to the first and third Persons of the Trinity

---

100. Larkin, *Very Nature*, 120–21.
101. Ibid., 123.
102. Ibid., 127.

to avoid falling into false worship and ultimate perdition. Instead, they were encouraged to think of God more abstractly, avoiding even images such as "light" in favor of concepts such as "truth" and "justice." Logically then, if God was to be conceived of as spiritual, then true worship should be done spiritually and not emphasize external displays of ritual: "And if your worship and adorations are exterior and are not . . . in spirit and in truth, your works will be poorer every day and more disagreeable in the eyes of God."[103]

Similar antipathy towards outward extravagance was shared by reformers in other areas. In 1774, for example, the newly installed priest of Yuririapúndaro was scandalized at the celebrations held for the image of Purísima Concepción. Processions were held at night and became occasions for drunkenness, theft, and even rape.[104] Similar accusations were made of other celebrations elsewhere.[105] Viceroy Revillagigedo, as we noted previously, sharply criticized the opulence of the Holy Week celebrations in Mexico City which were accompanied by people in elaborate costumes or penitentials, thus exposing the faith to ridicule.[106] An inquiry was held regarding religious confraternities in 1775 as the cost of the celebrations as well as their content were thought suspicious. It was found that many Indian villages lacked collective funds since their resources had been devoted to Church ceremonies, festivals "and other useless and harmful things."[107] Bishop Fabián y Fuero of Puebla in 1767 issued an edict ordering the simplification of music performed in the cathedral of Puebla—the ornate baroque music was inappropriate and hindered the role of music in conveying the meaning of the words sung by the choir. His attack on the music performed flipped the baroque argument in favor of sensuous display, criticizing it as moving the listener to concupiscence and worldly thoughts.[108] In 1793 Bishop San

---

103. Quoted in ibid., 128.

104. Brading, *Church and State*, 164–65.

105. Ibid, 166–70.

106. Ibid., 167.

107. Brading, "Tridentine," 12; the Council of the Indies sought to curb the number of confraternities and their celebrations but this was not only opposed by the people, particularly Indians, for whom the celebrations were an integral part of communal devotion, but also by parish priests. The confraternities raised money to meet the cost of ceremonies and liturgies and thus provided a source of income for the priests. Brading, "Tridentine," 14, cf. 19.

108. Larkin, *Very Nature*, 136–37.

Miguel banned the procession of images during Holy Week in Silao as they led to disorderly conduct and impoverished the Indians.[109] When Archbishop Lorenzana banned dancing and representations of Christ's passion during Indian religious festivals he denied the then-accepted notion that faith for the natives came about easier through visual displays such as processionals, images, and dances. What he and fellow reformers were doing was overturning centuries of Catholic tradition by toppling the role of the visual and prioritizing the spoken word in worship and formation.[110] To this end, the Fourth Mexican Provincial Council of 1771 sought to regulate preaching, ordering that priests deliver homilies regularly for about half-an-hour upon a point of doctrine and that it be delivered in a simple rhetorical style that sought to persuade listeners rather than impress or accuse them. Additionally, the catechism commissioned by the Council emphasized the content of faith in the Creed and the Commandments rather than the performance of the faith as in previous catechisms.[111]

According to reformers like Nuñez de Haro, true piety is found within. It is an act of the heart—not as the seat of emotion or feeling but, following medieval and early modern tradition, the place of the rational soul. True worship was therefore an act of the interior qualities of intellect and will, not that of prostrations, processions or penintentials. Spiritual piety, the reformers posited, was a relationship between the individual's interior disposition and God. At best, external piety and the splendor of worship could express the inward faith of the person but could never cause or excite faith, much less make the Divine present.[112] Relics, the mediation of the saints and places of pilgrimage were therefore redundant. Instead, reformers sought to put forth the saints as models of Christian virtue rather than go-betweens between a distant God and sinful humanity.[113]

---

109. Brading, "Tridentine," 18.

110. Larkin, *Very Nature*, 137.

111. Ibid., 131–32.

112. Larkin, *Very Nature*, 129–30, cf. 131–42. It can be argued, as Voekel and Larkin both do, that the reformers's emphasis of internal piety versus external, communitarian display represents the birth of the modern concept of the autonomous individual who stands alone with her or her conscience.

113. Voekel, *Alone before God*, 55–56.

Catholic reformers in Mexico also attacked the cult of the saints as being irrational and superstitious. Archbishop Lorenzana, for example, upbraided the people who thought they would be protected against accidental death by pinning scraps of paper with Scripture upon them or painting sacred images on themselves.[114] Further, the saints as mediators were unnecessary if the grace of God worked its sovereign pleasure upon the human heart as per Augustine, Jansen and contemporary reformers. God was already present in the believer's life. "An all-powerful God, 'a God who was everywhere,' to quote Mexico's Archbishop Francisco Javier Lizana y Beaumont (1803–11), a God who illuminated men from within, had no need for dramatic explosions into the mundane world, displays that contravened reformers' and Augustine's most fundamental notion of how man knew God: 'Do not go outward; return within yourself. In the inward man dwells truth.'"[115]

The emphasis upon the individual's relationship with God through his unmediated grace naturally brought into question the ministrations and the role of the Church. If salvation depended upon the work of grace and the outpouring of charity that resulted from it, how could Masses, alms, candles, and other instruments assist one, especially after she had passed on to her ultimate destiny? Voekel states that, in particular, papal authority came under attack. After all, what power does the pope truly have in the face of the individual's conscience before God? As a result of this questioning of papal power and the apparatus of the Church, some reformers called for renewal based upon the Church Fathers and the Councils of the Church.[116] Thus another feature of the Enlightenment in the Americas, following European trends, was a return to patristic studies, above all the study of Saint Augustine of Hippo as well as a renewal of Thomistic studies encouraged by the Dominican Order.[117]

Brian Larkin has noted the decline of the confraternities in eighteenth-century Mexico City. As we have seen, confraternities were an important part of colonial society through the distribution of charity, their participation in funerals and death rituals and their role in the public celebrations of Christ and the saints. Confraternities, through their collective nature, brought about a sense of Christian unity among their

---

114. Ibid., 55.
115. Ibid., 54; Larkin, *Very Nature*, 135–36.
116. Voekel, *Alone before God*, 56–58.
117. Saranyana, *Teología*, 2/1:41.

members who supported one another in their quest for salvation. Whereas in the beginning of the century confraternities remained a large part of death rituals, by the end of the century Spanish testators downplayed the role of the confraternities in their desired commemoration of the dead.[118] This suggests, as Pamela Voekel had also pointed out in her discussion of funerary rites and last wills, that a sense of the individual apart from the community had emerged in late colonial Mexico. Consequentially, the traditional communal network that assisted the person's quest for heaven (saints, confraternities, perpetual Masses, etc.) became unnecessary in light of the individual's own relationship with God.

A preoccupation of the Catholic Enlightenment in New Spain, as in the Mother Country, was the interest in reforming educational institutions and removing barriers towards obtaining an education. In 1755, for example, the Company of Mary opened a free public school for girls (of all races), a novelty of the time. The teaching staff would come from the convents and classes on writing, mathematics and sewing were conducted in Latin and Spanish. The effort was deemed a success and similar schools were established throughout Mexico by the early 1800s.[119]

The Enlightenment in New Spain was also seen in the Society of Jesus, who, farther from the political intrigues of the Spanish Court, from the 1740s on sought to reform the teaching of philosophy in their schools. They rejected scholastic theology and tried to incorporate Enlightenment thought such as that of Descartes and Newton. Some Jesuits, such as the polymath Francisco Xavier Alegre (1729–88), also promoted the study of the natural sciences and history. Their efforts, however, came to a halt with their expulsion from the Spanish colonies and eventual suppression.[120]

Additionally, Enlightened Church leaders sought the reform of the Church through the renewal of its clergy. The emphasis on pastoral oversight and reform is clear in some of New Spain's prelates. Francisco Antonio de Lorenzana y Buitrón (1722–1804), archbishop of Mexico, ordered the parish priests to teach Christian doctrine in a clear manner to their congregants and sought to curb abuses of church ceremonies. In a

118. Nesvig, *Local Religion*, 189–213; a related matter dealt with the appropriation of the civil power of the final resting place of the dead. Traditional church burials reinforced society's hierarchical structure with clergy, magistrates and the wealthy being buried closest to the altar while the poor where interred towards the doors. Civil cemeteries, where the rich and the poor lay side by side, reinterpreted societal structure.

119. Borges, *Historia de la Iglesia*, 802–3.

120. Peláez, *Historia*, 103–4.

pastoral letter issued in 1767 shortly after the expulsion of the Jesuits, he attacked the moral laxity of the clergy and the people, attacking probabilism for watering down both the moral demands of the Christian faith as well as the laws of the State. In his Eucharistic theology he sounds like a Jansenist reformer, urging fewer but more sincere confessions, and that not even members of religious orders should take Communion daily unless they were of extraordinary virtue and piety.[121] In the matter of clerical reform he sought to establish academies whereby priests and prelates could attend conferences upon moral issues, and liturgical and pastoral training.[122] As an Enlightened Catholic Lorenzana went beyond his clerical responsibilities, overseeing the composition of indigenous grammars, advocating for improved sanitation and even forming a collection of Aztec artifacts and wonders from natural history.[123]

Other clergy who were part of the Catholic Enlightenment included the moral philosophers Juan Benito Díaz de Gamarra y Dávalos (1745–83) and his disciple José Ignacio Fernández del Rincón who, in their writings, interacted with European philosophers such as Locke, Hobbes, and Rousseau.[124] José Pérez Calama (1740–93), an educator, promoted the creation of libraries and sought to improve the educational level of the priests under his care in Puebla and Michoacán, particularly in the field of theology where he criticized a curriculum dictated by Aristotle and medieval philosophers and suggested that students return to the classics to learn proper Latin. Far from being solely concerned with ecclesiastical matters, Calama, in a 1786 essay, sought to analyze the causes of a famine and suggested the establishment of public granaries in the larger cities of the diocese.[125] In 1784 this priest and dedicated teacher promoted a theological contest which a young Miguel Hidalgo y Costilla, the Father of Mexican Independence, won.[126]

---

121. Saranyana, *Teología*, 2/1:599, cf. Morales, *Clero y Política*, 23–31.

122. Saranyana, *Teología*, 2/1:600–601.

123. Ibid., 594–95 n.140.

124. Ibid., 607–16, 616–19. Brading, *Church and State*, 194–96. The very fact that these writers had access to these philosophers attests to the relaxed state of the Inquisition in New Spain as regards the censorship of books.

125. Ibid., 619–29.

126. Ibid., 628–29.

RELIGIOUS ROOTS OF MEXICAN NATIONALISM

An offshoot of the Enlightenment in New Spain was the growth of an incipient nationalism in part due to new historiographical approaches, the growth of new sciences such as archaeology and, perhaps most importantly, the appropriation of religious symbols to foster a distinct Creole patriotism. The roots of nationalism had already been forming since the late sixteenth century. Let us remember that society in New Spain, particularly from the seventeenth century on, was structuralized, and at the apex stood the European-born Spaniards, often referred to as *peninsulares* or *gapuchines*. Below them were the American-born Spaniards, Creoles.[127] Brading describes the animosity that arose between the two groups; perhaps due in part to the fact immigration to the New World at this time was almost totally male, thus forcing the *peninsulares* to seek Creole wives.[128] Since the Creoles were excluded from high office, the stereotype was perpetuated that it had something to do with Creole character—affected negatively by the American heat and humidity. Referring to the Creoles, a Spanish capuchin, Francisco de Ajofrín wrote in 1763:

> The understanding of the natives is clear and comprehensive and in consequence fit for all faculties and sciences, advancing rapidly with admirable progress to the point that in Europe it is not attained save after much time and at the cost of much toil. But at a certain age, at about thirty years, they decline, in part because of their delicate constitution and lack of health, but also through the lack of encouragement and of places to which they could be appointed. This is the reason, lacking incentives, that they become idle and abandon their books.[129]

This accusation was echoed by Antonio Joaquín de Rivadeneira, a Creole lawyer and member of the *audiencia* in Mexico, who wrote in 1771:

> It is not the first time that the reputation of the Americans has been maliciously attacked and that they have been regarded as unsuitable for honors of any kind. This is a war we have suffered since the discovery of America. The Indians, the natives born and originating in America, have even had their rationality questioned, against all the evidence. With equal injustice it is also claimed that those of us born here of European ancestry lack enough reason to

---

127. Lafaye, *Quetzalcóatl and Guadalupe*, 7–11.
128. Brading, *Origins*, 9–10.
129. Quoted in Brading, *Origins*, 10.

be really men. We have been depicted as suspicious creatures, full of our own opinions, resentful of reproof, and—the ultimate insult—it has been alleged that Mexico is apparently moribund.[130]

By 1700 the children of the conquistadors were facing disappointment. They were simply not the lords of the land as their ancestors had hoped. The high mortality rate of the Indian population along with the animosity of the Crown reduced the value of *encomiendas*, the grant of Indians to the conquerors (and presumably their heirs) to work the land in exchange (in theory) for their wellbeing and evangelism. Further, a new generation of immigrants had become successful in silver-mining and overseas commerce.[131] To answer this, Creoles looked to the Conquest and, more specifically, to its critics such as Bartolomé de Las Casas, and concluded that the "The crimes of the conquerors were punished in the poverty and misery of their descendents."[132] In addition to lamenting the sins of the fathers, this new generation of Creoles lifted up the Indian past, comparing Aztec society, for example to classical antiquity, noting that despite their bloody religion, they had, as visible in their laws and ruins, attained true civilization.[133] Creole apologists would return to the indigenous past again and again, forming a mythical bridge, as it were, between themselves and the Aztecs and Maya. Carlos Sigüenza y Góngora (1645–1700), a contemporary and friend of Sor Juana Inés de la Cruz, is an example of this kind of Creole scholar. This poet, philosopher, historian, and cartographer sought to infuse Creole patriotism with an extolling of the indigenous past.[134] He became heir to the manuscripts prepared by Juan Fernando de Alva Ixtlilxochitl (1568–1648) who had been commissioned by the viceroy to write the history of the indigenous peoples of New Spain.[135] Sigüenza y Góngora pored over these codices to decipher their hieroglyphs, referring to their author as a Mexican Cicero. Additionally, he became the first to conduct an archaeological excavation of the Pyramid of the Sun in Teotihuacán.[136]

130. De Rivadeneira, "America for the Americans," 59.
131. Brading, *Origins*, 4; Brading, *First America*, 293–301.
132. Brading, *Origins*, 5; cf. Brading, *First America*, 306–10.
133. Brading, *Origins*, 8–9; cf. Brading, *First America*, 184–212.
134. Lafaye, *Quetzalcóatl and Guadalupe*, 59–68, Brading, *First America*, 371.
135. Brading, *First America*, 273–75.
136. Brading, *First America*, 362–72, Cleere, *Approaches*, 90.

HISTORY, RELIGION, AND NATIONALISM

A decidedly Catholic interpretation of the history of New Spain contributed to the rise of Creole pride and nationalism. Early explorers and missionaries wondered how the Americas could have been "missed" by the Bible, unmentioned by the chroniclers of Genesis in recording the origins of the nations of the world. More importantly, if the apostles had been charged with spreading the gospel to the entire world, how could an entire continent have escaped their notice?[137] After all, similarities between Christianity and indigenous religion were present in the Americas. Cruciform shapes had been found in some sacred sites and codices.[138] There were also coincidences between native religious rites and Christian ones; "confession, fasting, circumcision; the belief in one creator God, in a virgin miraculously made mother, in the universal Deluge."[139] In their quest for an evangelistic precedent, missionaries and colonial scholars hit upon the person of Quetzalcóatl, the plumed-serpent god and the mythic king of the Toltecs who had taught the people agriculture and culture. Cortéz's coming had been interpreted by some as the return of the white-skinned Quetzalcóatl, though records of this belief come from post-Conquest sources (thus making it debatable as to whether this was *post hoc* rationalization of the Conquest). Missionaries took hold of these facts to propose an apostolic evangelization of the Americas. After all, did not some images of Quetzalcóatl show the god wearing a cross on his mantle? And didn't his name figuratively mean "precious twin?" Taking these clues, Sigüenza y Góngora attached Quetzalcóatl to Saint Thomas, whose Greek name, Didymus, means "twin."[140]

According to what became popular legend, Saint Thomas, after evangelizing India, made his way to the Americas where he preached the Gospel.[141] For Creoles this link was extremely important. Spain and other European nations claimed for themselves some form of apostolic evangelization from Saints Peter and Paul in Rome to Joseph of Arimethea in England to Saint James in Spain. Lafaye notes that between the religious categories of Christians and unbelievers was the inferior and spiritually

---

137. Lafaye, *Quetzalcóatl and Guadalupe*, 156–57, cf. 182.
138. Ibid., 153–55.
139. Ibid., 190.
140. Ibid., 156; Brading, *First America*, 365–66.
141. Lafaye, *Quetzalcóatl and Guadalupe*, 180–92; Brading, *First America*, 273–74.

dependent category of newly converted barbarian. Wasn't Spanish society in the Renaissance divided between "old Christians" and *conversos*, persons who had or whose recent ancestors converted from Islam or Judaism? And spiritual subjection led to political subjection. The New World's apostolic credentials in Saint Thomas could bypass the violence of the Conquest and allow the American people to change their spiritual status and stand as equals by their European brethren.[142]

THE CREOLE VIRGIN

A more potent figure stands in the center of the religious roots of Mexican nationalism, however. In 1648, Miguel Sánchez (d.1674), a popular preacher and chaplain, wrote a tract known as the *Imagen de la Virgen María* (Image of the Virgin Mary).[143] Written in Spanish, this account of the 1531 apparition subverts the prerogatives assumed by *peninsulares* by recreating the Spanish apparition stories on American soil. Designed to appeal to Creole feelings toward the Mexican homeland it begs the question, how can the New World and the Creole people be inferior to the European when the Virgin Mary herself has appeared in Mexico as a native of the land? A year later, the *Nican Mopohua*, the Nahua account of the apparition of the Virgin of Guadalupe to the Indian Juan Diego, written by Luis Laso de la Vega would further subvert the myth by returning it to its indigenous roots.[144] Particularly among the Creoles and indigenous, public devotion to this Virgin and her image gained in popularity.[145] Poems, panegyrics, and sermons followed, extolling this American Madonna. The lauds given to the Virgin of Tepeyac Hill would come to fruition in her assignation as Patron Saint of New Spain by Pope Benedict XIV in 1756.

---

142. Lafaye, *Quetzalcóatl and Guadalupe*, 192.

143. *Imagen de la Virgen María, Madre de Dios de Guadalupe, Milagrosamente aparecida en la ciudad de México: Celebrada en su historia con la proefecia del capítulo doce del Apocalpsis* (Image of the Virgin Mary, Mother of God of Guadalupe, (who) Miraculously appeared in the City of Mexico: Celebrated in her story with the prophesy of chapter twelve of the Apocalypse).

144. Found in *Huei Tlamahuiçoltica omonexiti in ilhuicac tlatocacihuapilli Santa Maria totlaçonantzin Guadalupe in nican Huei altepenahuac Mexico itocayocan Tepeyac* (By a great miracle the Heavenely Queen, Saint Mary, our precious Mother of Guadalupe, appeared here near the great Altepetl of Mexico, in a place called Tepeyac).

145. On the publishing of the account see Brading, *Mexican Phoenix*, 81–95.

The Virgin of Guadalupe represented a founding myth, the spiritual foundation of the Mexican Church and nation. She chose to appear to an Indian and in the brown-skin of an Indian, magnifying the American quality of the story. Implicitly, Mary's apparition undermined the peninsular roots of the Church, connecting the people of Mexico—the Indians and the Creoles, with a spiritual pedigree that went far beyond apostolic credentials. Indeed, the Latin inscription attributed to her from Psalms 147:20 *non fecit taliter omni nationi* (He/She has not done this for any other nation) dates from this era and attests to Mexico's favored place in the spiritual economy. Here one poet compares her apparition with that given to John, the author of the book of Revelation.

> The world wonders,
> Heaven, the birds, angels and men
> Suspend their echoes,
> Hold still their voices
> That in New Spain
> From another John is heard
> A new Apocalypse,
> Although the revelations differ.
> From America in the desert,
> And in the crags if a hill,
> Patmos of New Spain
> Hides another John . . .
> A great Sign in the heavens
> Of Guadalupe, there unfolds
> A Conception in roses,
> Which has idols at her feet . . .[146]

An Italian historian, Lorenzo Boturini Benaduci (1698–1755) spent six years in New Spain touring Indian villages, collecting documents, maps, and codices on Mexican history and the Virgin of Guadalupe. The Jesuits had even given him access to Sigüenza y Góngora's papers. Once in Spain, Benaduci was deported to Spain for not having the correct papers, but through the help of powerful patrons, was appointed Chronicler of the Indies.[147] The result of his New World peripatetic wanderings and research, his *Idea de una nueva historia de América Septentrional* (Idea regarding a new history of North America) published in 1746, would consolidate these disparate threads. He modeled his history on

---

146. By Felipe de Santoyo García quoted in Brading, *Mexican Phoenix*, 99–101.
147. Brading, *First America*, 381.

recent Enlightenment historiography, most notably that of the Italian Giambattista Vico (1668–1744) seeking to explain the origins and progress of Mexico's indigenous who, for him, ascended through the stages of rule by gods, sages, and men.[148] Following Sigüenza y Góngira he asserted the identity of Saint Thomas with Quetzalcóatl and amassed documents dealing with Guadalupe.[149] These and similar historical efforts as well as the birth of Mesoamerican archaeology during the Enlightenment gave Creoles the sufficient scholarly tools to assert their own distinct patriotism and to dismiss remaining assertions of American inferiority, weakness, or corruption.[150]

The reforms of Charles III in the latter half of the eighteenth century put a spotlight on the administration of the Americas. The Bourbon monarch insisted on the Americas' submissive status as colonies to enrich the Mother Country.[151] Emboldened by a new sense of patriotism Creoles called for a change in the dominant system, asking that American Spaniards should be appointed to the highest ranks and railing against *peninsulares* who came to America to govern with no previous knowledge of the lands, customs, laws or peoples.[152] Creole elites both at home and abroad appealed to the natural wonders of the Americas and to the civilization of the Aztec and Inca peoples as equal to Europe's over against crude stereotypes of the Americas.[153] The resentment over absolutist claims favoring European Spaniards was exacerbated with the expulsion of the Jesuits in 1767. Some resisted the order and sought to defend the members of the Order and suffered penalties, in some cases severe.[154] The decree resulted in several riots in missions and wherever the Jesuits were popular, especially among the Creole elite, many of whom had been educated in Jesuit schools.[155]

---

148. Ibid., 382.
149. Ibid., 386.
150. Cleere, *Approaches*, 90.
151. Meyer and Sherman, *Course*, 280–81ff.
152. Brading, *Origins*, 15–17.
153. Ibid., 19–23; cf. Brading, *First America*, 514–34.
154. Peláez, *Historia*, 108–16.
155. cf. Lutteroth, *Hacia Una Historia*, 74–75; Meyer and Sherman, *Course*, 138; Dussel, *Tomo V*, 171.

FRAY SERVANDO ON FAITH, POLITICS, AND THE CHURCH

A figure that ties many of these threads together, the religious and the patriotic, was Fray Servando Teresa de Mier (1765–1827). This Dominican priest, controversial in his own time, interests us as he straddles the colonial New Spain and the early Mexican republic. He exemplifies the religious side of Creole Mexican nationalism, rooted in his particular interpretations of the Guadalupe story and its ramifications for public life. Additionally, his arguments as well as the reflections contained in his memoirs bring to light the mirror side of Spanish regalism, the desire for the colonies to gain independence and with them, a Mexican Church.

Born José Servando Teresa de Mier Noriega y Guerra in 1765 and ordained in the Dominican order, he gained popularity as a preacher. He was still relatively young when called to preach before the viceroy, archbishop, and Mexican dignitaries on the feast day of Our Lady of Guadalupe in 1794 at the newly restored sanctuary. Here he delivered the sermon of his life, a turning point that would forever alter his path. Mounting the pulpit, Fray Servando put forth four propositions that stunned his audience:

- the image of Guadalupe had been imprinted on the mantle of Saint Thomas and not on the tilma of Juan Diego.
- Saint Thomas had hidden the image after the Indians had fallen into apostasy.
- the Virgin Mary had indeed appeared to Juan Diego but to reveal to him the whereabouts of the image.
- the Guadalupe image was still miraculous in origin as the Virgin, while still alive had imprinted it on Saint Thomas' mantle.[156]

The ramifications were obvious to Servando's listeners. By moving the apparition to the first century rather than in the more recent colonial past, the friar had given New Spain an apostolic and supernatural credential that was the very equal, if not superior, of any in Europe. Further, by asserting that the Mexican Church had been established (as was visible in the relics and antiquities of the Aztecs recently unearthed that demonstrated Saint Thomas as Quetzalcóatl) in the years immediately after Christ's death and resurrection, Servando undermined the entire Spanish

---

156. Brading, *Mexican Phoenix*, 201–2; Michael, *Vida*, 85.

colonial enterprise. Recall that the entire justification of the Spanish Conquest of the Americas was the evangelization of the native peoples. In other words, if Saint Thomas had evangelized the Americas with the miraculous image of Mary, what need was there for the Conquest and subsequent occupation/colonization of the Americas? Brading notes, "Among his notes was an extraordinary invocation, his coup de grace to his incendiary sermon, which he may or may not have delivered, in which he addressed Mary as 'Teotenantzin entirely Virgin, trustworthy Tonacayona . . . Flowery Coyolxauhqui, true Coatlicue de Minjó.'"[157]

The reaction of his listeners was immediate. Having grasped the import of his message some sought to act violently against him. For his efforts Servando was jailed and sentenced to perpetual exile in Spain. Though exonerated from the archbishop's punishment after a successful appeal to the Council of the Indies, Servando was subjected to further confinement based on rumors that he welcomed the news of the French Revolution and opposed the rights of the king.[158]

Fray Servando describes his European journeys and reflections in his *Memoirs*.[159] The details of his adventures are best left to his biographers, but what concerns us is the evolution of his ideas, partly reflected in the company he kept during those years before his return to Mexico. In 1801 he was welcomed in France by Henri Gregoire, the leader of the constitutionalist clergy. He emerged as a partisan and theorist in support of the Mexican insurgency in the early 1800s. This is no surprise as Brading notes that nearly all the men he associated himself with in his *Memoirs* belonged to, or was accused of being, a Jansenist. Gaspar Melchor de Jovellanos, Charles III's Minister of Justice and a Jansenist, had been recommended to Mier after an attempted escape in 1796, for example.[160] By this time, as we have noted above, Jansenism had become synonymous with episcopalism as regards church governance, appealing to church councils vis-à-vis the papacy, and regalist as concerning the power of the king to reform the church, thus setting the stage for a

---

157. Brading, *Mexican Phoenix*, 204; according to documents the archbishop feared that the congregation would try to stone Fray Servando; cf. de Mier, *Apologia*, 55–123.

158. Brading, *First America*, 584–85.

159. De Mier, *Memorias*; de Mier, *Memoirs*. See also de Mier, "Borradores del sermón."

160. Brading, *First America*, 587–88; Brading, *Origins*, 32; Michael, *Vida*, 166.

national church. The movement was popular among some of the enlightened monarchs of Europe including Emperor Joseph II of Austria.[161]

Mier followed many of the Jansenist ideas of Grégoire who believed that the priests were the heirs of the apostles and should govern the Church together with the bishops. He supported the French Revolution, voting for the end of the monarchy in the National Assembly. However, he did not favor the execution of Louis XVI. He also accepted the Civil Constitution of 1791 that called for the election of bishops by all the voters. Whereas many clergymen reacted against the excesses of the Revolution and favored a return to the monarchy, Grégoire strove to reconcile Christianity and democracy.[162]

For Mier, a Mexican Creole, the regalist impulses in Jansenism were turned on their head. He supported the Mexican insurgency and, while in London, quarreled with the Spanish newspaper *El Español*, calling into question the Donations of Pope Alexander in 1493 and arguing that the papal monarchy was based on forged documents such as the Donation of Constantine.[163] In this way it is obvious that he undercut not only the Spanish colonial enterprise but that the papacy had no right or authority to condone the Conquest. In other words the Mexicans were only taking back what was rightfully theirs.

After Mexico won its independence, de Mier was apprehensive about establishing relations with the papacy. While acknowledging the spiritual authority of the pope, he nonetheless presented the French Constitution of 1791 as appropriate for Mexico, arguing that the people should vote for their bishops and that each see had the power to consecrate them without referring to Rome.[164] "'Each church has its divine founder, with all the powers necessary to conserve and propagate itself without any necessity of going to Rome.' In a word, Fray Servando advocated the establishment of a national Catholic Church in which Mexico's absent Spanish bishops would be replaced by a popularly elected episcopate."[165] His fears appeared justified when in 1824 Pope Leo XII issued an encyclical exhorting Spanish Americans to renew their allegiance to the Spanish king. Mier rejected the papacy's airs in meddling in political affairs and reminding

161. Brading, *Origins*, 33.
162. Ibid., 35, Michael, *Vida*, 179ff.
163. Brading, *First America*, 588.
164. Saranyana, *Teología*, 2/2: 221.
165. Quoted in Brading, *Origins*, 36–37; cf. Michael, *Vida*, 653.

his readers that the Holy See had unleashed "atrocious torments" in the Americas through the Donations of Pope Alexander.[166]

> It is just to obey the head of the Church; but only in the spiritual limits of his sphere, and even regarding this your obedience ought to be reasonable, as the Apostle instructs us: *rationabile obsequium vestrum* (Romans 12:1). Be alert therefore! Mexicans, be alert! Don't ever forget that in the name of a papal bull all of America drowned in blood. Millions and millions of innocent Americans perished at the edge of a sword, in flames and through all sorts of atrocious torments, and the rest have been slaves for three hundred years. Remember and always remember the butchery, the time and the labor it has cost us to free ourselves. *Et nondum statim finis.*[167]

Mier considered himself a good Catholic to the end of his days. He opposed the revocation of priestly rights and religious toleration in the new Mexican republic.[168] However, his Catholicism had imbibed from Jansenist sources and, combined with his Creole sympathies, had turned him into a fierce advocate of a national church. Though admitting to the authority of the pope in spiritual matters, he was opposed to papal power in the temporal administration of the Church and presumed papal prerogatives to interfere in the political sphere. He noted the dangers of such power to the health and well-being of the regional/national Church and fought the ultramontanist papal claims that were to dominate Roman Catholicism in the latter third of the nineteenth century. In the meantime, the question of the role and authority of the State vis-à-vis the Church and the papacy would take up the much of the energies of the new Mexican nation as it sought to define itself and its government in the decades after the Wars of Independence.

---

166. Brading, *First America*, 590; Michael, 665; cf. Saranyana, *Teología*, 2/2: 222.
167. Quoted in Saranyana, *Teología*, 2/2: 226.
168. Saranyana, *Teología*, 2/2: 224-25.

6

Church and State II

The National Patronage (1824–50)

> "America is ungovernable. Those who serve
> the Revolution plow the sea."
>
> —*Simón Bolivar,* 1830

THE STILLBORN REVOLUTION

BY 1820 THE INEPT twice-king of Spain, Fernando VII (1784–1833), faced insurrections not only in Mexico, but in the Caribbean and South America as well. He prepared an army to deal with these overseas rebellions but apparently did not keep in mind how unpopular his efforts to establish absolute rule were. Colonel Rafael del Riego (1784–1823), supported by his troops, established a revolt against the king. They demanded that Fernando swear allegiance to the 1812 Spanish Constitution that had proclaimed the liberty of the people and enacted liberal reforms, including a bill of rights. The Spanish monarch yielded in 1820 but when conservative Creoles in Mexico learned of this capitulation, many of them decided to join the insurgent Mexican Independence movement as a means to preserve their status and colonial institutions.

The Mexican viceroy chose Agustín de Itúrbide (1783–1824), a career military man, to lead the forces against Vicente Guerrero (1732–1821) and the insurgents. Realizing that he could not defeat Guerrero's army, Itúrbide did an about-face and proposed a truce. A series of conferences between the two resulted in the *Plan de Iguala*, a document outlining the principles of the new Mexican government designed to gain support among the conservatives, who feared the loss of their traditional powers and privileges. Itúrbide declared that Mexico, after three hundred years under Spanish tutelage, would now be independent but be organized as a constitutional monarchy under a Bourbon ruler. He also guaranteed the spiritual monopoly of the Roman Catholic Church, thus ensuring the support of that vital institution. Finally, Itúrbide's plan declared the equality of *peninsulares* and *criollos*. With these three guarantees, and with the military behind him, Itúrbide changed the terms of the insurgency. It was no longer the social revolution that Miguel Hidalgo and José Morelos had initiated in 1810, but a broader movement designed to appeal to the conservatives with their desire for a monarchy and the liberals who favored a constitutional government. It worked. Within months the new Spanish viceroy recognized the independence of the colony and signed the peace treaty with Itúrbide. This Treaty of Córdoba had one important and calculated modification introduced by the general: if no suitable European monarch would accept the Crown of Mexico, the Mexican congress could choose a Mexican one. Less than a year later, after a staged demonstration involving the military, Itúrbide was crowned Emperor of Mexico in the National Cathedral.[1]

In the months that followed the formal independence of Mexico, cracks began to appear in the national structure as the divisions panned over by the Plan of Iguala began to manifest themselves. Some, federalists, wished that the momentum of Independence could move forward into economic, political, and social reforms. Others, centrists, sought the preservation of colonial privileges and institutions. Adding to the political fault lines of the 1820s and 1830s was the fact that political and clandestine groups grouped around the Masonic lodges, most notably those of the York rite (*yorkinos*) and those of the Scottish rite (*escoceses*). Since Masonic meetings were secret and inviolable all manner of conspiracy and plan could be hatched within them. The *yorkinos* attracted

---

1. Meyer and Sherman, *Course*, 294–303. The Plan of Iguala and the new government was a hundred and eighty degree turn from the movement initiated by Hidalgo that has called for the equality of all Mexicans, Indians as well as Creoles. "(The rural Mexican) could take little solace in the fact that the politically articulate groups in Mexico City that overlooked his interests demonstrated precious little ability to govern even themselves." Ibid., 297.

liberals and radicals who feared Spain's designs to regain the country. These sought a federalist government that gave more power to the states. Their opponents, who sought a centrist government that would recreate political and social structures similar to those of the colonial era coalesced around the Scottish rite.[2] The struggle between these Liberals and Conservatives, as these feuding parties would become known, would haunt Mexico for the next quarter century and have important ramifications on the Church and its relations to the State.

THE DEBATE BEGINS

The Spanish Constitution of 1812 that had instigated Itúrbide's and the conservative rebellion against the Crown included some measures designed to curtail the power of the Church, including the confiscation of some of the Church's property, the elimination of the Inquisition, the seizure of clerical tithes, and the establishment of a free press. The Mexican clergy, fearing that these statutes would be enacted, began to advocate for the independence of the colony. Fearing that liberal revolution would lead to an attack on the Church itself, her doctrines, or even her very existence (as in the French Revolution), clergy supported Itúrbide and the Plan of Iguala.[3]

Central to the status of the Church in the fledgling nation was the matter of patronage. This issue had been discussed soon after independence as the sees of Michoacán, Linares, and Chiapas were vacant due to either attrition or desertion by bishops loyal to the Spanish Crown.[4] In December 1821 a committee on foreign affairs stated that since patronage had been a right of the monarch and not of the individual king (whoever that may have been), when Mexico achieved its independence that right fell to it as a sovereign nation and as the protector of the Church. Until a monarch was found under the Plan of Iguala, the right of patronage should be exercised by the Regency, whose president was Itúrbide.[5]

Itúrbide assembled a provisional junta to resolve the matter and to address the issue of ecclesiastical vacancies, many of which remained

---

2. Meyer and Sherman, *Course*, 317; Meyer, *Oxford*, 296. For the relationship between masonry, liberalism and Protestantism in Latin America see Bastian, *Protestantes, liberales*.
3. Mecham, *Church and State*, 340–41.
4. Peláez, *Historia*, 136.
5. Costeloe, *Church and State*, 110–12.

unfilled since their holders fled to Spain at the beginning of the insurgency. Assuming that the new nation inherited the rights of patronage, it suggested that lists of candidates should be compiled by the junta. Itúrbide then asked the Archbishop of Mexico, Pedro José de Fonte y Hernández Miravete (1777–1839) his opinion the matter. The Archbishop consulted his chapter and the bishops, the two groups concluding at last that with the winning of independence the royal patronage enjoyed by Spain had come to an end. If the Mexican government wished to take up the privilege, it had to receive it from the pope.[6] Archbishop Fonte, however, did not think that the matter was pressing at the time.[7]

A great part of the Mexican clergy supported Itúrbide's imperial pretensions as he declared himself a champion of the Church, defending the traditional rights, or *fueros*, of both secular and regular clergy. However, Archbishop Fonte, having considered independence treason, upon Itúrbide's creation of the Mexican Empire abandoned his see to return to Spain. Without the Archbishop of Mexico, all of sudden the issue of patronage became very important.[8] When the Mexican government sought to declare the see vacant it was ignored by the pope.[9]

The Mexican Empire lasted less than a year. The economy, dependent on agriculture and mining, had never recovered from a decade of conflict. Trade with other nations was not forthcoming quickly enough and in the economic stagnation the people, including Congress and the press, began to realize that the emperor wore no clothes. In October Itúrbide dissolved the Congress and an antimonarchical plot formed in Veracruz led by Antonio López de Santa Anna (1794–1876). In December, 1822, Santa Anna declared a republic and, with the military at his side, rode into Mexico City, forcing Itúrbide to abdicate his throne in February, 1823.[10]

A Constitutional Congress was called to draft a new form of government. Those favoring a republican form of rule outnumbered the monarchists but they were divided between those favoring centralist and federalist government. Generally, those favoring a centralist constitution were supported by the clergy, the landed aristocracy and the military

6. Mecham, *Church and State*, 342–43, Costeloe, *Church and State*, 44–45.
7. Costeloe, *Church and State*, 46.
8. Mecham, *Church and State*, 342.
9. Ibid.
10. Meyer, *Course*, 304–7.

while the federalists drew encouragement from the intellectual liberal Creoles and mestizos who looked to the United States Constitution and the Spanish Constitution of 1812 as models. Mecham notes that clerics were represented in both these camps, Miguel Ramos Arizpe (1775–1843) in the federalist and Servando Teresa de Mier among the centralists.[11] Citing the three hundred years of colonial rule and the recent months of despotic imperialism, the congress adopted a federalist Constitution in 1824. This document protected the status of the Catholic Church as sole recognized religion as well as the preservation of ecclesiastical rights. However, it also added the provision that the federal government had the power to establish concordats with the pope, grant or refuse promulgation of papal bulls, and exercise national patronage. In short, the Mexican government assumed unto itself the privileges of the patronato.[12]

Guadalupe Victoria (1786–1843), the new president of Mexico, sought to establish relations with Rome shortly after his taking power. The Committee on Foreign Affairs at first took a regalist view and asked that the pope recognize national patronage. However, by early 1825, the canonist argument took the upper hand and simply called for the pope to *authorize* Mexico's patronal rights. Leo XII (1760–1829), however, issued an encyclical calling for the American clergy to swear loyalty to the king of Spain and urge their congregations to do the same.[13] This lack of recognition of the newly independent Latin American nations on the part of the papacy could prove disastrous for the Church in Mexico as the country needed the papacy's approval of any candidates it sent forth to fill increasingly vacant church positions. By 1827 Mexico had no bishops, making it impossible to ordain new parish priests. The Mexican Congress, along with many clergy and newspapers, thought that the pope's encyclical was either a fraud or that His Holiness had been coerced in some fashion by the Spanish king.[14] Teresa de Mier issued a pamphlet calling for a National Church saying: "As long as it has its bishops and priests, every Church has within itself the things needed for its preservation and expansion. Let us have recourse, if Rome remains obdurate, to the same method which in similar circumstances, every Roman Catholic nation

---

11. Mecham, *Church and State*, 343; Meyer, *Course*, 313; Teresa de Mier, as we noted in the last chapter, advocated the creation of a national Church independent of Rome.

12. Mecham, *Church and State*, 344, Morales, *Clero y Política*, 114–15.

13. Costeloe, *Church and State*, 91, Mecham, *Church and State*, 346.

14. Costeloe, *Church and State*, 92.

has tried. Let us return to the ancient and sacred discipline of the Church; to rule ourselves by those true and legitimate canons."[15]

In February 1826 a senate committee, dominated by regalists, authorized the national patronage since the Roman hierarchy had long since usurped the rights of the diocesan bishops and the State's rights to not only protect the Church but to safeguard it. Having recently freed itself from the tyranny of Spain, it was now time to shake off the shackles of Roman despotism. The document goes beyond just the right to present candidates for ecclesiastical office. It also reserves the right of the government to enact discipline and control Church revenues. Additionally, it called for the pope to summon a general council and for Latin American nations to agree on common policies to be presented to Rome.[16] This report, in short, called for the establishment of a Mexican National Church independent of Rome in matters of polity. The reaction was immediate. Whereas regalists and their supporters hailed the document as a new revolution, canonists perceived this effort to establish a national Church as nothing less than schism.

As a result of this measure combined with the pope's negative encyclical, liberal reformers on both the federal and state levels were emboldened to enact legislation even without a papal concordat. The Arenas Conspiracy, discovered in January 1827, which sought to restore Spanish rule, involved a number of religious and contributed to an anticlerical atmosphere and for further calls to act on national patronage.[17]

In late April, José María Alpuche e Infante (1780–1840), himself a cleric, a mason, and representative of Tabasco in the senate, published a law he had drafted against papal power. He recognized that he would be called a Protestant and a Jansenist but averred that his proposals were no different than from what other Roman Catholic countries already exercised.[18] In effect he set forth the plans for the establishment of a Mexican Church independent of Rome. It gave enormous powers to both the government and the people. The Mexican nation would now exercise the privileges held by Spain in the colonial era with some modifications: parish priests would be elected by the people and clergy of each parish while bishops were to be chosen by the parishioners of the diocese with

---

15. Quoted in Costeloe, *Church and State*, 93.
16. Costeloe, *Church and State*, 96–97.
17. Ibid., 99ff.
18. Ibid., 102.

the governor choosing from the top three candidates. The archbishop would be chosen by the president from a list of candidates chosen by the Congress. All ecclesiastical buildings and institutions, churches, schools, monasteries, seminaries, and convents would fall under the control of the State. Congress would fix all clerical salaries but the administration of monies would be handled by local authorities. Additionally, no fees would be charged parishioners for any ecclesial services such as masses, marriages, and funerals.[19] This was a plan that, admittedly, would be impossible to implement, but Alpuche, along with other reformers, had published or introduced such plans and proposals so as to put pressure on Congress to act on patronage issues as the questions of Church wealth and clerical needs of the Church, became more urgent.[20] Canonists were quick to respond to the regalist proposals and calls for action, however. In several newspapers they set forth their position that the Church was an entity separate from the civil power and that the appointment to clerical offices and regulation of the Church's wealth belonged to that institution and not the State.[21]

A propaganda war ensued between the members favoring either position and this resulted in the Congress vacillating on positions or becoming indecisive on what course of action to pursue. In the end, the senate avoided a direct statement of national patronage but, as the canonists pointed out, the language strongly implied, or left the door open for a national patronage. In October 1827 the Senate voted to implement the original 1825 report asking for simple authorization from the pope for the rights of patronage.[22] For the time being, regalist hopes for a declaration of patronage were squashed.

THE LIBERALS STRIKE BACK

The next major stage of the Church/State, liberal/conservative battle occurred in 1830 after the short-lived presidency of liberal president Vicente

19. Ibid.
20. Ibid., 103.
21. Ibid., 107.
22. By this time also international matters had changed leading to a more conciliatory position on the part of the pope. The powerful Spanish ambassador to Rome had died, Spain was defeated militarily in the New World, and Great Britain recognized the independence of Mexico, Colombia and Buenos Aires and the Spanish surrendered the fortress of San Juan de Ulúa off the coast of Veracruz. Ibid., 110.

Guerrero. Anastasio Bustamante (1780–1853), a conservative, sought to stamp out liberal and radical ideas and preserve the rights of the propertied class. Pressure was put upon political rivals, military rebels, authors, and newspapers that disagreed with the president's direction.[23]

In order to build a stronger Church, Bustamante determined for bishops to be appointed to the vacant sees. He thus abandoned any claim to national patronage and had the Congress draw up a list of candidates' names that were presented to the pope not in recognition of any kind of patronage nor even in hopes of acquiring it but for the pope to approve them out of his own compassion for the faithful. These were approved by Gregory XVI. Mecham believes that this move demonstrated the government's abandonment of the right to patronage, but in a way it was quite the opposite as the Mexican government did indeed present the names to the pope for his approval, thus implying the right of presentation.[24] However, the canonist side of the argument appeared to win a battle when Bustamante enacted a law in May 1831 allowing the clergy the right to elect the canons of the cathedral chapters. Here Bustamante clearly forfeited the patronal right.[25]

In 1833, Antonio López de Santa Anna, the illustrious and decorated war hero, was elected president. His vice-president was Valentín Gómez Farías (1781–1858), a liberal. Shortly after his election Santa Anna, complaining of ill-health but most likely bored of day-to-day administration, returned to his estate and left the presidency in the hands of Gómez Farías. As a good liberal he began to institute reforms in the army and the Church. He reduced the size of the military and abolished the military *fueros*, including the right to military trials. On the ecclesiastical side, clergy were advised to keep their sermons and directives to the spiritual sphere instead of speaking out on matters of State. When this did not provoke a reaction, Gómez Farías and other liberals, José María Luis Mora (1794–1856), a cleric himself, and Lorenzo de Zavala (1789–1836) sought to secularize education, even closing down the University of Mexico because the majority of its teaching staff were priests. Better that the students, including children, be deprived of an education than that it be administered by a cleric! In this matter, as in others, the liberals showed themselves to be impractical if not short-

---

23. Mecham, *Church and State*, 347, Costeloe, *Church and State*, 117–18.
24. Costeloe, *Church and State*, 117–20; Mecham, *Church and State*, 347.
25. Mecham, *Church and State*, 347, Costeloe, *Church and State*, 123–24.

sighted. In addition, the mandatory nature of the tithe was abolished; parishioners would now contribute freely as they wished. Monks, nuns, and mendicants would have the power to forswear their vows and rejoin secular society in the name of individual freedom. They also took up the idea of national patronage again, with all the regalist implications of subordinating the Church to the State, decreeing that future clerical appointments would be made by the government and not the papacy.[26] This came on the heels of the expulsion of the Spanish bishops of Linares, Durango, Chiapas, Michoacán, and Puebla, who had refused Gómez Farías's efforts to appoint parish priests to these dioceses.[27]

The response was immediate and predictable. The army, the Church, and other interested groups rallied to the cry of *Religión y fueros* and Santa Anna, sensing once again in which direction the winds blew, joined with the conservative cause to depose his own vice-president. Santa Anna took the reins of power to the ringing notes of *Te Deums* sung in the cathedral as he was hailed as the restorer of liberty and savior of the Church. Under the new Santa Anna presidency, the government would be conservative, centralist and Catholic. A new constitution was promulgated in 1836 known popularly as the *Siete Leyes* that revoked the Farías reforms. Among other things this constitution reverted back the ecclesiastical patronage matter to the way it had been in the Constitution of 1824. This displeased the clergy as it still held the door open for a resumption of national patronage at the conclusion of any concordat with the papacy and reserved the right of the government to promulgate or withhold any papal communication. However, the revocation of the liberal reforms and return to the status quo were good enough for Pope Gregory XVI who, in 1836, recognized the Mexican nation. He did not negotiate a concordat with Mexico, though. Unwilling to countenance national patronage the pope himself filled the vacant Mexican sees.[28]

Anastasio Bustamente, friend of the Church, returned to the presidency in 1837, but aroused clerical opposition in seeking a loan from the Church for covering government costs. Having already suffered the liberal tendency to avail themselves of the coffers, the Church hierarchy imagined that the loan would only establish the precedent and founda-

---

26. Meyer and Sherman, *Course*, 325–26; Costeloe, *Church and State*, 129–35; Mecham, *Church and State*, 351–52.

27. Peláez, *Historia*, 137.

28. Mecham, *Church and State*, 354–55.

tion for the wholesale confiscation of the Church's properties and wealth. In the decade to come, national patronage would take a back seat to the more pressing matters of financing wars with France (1838), the state of Texas (1835–36), and then the United States (1846–48). To resolve face these military challenges, the State tussled with the Church as loans were forced upon the Church, effectively mortgaging its properties and pinning them on hypothetical future re-payments. During the Mexican-American War, the Church refused to aid the government financially. Its wealth had already been depleted greatly as a result of government need. At this unfortunate time, the Church resisted further monetary extractions. It would, with the conclusion of the war, lead to rumors of ecclesiastical collusion with the North Americans, accusations of being unpatriotic, and stirrings of anticlericalism.[29]

Additionally, the political uprisings across Europe in 1848 and the 1849 declaration of the Roman Republic had forced Pope Pius IX (1792–1878) to flee the city. On returning to Rome he repented of his previously liberal views and definitely was not inclined to cede to Mexico on the matter of patronage. President José Joaquín Herrera (1792–1854), a moderate, was able to pass a temporary law that allowed the chapters of vacant sees to present a list of candidates from which one would be selected to be presented to the pope. In this way Herrera sought to fill the many ecclesiastical vacancies until a concordat was signed. However, the clergy, desirous that the Church should be free of any temporal power, opposed the law as it implied the government's right to present candidates. They submitted the lists, however, and the pope recognized the candidates.[30] The matter of patronage however, was still an issue that the papacy refused to concede. Ignacio Valdivielso, the Mexican envoy to Rome wrote:

> The Pontifical Court does not consider valid the titles to the patronage that Mexico alleges, nor will it recognize that the patronage is an acquired or inherent right in any nation: and even if it is requested as a concession, it would not be allowed in a form as broad as that exercised by the kings of Spain. Also it would certainly not be agreed to without the condition of reestablishing civil enforcement of the collection of the tithe and probably

---

29. Dussel, *Tomo V*, 206–8.
30. Mecham, *Church and State*, 358.

without securing its right of representation in Mexico by way of an Apostolic Nuncio.[31]

In the end the Church in Mexico, assisted in great part by the refusal of the pope to grant or recognize the patronage, resisted the efforts made against its wealth and authority and stood strong. The State, however, had no reason to complain either. The law enacted in 1850 allowed for a compromise position, much like the established status quo without touching the matter of patronage. Both the chapters and the state governors were able to participate in the process of short-listing candidates for vacant positions as well as enabling the Head of State to present the final candidates to the pope while ensuring the needs of the diocese were being considered.[32] For some parts of the Mexican government, the matter of national patronage, was far from settled and a new and bloody chapter in the relationship between the Mexican State and the Roman Catholic Church would follow in the years to come that would provide the immediate backdrop for the attempted formation of a Mexican National Church.

---

31. Quoted in Costeloe, *Church and State*, 168–69.
32. Ibid., 170.

7

The *Iglesia de Jesús* (1859–72)

EARLY PROTESTANTISM IN MEXICO

IN NEW SPAIN, PROTESTANTISM, often better known as the "Lutheran heresy," arrived both through the dissemination of books and pamphlets and by way of unfortunate strangers—English pirates or traders—who somehow made their way to the colony. The main body charged with combating Protestantism in the colony was the Inquisition, following Pope Paul III's 1538 bull prohibiting the admittance of apostates in the New World territories. Despite this, it is probable that many people otherwise forbidden made their way to the American colonies, including crypto-Jews fleeing religious pressure in Spain and subjects of Charles V's German and Flemish lands. Under Charles' son, Philip II, the policy became more stringent and foreign emigration to the Spanish colonies was forbidden.[1]

Beginning in 1535, with the case of Andrew Alemán, the Inquisition (the episcopal tribunal rather than the Holy Office, which was not established until 1571) began to try cases of suspected Lutherans. Admittedly, it is difficult to gauge just how many of the defendants were actually Protestant in their religious convictions. Some of the accusations ranged from denials of Catholic belief in purgatory or the presence of Christ in the Eucharist to criticisms of indulgences, an act that was not exclusive to Protestantism but also part of the Council of Trent's reforms. The term "Lutheran" was thus not necessarily descriptive of individuals

---

1. Bastian, *Historia*, 95–96.

who subscribed to the Formula of Concord or even Protestant belief in general, but tended to be a blanket accusation for most forms of heterodoxy. Consequentially, it is difficult to entangle true Protestants from people who were simply ignorant of Catholic beliefs.[2] The records of the Holy Office, however, reveal a fear of Protestant penetration in the Americas—the Red Communists or Islamic terrorists of the sixteenth century, as it were. And, as the New World boogey-man, the specter of Lutheran heresy allowed society to circle the wagons and establish the identity of friends over against the outside enemy, represented not only by Protestant preachers and books, but also English pirates who threatened the smooth flow of American wealth and Spanish goods on the open seas.[3]

The Bourbon reforms enacted in New Spain greatly reduced the power of the Holy Office. The expansion of the commercial enterprise to foreign markets greatly facilitated the penetration of heterodox materials and persons. Most of the accusations against Lutheranism occurred in the 1760s during an economic downturn and internal tensions that culminated in the expulsion of the Jesuits.[4] Meanwhile, the dissemination of Protestant and Enlightenment (which was associated with Protestantism) books, including the works of John Calvin and vernacular translations of the Bible, increased in the eighteenth century. The Crown, however, was more concerned with the influx of certain strands of anti-regalist French Enlightenment thought than strictly Protestant doctrine. Here the Holy Office, increasingly an arm of the State, moved from religious to socio-political censorship in fear of rebellion and insurrection.[5]

This period also saw the westward expansion of the United States and its accompanying territorial and economic growth. From a Mexican perspective, this encroachment of a Protestant United States on Mexico's doorstep further heightened the sense of a real danger from without— one that would come to bloody fruition in the decade of the 1840s. Meanwhile, the various religious denominations in the United States perceived of the annexation of Texas and the westward migration as opportunities for evangelistic work into Catholic Mexico. However, these dreams were delayed first by the inter-denominational struggles over the question of

2. Ibid., 71.
3. Ibid., 73–76.
4. Ibid., 85ff.
5. Ibid., 88.

slavery and by the subsequent Civil War. With the conclusion of hostilities, the reunion of the North and South, and the reconstruction of the social, political, and economic infrastructure of the nation, the Protestant churches could once again set their eyes upon their neighbor to the south. By the time the first missionaries arrived in the 1870s, however, they discovered that the fields were not altogether barren and devoid of evangelistic work.

During the Mexican War, an agent of the American Bible Society, William H. Norris, accompanied the invading troops. Although there to minister to the U.S. troops primarily, Norris also distributed Bibles to the Mexican people. This effort had the unintended negative effect of connecting the Bible with the invading enemy. However, it was not devoid of positive results. Individuals and groups discovered the Bible, resulting in small circles of study groups, some of which became receptive both to the reform movements within the Mexican Church as well as to the later arrival of Protestant missionaries. Presbyterian missionary and teacher, Melina Rankin (1811–88), who lived on the near Brownsville on the border, created an institute for young Mexican women in 1852 to compete with a newly opened Catholic convent. Upon Mexico's establishment of the freedom of religion in 1857 she began to distribute Bibles and tracts supplied by the American Bible Society. Rankin established herself in Matamoros in 1859 and came into contact with an agent of the American Tract Society, James Hickey. Together they organized an evangelical society in Monterrey in 1864, the first Protestant mission in the country. His work was succeeded by Thomas Westrupp who eventually brought the congregation under the Baptist Missionary Society. Also in 1859, G. Maller Prevost, an American doctor and businessman established congregations in the state of Zacatecas that were eventually adopted by the Presbyterians in 1872.[6]

LIBERALS AND RELIGION

Conventional wisdom states that the Liberals who sought the curtailment of the rights and privileges of the Catholic Church in nineteenth century Mexico did so out of anticlerical or antireligious motivations. Martin Nesvig notes that in North America scholars tend to take the approach, consciously or unconsciously, that as nations move to modernize they

---

6. Dussel, *Tomo V*, 228–29, López and Guerra, *Protestantismo*, 17–20.

become secularized. Further, religion is perceived to be something marginal at best or a liability at worst, a holdover from colonial superstitions and worldviews that have no real place in the discussion of the modern state.[7] This kind of accusation is made even when some members of the Liberal movement, such as José María Luis Mora, were themselves clerics. Some Mexican writers take on a similar approach when approaching the Liberal movement of the nineteenth century. Assuming that because of their connection with the Masonic lodges and the legislation curbing the traditional rights of the Church, the Liberals were not only anticlerical but also anti-Catholic.[8]

Pamela Voekel has done research into the motivations of some of the Liberal leaders and come up with a vastly different interpretation, one that links these men with the Catholic reformers of the eighteenth century. "In place of Roman excess they envisioned not a secular society but a Godly alternative."[9] At the root of this lay the question as to the nature of salvation and the Church, the very means of salvation. Much like the Jansensists and Enlightened Catholics had previously done, these Catholic Liberals countered the hierarchical, sensory, and mediating nature of the ultramontane Church with their own answers.

Melchor Ocampo (1814–61), for example, Benito Juárez's Minister of the Interior, had come to fame when as governor of Michoacán he battled the clergy over the case of a local priest who refused to bury the body of a poor man because his wife could not afford the sacramental fee.[10] Ocampo attacked the idea that the mediation of the Church and the saints was indispensable for salvation when he countered that God has already given human beings "moral instincts by which each man sees inside himself his duty, on each occasion given by and in accordance with the infallible light that, as a general rule, God has deigned to give him."[11] This, in effect, is Jansenism shorn of Augustine—the gift of Divine grace for the elect has been replaced here with the gifts of reason and conscience given to all humanity to guide the individual into acts of charity and love.

---

7. Nesvig, *Religious*, 3.
8. Peláez, *Historia*, 136.
9. Nesvig, *Religious*, 78.
10. Meyer and Sherman, *Course*, 373–74.
11. Quoted in Nesvig, *Religious*, 79.

The Liberals of the nineteenth century have often been accused of anticlericalism—and that was probably the case with many of them. However, anticlericalism is not the same as anti-religion or even anti-Catholicism. Liberal attacks on the clergy focused on the power—spiritual, economic, and political—that the Church had held for centuries, often at the expense of the poor. José Luis Mora stated that "The Church can be considered under two aspects: as a mystic body or as a political association; under the first aspect it is the work of Jesus Christ, it is eternal or indefectible, eternally independent of the temporal power; under the second aspect it is a civil work; it can be altered or modified, and the privileges it owes to the social order can even be abolished, as they can with any other political community."[12] Pedro Echeverría satirized the Catholic catechism, having the pope take action against the Liberals in the name of "the aristocracy, tyranny and Mammon."[13] For Echeverría and others, the papacy and Church hierarchy were complicit with the nobility—a relationship of the feudal past that was simply passé in the nineteenth century when democracy was taking hold of modern nations.

It was not only the Church's political ties that the Liberals attacked but also the emphasis upon outward displays of religion that both opened the door to fraud and distracted the faithful from Christ and His moral precepts found in the Bible. In a world where the Divine manifested itself in the daily, the Liberal media, the newspapers of the day, took pleasure in exposing fraudulent miracles and superstitions including prayers to make prisoners invisible to guards or chants to find lost objects.[14] They also pointed out the inconsistencies between the Church's duty to care for the poor and its actions. It is worth noting in full the quotation from the Mexico City newspaper *El Monitor Republicano*:

> It would be better indeed to see inside a church on the day of its patron saint celebration curtains of rich silk, chasubules, gilded objects, ornaments of pure gold, branches of bright silver, incense holders, and chalices of emerald and other precious stones while there exists in the porticos of the same temple dedicated to the God of Love (*Dios de la Caridad*) a multitude of blind men, lepers, and the sick pallid with hunger, exhausted by misery, pulling themselves along the ground and extending their squalid hands

---

12. Quoted in López and Guerra, *Protestantismo*, 43.
13. Ibid., 80.
14. Ibid.

> for a handout, for the charity that one asks for in Christ's name and in the name of the same saint in whose honor they pay the noisy orchestra, Italian singers, and fire works . . . cover your face Holy Charity (*caridad santa*)! . . . nothing is true, nothing is just, nothing correct, nothing legitimate, especially not for the Christian clergy, without love (*caridad*) and good works.[15]

With their emphasis upon works of love and charity Catholic Liberals, like their eighteenth-century precursors, posited an alternative to the confradías and religious festivals that had previously served as society's social cement. The religious alternative they imagined would not be a purely individualistic one—the individual vis-à-vis her relationship to God via divine grace/conscience—but one that involved the greater community through the doing of good works to assist others. The aim of the Liberals was then not to abolish the Church, but to reform it for the good of the nation.

> The liberals imagined many grand changes that would improve the economic condition of Mexico. They wanted to extend the means of communication and were ready to concede great subsidies to manufacturers of trains, canals, telegraphs, etc. They sought to increase agricultural production and proposed removing the latifundos of the Church in order to divide them into smaller properties. In the same manner, they wanted to attract foreign capital, encourage industry, develop mining, increase internal security, pay the national debt, lift the sales tax, stimulate colonization from non-Catholic nations, and finally, inculcate in the Mexican citizen a trust in its own initiative.[16]

It has been estimated that about 2,000 Bibles entered Mexico during the colonial era, most of these being the Latin Vulgate.[17] The Constitution of 1824 facilitated the importation of Bibles into the nation but its possession was still prohibited. However, some people, including a few in the seats of government, began advocating for a greater access to the Bible among the Mexican people. This was not done in an effort to introduce Protestantism but to inculcate morality and faith among the people and in the hopes that knowledge of the Bible would foster prosperity much

---

15. Quoted in Nesvig, *Religious*, 81.
16. Quoted in López and Guerra, *Protestantismo*, 47.
17. Dussel, *Tomo V*, 288.

as it supposedly had for the United States and Great Britain.[18] An article published in the state of Oaxaca articulates this well:

> Sirs: Our Lord Jesus Christ, in establishing his religion, had as his principal goal the moralization of humanity, and we know how civilization has advanced as a consequence of the promulgation of his doctrines both in Europe as in America. But in Mexico, our conquistadors brought Catholicism, that is, the disfigured doctrine of Jesus Christ . . . Every Mexican who desires the well-being of his country should work with every means within his grasp so that every shadow of ignorance disappears . . . It is necessary to establish a society that has, as its goal, our instruction in the doctrine of Christ Jesus. Once the freedom of worship is established in Oaxaca, this society will become a reality, and, without doubt, if we stand firm, constant, and do not forget ourselves, our people shall progress.[19]

An indication of this Liberal religious mindset can be encountered in the activities of José Mora as regards his support of James "Diego" Thomson (1788–1854), an agent of the British and Foreign Bible Society and representative of the Lancasterian model of education. Liberals in particular appreciated this educational method as it did not depend on the clergy as instructors but rather, was a self-propagating system whereby teachers instructed others who in turn, became teachers themselves. This effectively placed education under government control. Adopted and encouraged by several Latin American governments throughout the 1820s and 1830s the Lancasterian system was a departure from traditional scholastic methods. It represented, to Liberal leaders, a break from the colonial past and the emergence into the modern world.[20]

Thomson, who used the Bible, or printed portions of it, as a pedagogical text in order to introduce it by stealth to Latin America, was well known among some circles in Mexico. He had already labored in South America after the Wars of Independence at the request of some of the government leaders there, including Simón Bolívar, to establish the Lancasterian model of education.[21] In 1827 he had made his way to

---

18. Cf. Ibid., 300.

19. Quoted in ibid. For examples of the influence of the Bible in Mexico see ibid., 288–90.

20. Argentina 1818–21, Chile 1821–22, Peru 1822–24; Schroeder, "Father José María," 380–81.

21. Schroeder, 382, 384, Dussel, *Tomo V*, 196–97.

Mexico to reinforce earlier introductions of the method and remained there until 1830.

In 1822, while Itúrbide was still Emperor, Mora was part of an committee formed to present a plan to Congress for educational reform. For the next decade and under various administrations, Mora labored to change the educational system, calling for a general education of the people and to close private schools if they did not improve. By the time Thomson arrived on the scene, Mora was already a veteran in education reform.

Mora and Thomson met in 1827 shortly after the latter's arrival. In Mexico City Thomson met many religious, including José María Alcantará, rector of the college of San Agustín along with many friars and nuns who supported his endeavor and the distribution of Spanish-language Bibles.[22] At first Thomson had little problem finding interested parties for his Bibles, including those published without the Apocrypha. However, as Mora and other Liberals, especially President Farías, stepped up attacks on the clergy and their privileges, resistance grew to Thomson's enterprise. Opposition to Thomson's Apocrypha-less Bibles grew and papal edicts against Bible societies caused Thomson's clientele to dwindle.[23]

In 1830 Thomson was forced to leave Mexico when warned by Mora of death threats against him. Thomson left behind numerous crates of Bibles with more on the way. Had Mora simply been interested in Thomson's educational work he may have left matters at that, but with Thomson's departure Mora tried to take over, in some respects, his friend's work. He maintained contact with the Bible Society in Great Britain and even tried to have his own translation of the Bible published as well as underwrite translations into the indigenous languages.[24] In 1834 Mora was forced into exile and, when arriving in London, offered his services to the Bible Society. For the next decade he lived in Paris, spending his time, among other things, in producing a Nahuatl transla-

---

22. Schroeder, "Father José María," 385, Dussel, *Tomo V*, 196.

23. Opposition to the Bible societies focused not on their being in the vernacular but that they were without doctrinal or catechetical notes that would guide the reader in his study. There was a fear that reading the Bible without ecclesiastical guidance could lead to error and danger to one's faith. Popes throughout the nineteenth century published edicts and encyclicals against the Bible societies. Schroeder, "Father José María," 388, cf. Jean-Pierre Bastian, *Disidentes*, 27.

24. Schroeder, "Father José María," 390.

tion for the Gospel of Luke.[25] Throughout those years, the Bible Society, unaware of Mora's financial difficulties including his precarious status as an exile, continued to hound him for monies owed. Shortly before Mora's death Thomson wrote a touching letter to the society informing them of all of Mora's contributions, and in light of his difficulties and work on behalf of Bible distribution, asked them to forgive his debt and demonstrate their appreciation.[26]

For Mora, as for many of the Catholic Liberals, the dissemination of the Bible was the means towards improving society beginning with the educational quality of its citizens. Since the Bible was a holy book, literacy as well as moral improvement and the dissemination of Catholic doctrine could be accomplished through the one means. Further, by allowing the people access to the Book, the spiritual reform of the people could take place. Like the Enlightened Catholics of the previous century, Catholic Liberals believed that education was the key to the destruction of superstition; except, that while the Enlightened Catholics focused on the education of the parish priests, the Liberals focused on the citizenry. "'Millions of souls will divorce themselves from the bad clergy,' the liberal press predicted, but not to become secular rationalists: to the contrary, they would 'conserve the most powerful connection, the belief in just one Book.'"[27]

The leaders of the Liberal movement were not the only ones who espoused religious beliefs that echoed those of Enlightened Catholicism. Alejandro Cortazar has taken inventory of novels written during or shortly after the Wars of Reform wherein the greed, gluttony, and exploitation of the Roman Catholic Church is contrasted with the heroic figure of a priest, sometimes Miguel Hidalgo himself, who converts "theology into charity" and lives and works among the people, doing good.[28]

Religious Toleration

The Constitution of 1824 had guaranteed the rights of the Roman Catholic Church as the sole religion of the land. Catholicism was perceived to be the integral glue that could hold the disparate regions and

---

25. Ibid., 392.
26. Ibid., 394.
27. Nesvig, *Religious*, 80.
28. Ibid., 106–28.

peoples of the nation together. Religious pluralism, it was believed by some, would only highlight the social and ideological differences among the people and lead to unrest or violence. However, the issue of religious toleration could not be held at bay for long. In its effort to establish trade with the United States and the European nations, some of which were traditionally Protestant (Germany, Great Britain), Mexico had to wrestle with the question of religious tolerance. Trade treaties with Protestant nations often stipulated that freedom of worship should be allowed for nationals living or conducting business in Mexico under the auspices of their respective embassies.[29] Already in the 1820s some Liberal publications were calling for a form of religious liberty. Juan de Dios Cañedo (1786–1850) was the only legislator to dissent from the 1824 Constitution's provision of Roman Catholic exclusivity.[30] Some Liberal leaders saw religious liberty as inherent in God's creation of humanity whereas others defended it as having its basis in the free preaching of the gospel.[31] Others perceived of religious liberty as essential to the growth and development of the Mexican nation. General Joaquín Parres said, "I would like my homeland to be in the state of being tolerant and our ports open to all foreigners because in this way the Enlightenment, the population, and industry will increase as far as is necessary to make us as happy as we can be in this world; sometimes I have lamented that this is not possible. I desire a less fanatical nation that nevertheless, does not cease from being religious."[32]

The matter became further complicated and controversial in 1831 with the publication of the *Ensayo sobre la tolerancia religiosa* (Treatise on Religious Tolerance) by Vicente Rocafuerte (d.1847), the Ecuadorian legislator and diplomat. In this treatise, written while in Mexico, Rocafuerte called for the separation of Church and State and for a dismantling of the privileges of the Catholic Church. He sought to establish a clause on religious liberty in the Constitution in order to encourage Protestants to migrate to Mexico and settle in sparsely populated areas. Though supported by some Liberals such as José María Luis Mora, Rocafuerte suf-

---

29. Cf. López and Guerra, *Protestantismo*, 42.
30. Matute et al., *Estado, Iglesia*, 182.
31. Ibid., 183–84.
32. Ibid., 185.

fered imprisonment before returning to South America.[33] The issue of religious freedom would not be settled until the era of Benito Juárez.

THE JUÁREZ REFORMS

The resilient Santa Anna was president again. After the debacle of the Mexican-American War of 1846 one would think that Mexico had seen the last of the general. But with the tenacity of a boomerang he was back in 1853, this time with the help of the Conservatives. During this tenure, Santa Anna was supported by the military and the church hierarchy, both groups vying to implement their own visions for the Mexican nation. In the process, religious leaders took on positions of power within the civil government.[34]

Santa Anna's final reign was a disaster. He funneled money to himself, sold off even more Mexican territory to the United States (the Gadsden Purchase) and declared himself, "Most Serene Highness" and dictator for life. Santa Anna wasted no time in uprooting Liberal leaders and retaliating against his enemies, real or perceived. One of those was a governor of Oaxaca, the Zapotec Indian lawyer Benito Juárez who had refused asylum to the General after his most recent humiliation.[35]

Santa Anna never forgot that rebuff and Juárez was sent into exile to New Orleans where he met other Liberal refugees including Melchor Ocampo, who led a group of men seeking to overthrow the Serene Highness's government. When, in 1854, the *Plan de Ayutla* was proclaimed, it met with considerable support from other parts of the country. Led by Juan Alvarez the rebellion made its way to Mexico City in 1855 where Santa Anna was himself forced into exile.[36]

The new Liberal government wasted little time in trying to reform the nation. Led by Alvarez as provisional president and Ignacio Comonfort as secretary of war, it also included Melchor Ocampo (treasury), Miguel Lerdo de Tejada (development), and Benito Juárez as minister of justice. Between 1855 and 1857 a series of laws were promulgated by the government seeking to secularize society without overtly attacking the Church.

---

33. López and Guerra, *Protestantismo*, 42.
34. Saranyana, *Teología*, II/2: 112–13.
35. Meyer and Sherman, *Course*, 375, Mecham, *Church and State*, 359.
36. Meyer and Sherman, *Course*, 376.

- Ley Juárez (1855) placed strong conditions on military and ecclesiastical courts, allowing these to have jurisdiction only over military and ecclesiastical cases. Members of the army or the clergy accused of violating civil or criminal law would stand trial in federal or state court.

- Ley Lerdo (1856) prohibited civil and ecclesiastical institutions from owning oradministering property not connected with day-to-day functions. This meant that the Church could maintain its churches, seminaries, and other buildings, but had to divest itself of properties such as rural estates. The government had no plans to take the land; they were to be sold and the owner could keep the profit.

- Ley Iglesias (1857) was the first law directed at the Church as it prohibited it from charging high fees to administer the sacraments and prohibited the Church from using the State to collect tithes. The poor would receive the sacraments freely while those who could afford to do so would pay a modest fee.

Additionally, in January 1857 the government issued a law secularizing the powers of the registry, taking the recording of births, marriages, and deaths out of the hands of the Church and placing them into those of the State. Furthermore, and in continuation with the cemetery reforms of the late 1800s, cemeteries would be taken out of the jurisdiction of the Church and placed under the Department of Hygiene.[37] The meaning of these acts was obvious—it would be the State, not the Church, that determined citizenship through birth, the legitimacy of marriages, and the legal state of the deceased.

The reaction to these laws was predictable. The military and the clergy dusted off the old battle cry of *religión y fueros*. Juárez defended the law, stating that it was not an attack on the Church but an effort to make all members of society equal in the eyes of the law. In the end, Alvarez relinquished the presidency to Comonfort, a more moderate voice among the Liberals.[38]

In reaction to Ley Juárez, a revolt broke out in December 1855 in the mountain village of Zacapoaxtla in the state of Puebla. Led by deserters from the army who sympathized with the Conservative cause, the rebel-

---

37. Ibid., 378; Bastian, *Disidentes*, 28; Brading, *First America*, 656; Mecham, *Church and State*, 360–64, cf. Voekel, *Alone Before God*.

38. Mecham, *Church and State*, 360–61.

lion was suppressed a month later. The government pointed the finger at the Bishop of Puebla, Pelagio Antonio Labastida y Dávalos (1816–91) who was accused of instigating the rebellion using diocesan funds. He was deported to Rome later that year where he heavily influenced Pope Pius IX's attitude towards Mexico.[39]

Ley Lerdo caused more of an uproar among the Church hierarchy. Archbishop Garza of Mexico declared that the State had no rights over the Church, even over its properties. Brading has noted that when it came to their rights and property even the most nationalist bishop turned from any vestiges of Jansenism towards an ultramontane position that effectively separated Church from State. The State should have no more right to legislate on the polity or property of the Church than the Mexican government had over any other sovereign entity.[40] Churchmen called down the higher power of thomistic logic to make their case against the liberal positions. Against the principle of the equality of all people they pointed to natural law and against national sovereignty they looked to God's sovereignty. Religious tolerance would open the door to Protestantism and communism. The clergy affirmed the hierarchical nature of the Church not only as sovereign of the State but also as the entity whose power and wealth had helped build Mexican society.[41]

The opposition of the clergy, however, did not cause the Liberals to back down. They allowed those who had taken religious vows to revoke them and rejoin secular society. The Jesuits, who had been readmitted into the country by Santa Anna, were expelled once again and the University of Mexico closed under the accusation that it had become a center of clerical propaganda and rebellion.[42]

---

39. Saranyana, *Teología*, II/2: 114ff. That was not the end of Labastida's career, however. During the Wars of Reform he was recalled to Mexico by General Miguel Miramón but was exiled once more in 1862. It was he who put forth Maximilian as a candidate for Emperor of Mexico. Named Archbishop of Mexico by the pope, Labastida was named to the Regency of the Empire and was part of the delegation sent to Austria to offer Maximilian the crown in 1863. He was replaced by the French over differences regarding ecclesiastical properties and likewise, became disenchanted with Maximilian when the latter proclaimed religious liberty. Retreating to Europe, he took part in the Vatican I Council of 1869–70 but was given permission by Juárez to return to Mexico in 1871.

40. Brading, *First America*, 656–57, Mecham, *Church and State*, 363.

41. Bastian, *Disidentes*, 30.

42. Mecham, *Church and State*, 363.

In 1857 a new Constitution was drafted that included the controversial reform laws. Because they opposed the Plan of Ayutla, Conservatives went underrepresented at the constitutional assembly. The Constitution of 1857 also included Mexico's first Bill of Rights, which for our interests is significant because of what it did *not* include: an article establishing the Roman Catholic Church as the State Religion. The Constitution did not provide for freedom of religion, but its silence on the spiritual monopoly of the Catholic Church opened a back door, as it were, for other faiths.[43]

The church hierarchy, in general, was vocal in its opposition to the new Constitution. They recognized the battle lines drawn against their privileges and traditional role in society. Not only did they threaten excommunication upon anyone who took advantage of Ley Lerdo to buy church properties, but the same punishment would be meted out on those who swore allegiance to the Constitution's objectionable articles.[44] Not only did the defenders of the Church seethe at Ley Lerdo and Ley Juárez, but they also found fault with several articles of the Bill of Rights. Freedom of education conflicted with the Church's mission to "teach all nations"; freedom from compulsory service would affect the regular orders, giving them a legal means to renounce their vows and freedom of the press could invite criticism of the Church.[45] One bishop urged armed rebellion against the government.[46] A writer, Bernardo Couto, eloquently penned a more nuanced and sublime defense:

> The Catholic Church is a universal society, given that man, by nature is divided into races that are antipathetic among themselves and in a thousand distinct societies, constituted upon opposing concepts. Christianity follows the contrary route as it forms, out of all humanity, of all origins, from all conditions, of all peoples, a single community . . . Catholicism is the greatest and most beautiful plan of association that has appeared on Earth. With its two characteristic features: unity and universality, it is intimately

---

43. Cf. Mecham, *Church and State*, 364.

44. Dussell, *Tomo V*, 216–17.

45. The proposed article on freedom of religion had been defeated by moderates and conservatives fearing that it would provoke anarchy and the disintegration of the family. Meyer, *Course*, 380.

46. Mecham, *Church and State*, 365.

linked to independence of each church in respect to the country in which it resides.[47]

As a result of this universal and independent body, any interference on the part of any government into the affairs of the Church constituted tyranny.

Even Pope Pius IX, influenced by the exiled Bishop of Puebla, chimed in:

> In order that the faithful who live there may know and the catholic world may understand that we energetically reprove all that the Mexican government has done against the catholic religion and its sacred ministers and pastors, against its laws, rights, and properties, as well as against the authority of the holy see, we lift our pontifical voice with apostolic freedom, in this full assembly to condemn, reprove, and declare null and void the said decrees, and whatever else the civil authority has put into effect with such contempt of ecclesiastical authority and this apostolic see.[48]

The conundrum for Mexican citizens was not merely theoretical or confined to newspapers or the floor of the Congress. The Church was the vehicle of salvation for good Catholics and to be deprived of the sacraments meant to be outside the grace of God, particularly at the point of death. The tension and dissonance between fealty to State and homeland on the one hand and the deep emotional and spiritual need to remain in the good graces of the Church (and all that implied in society) must have been enormous. Civil servants, for example, could be denied treatment at a Catholic hospital, but if they did not swear allegiance to the Constitution they could be deprived of their jobs. Similarly, priests who administered the sacraments to those who had not forsworn the Constitution would be suspended. The Laws of Reform and the Constitution brought forth the simmering tensions within a society that at once wanted to hold on to tradition and yet emulate modern, prosperous nations. The positions were uncompromising and would lead, yet again, to civil war.[49]

---

47. Quoted in López and Guerra, *Protestantsmo*, 65–66.

48. Meyer and Sherman, *Course*, 381; Mecham, *Church and State*, 363. For more on Pius IX's reactions to Mexican Liberalism of this time see Dussel, *Tomo V*, 218–19, 225.

49. Meyer and Sherman, *Course*, 381.

LIBERAL FATHERS

The presence of clergy who would give their support to the Juárez reforms might seem surprising to those who perceive of the Mexican Church as a particularly conservative institution, concerned with holding on to their colonial power, rights and privileges. Indeed, there is ample evidence suggesting this: the hierarchy's collaboration with the Conservative factions and their refusal to aid the Liberal government during the war with the United States, to cite two significant instances. Later, sectors of the clergy would win the spite and disdain of a great part of the Mexican people through their encouragement and backing of the foreign occupation under Maximilian.

Reality, however, is not so easily divided into the black and white hats and the attitude of the Catholic Church, its hierarchy and its priests, like that of any other institution, could be much more diverse. Alongside the more conservative attitude towards the State run other threads in the clerical history of the Mexican nation, namely members of the Catholic episcopate who sought to adapt and accommodate to the reality of the new republic as well as priests who more openly sided with the Liberal agenda. In the decades between Independence and the Wars of Reform the response of the Catholic Church in Mexico towards the government varied, often depending on how far the Liberal agenda sought to curtail the assumed role and rights of the Church in society.

Despite the alarm with which Church officials viewed the revolt of 1810 and its subsequent support of royalist forces during the Wars of Independence, by the 1820s the Catholic Church argued that it was compatible with whatever political structures the City of Man may devise on Earth. Thus by definition, Catholicism was not incompatible with Liberalism or federal forms of government. The Bishop of Puebla, for example, removed the ecclesiastical governor because of his lack of support of the 1824 Constitution. Despite the reservations of some over certain anticlerical clauses in the Constitution, and despite occasional clashes with parish priests who opposed the Constitution, Church authorities proceeded afoot in their alliance with the Liberal government.[50]

The adaptability of the Church in this new era extended to the use of Liberal language and law to both defend its interests and to promote its relevancy in the fledgling Mexican society. Connaughton cites the

---

50. Connaughton, "The Enemy Within," 184.

example of the ecclesiastical governor of the Diocese of Guadalajara. In 1826 Miguel Gordoa protested the State of Jalisco's intention to exclude some clerics from Church appointments based upon a perceived lack of patriotism, stating that such an act would violate due process and was incompatible with the liberal government and its guarantees of a citizen's legal rights. When later, the government sought to control the use and sale of Church lands in the 1830s, one writer was able to summon forth the Liberal tradition and the Constitution to accuse the State itself of violating its own values.[51]

In the beginning of the 1830s, when cracks were more noticeable in the national alliance, Church spokesmen hesitated at attacking the Liberal State or liberalism outright, instead directing their invective against extreme positions, against Masonic intrigue and anticlericalism. To the contrary, the Church continued to use the language of "freedom" and "independence" to stake for itself the rights enjoyed under Liberalism. Nonetheless, the tensions that developed between the State and the Church in the 1830s, particularly over matters of Church property, began to convince some Church leaders that the nation was on a path towards a form of ultraliberalism that marginalized the Church's role in society (primarily to a lending institution to the government) in favor of a more humanistic or secular view of the citizen and her role in society.[52]

Tensions between the government and the Church only increased in the 1840s as an increasingly leftward-leaning State exerted pressure to take over ecclesiastical wealth in order to relieve the national debt as well as make clergy dependent upon an established salary like any other civil employee. Church authorities pored over the 1842 Constitution and objected to the clauses establishing freedom of expression and private education. Additionally, language in the Constitution appeared to imply that the rights of patronage belonged to the Mexican State, limiting the propagation of papal communiqués and abrogating to the government greater power over Church properties and authority.[53]

As the war drums between the United States and Mexico beat to a deafening rumble in 1847, the pressure increased on the Church to

---

51. Ibid., 185.
52. Ibid., 183, 185–87.
53. Ibid., 187–88.

advance the government loans to run the war while still forbidding the Church to sell its possessions. According to Connaughton, despite the feeling that anticlerical and ultraliberal factions were taking the government hostage and determining policy, Catholic leaders continued to call upon the 1824 Constitution in defense of its property rights and role in Mexican society, demanding not special rights but the same equal rights afforded to any citizen under the Constitution. Despite this appeal to Liberal and republican values, the specter of the Church's lack of cooperation with the State in the face of North American invasion would return to haunt it during and after the French occupation of the country in the 1860s.[54]

The attitude of Church leadership vis-à-vis the State up through the 1850s appears to have been one of adaptation and accommodation in an effort to maintain relevant in Mexican society. While struggling with the government over the rights of patronage and the traditional place of the Church in Mexican society (along with the attendant issues of religious freedom, private education and the national registry), Church authorities, some of them coming from an Enlightened Catholic tradition, continued to dialogue with the Liberal governments and avail themselves of the republican tradition to stake a claim in the life of the nation. Sermons and pamphlets repeatedly spoke of the alliance between the Church and the government and of the Church's dedication to ideals such as progress, civilization, freedom and true democracy. When battle-lines were drawn over particular issues or actions against the Church, the enemy was not Mexican liberalism per se, but rather, perceived extreme factions within the Liberal party that conspired to act in a regalist and definitely non-republican manner against the Church.

The views of Church authorities are one matter. The perspectives of the parish priest, in some cases, could be different altogether. As early as the 1820s some priests were advocating for a stronger balance of power in favor of the State. José de Jesús Huerta, a parish priest of Jalisco argued in favor of the national patronage and attacked clerical authorities. Father Francisco Delgadillo of Colima demanded in 1830 that the government enact a law setting out the responsibilities of the Church under the Nation. Removed from his post because of his outspokenness, Delgadillo continued to complain against the "yoke" of the Church's power.[55]

54. Ibid., 187.
55. Ibid., 190.

Some priests escalated their rhetoric in favor of freedom and liberty. Connaughton has noted the activities of some clerics in Colima and Guadalajara in the mid-forties who rallied the people in speeches, pamphlets, and sermons that combined religious, social, and political issues ranging from a return to Christian virtues to a reform of the educational and legal systems to a defense of the State's authority over Church wealth and property.[56]

In the years before the Reform Laws and the 1857 Constitution matters of religious tolerance, public education, and the ever-present frustration over the appropriation of Church wealth continued to tear at the national alliance. Added to the frustrations of Church hierarchy were the presence of dissident priests, the eroding role and power of the Church in society, and the antagonism of those in government and in public who adopted more extreme, even anticlerical positions.[57] Considering the overall historical context, the outright opposition of the Catholic Church towards the Juárez Reforms was the proverbial frosting on the cake, the eventual outcome of ever-increasing tensions and antagonisms between the Mexican government and the Church.

The clergy who did support the Constitution appear to be exceptions that prove the rule. The Bishop of Oaxaca, Juárez's home state, accepted the Constitution and had a Te Deum sung in its honor. The Vicar Capitular of the cathedral in Tabasco also gave his support. One priest in Tampico published an article defending the Constitution and denouncing priests who used the pulpit to encourage resistance to the law. A priest in Jalisco went even further, saying that it was not always necessary to obey the bishops in matters outside doctrine. Seven priests took up arms in defense of the Reform. In response to the threat of excommunication, five clerics promised to absolve anyone who had sworn loyalty to the new Constitution. In Monterrey, a public reading in the churches of the circular letter prohibiting fealty to the Constitution was forbidden by the local clergy.[58]

56. Ibid., 190–92.

57. For example, a drop in religious vocations in the decades after Independence and a greater acceptance of secular activities apart from religious ones (such as the opening of an opera in Guadalajara during Lent or non-religious Independence Day events) that could be interpreted as a rejection of the religious role in the public sphere or evidence of a modernity in Mexico that makes a greater distinction between the religious and the secular. Ibid., 188, 192.

58. Greenland, "Religious Reform," 10; Peláez, *Historia*, 158; Dussel, *Tomo V*, 219; cf. Connaughton, "The Enemy Within," 191.

The presence of parish priests who broke ranks with their superiors in support of the more radical aspects of the Liberal agenda (freedom of the press, public education, etc.) including the Laws of Reform and the 1859 Constitution call for some sort of explanation. Why would they hold positions and ideas that placed them in disagreement or even outright antagonism with some of their superiors? One explanation may lie with their very position. As parish priests they were simply closer to the grassroots—their personal backgrounds, their connections, and of course their ministries brought them closer to the personal and ideological currents of the times. Like Hidalgo and Morelos before them, these parish priests could sympathize with the needs and desires of the people around them and perhaps conclude that certain ideas would serve the nation better. Conversely, parish priests had less to lose. During the rising tensions of the 1840s, particularly under the presidency of Valentín Goméz Farías, the group most affected was the higher clergy. During this period their power was continually curtailed by the State through a series of laws revoking the ecclesiastical courts, abolishing the clerical monopoly over education and enacting the freedom of the press without ecclesiastical censure. Clergy were forbidden to address political issues in their sermons and monks and nuns were allowed to forego their monastic vows in the name of freedom. In a strike to the Church's coffers, the compulsory tithe of 10 percent was abolished and individuals were instead encouraged to give to the Church whatever their consciences and piety led. Additionally, the expulsion in 1833 by Farías of several bishops recently appointed by Pope Gregory XVI was a definitive blow in the name of National Patronage and served as a shot across the bow against the Church hierarchy.

It appears then that the increasing pressure against the Church in the years leading towards the 1857 Reform Laws was directed mainly at the power of the higher clergy rather than against the clergy as a whole and represented escalating skirmishes in the greater war over episcopal patronage and ultimately, the power of the State vis-à-vis the Church. These struggles led Church leaders to dig in their heels and hold their positions while parish priests felt more at liberty to express dissident opinions supporting the power and prerogatives of the government.

THE CONSTITUTIONALIST CLERGY

The Plan of Tacubaya began the Wars of Reform (1858–61) when conservative general Féliz Zuloaga (1813–98) dissolved Congress and suspended the Constitution of 1857 without firing a shot. Comonfort decreed to himself extraordinary powers, a move that alarmed both his enemies and his allies. Zuloaga's forces took many people prisoner during the inevitable unrest, including Benito Juárez, who was next in line to the presidency. Zuloaga pressured Comonfort to resign, which he did in January 1858. Juárez, who had escaped north to Querétaro, was proclaimed president. Establishing their capital in Veracruz, in the latter half of 1859 the Liberal government issued decrees that took the reform even further. Births and marriages became civil ceremonies, monastic orders were outlawed, and all church properties were nationalized.[59] The number of religious holidays was reduced as well as the public display of religion such as processions or festivals. The absolute separation of Church and State was promulgated as was the freedom of worship.[60] These laws were aimed directly at the Church's role in society (including its continual role in supporting the Conservatives) and were perhaps meant more for moral effect than for execution at the time.[61]

The Church gave three million pesos in their support of the Conservative armies against the Liberals. Between 1858 and 1860 several prominent churches were sacked and robbed of hundreds of thousands of pesos by some of Juárez's generals but the President made them return the monies. During and after the civil war, forty churches, in addition to various seminaries and convents dating to the early years of the colony were sacked or even demolished by Juárez's supporters. During the War of Reform, Conservative forces killed two priests while the juaristas killed ten.[62]

A small group of clerics however, did, in 1859, lend their support to the Laws of Reform and the Constitution. This circle, though never very large, was led primarily by four priests, Manuél Aguilar Bermúdez, Rafael Díaz Martínez, Francisco Domínguez, and Enrique Orestes.[63] Biographical data on these men is very scarce save what might be revealed in their few existing letters, but their activities and careers were centered on Mexico City, the states of Mexico and Oaxaca. Their aim in

59. Saranyana, *Teología*, II/2: 116–17.

60. Meyer and Sherman, *Course*, 383, Bastian, *Disidentes*, 32, Mecham, *Church and State*, 367–70.

61. Mecham, *Church and State*, 367.

62. Peláez, *Historia*, 156–57.

63. Bastian, *Disidentes*, 32. Martínez had publicly supported the 1855 law dissolving ecclesiastical courts and, in 1856, Ley Lerdo. López and Guerra, *Protestantismo*, 64.

gathering was not only to support the Liberal government but to reform the Church. We must remember from the examples of dissident clergy in the previous decades that these two emphases were not exclusive of one another. The Constitutionalist Clerics appear to have had a nationalistic streak, maintaining that the Mexican Church should be indeed, a *Mexican* Church, and independent of Rome in the tradition of the Enlightened Catholics and more recently, Servando Teresa de Meier.

Fay Greenland suggests that some members of this group had met as early as 1857, composed of seven curates and four itinerant vicars, later joined by nine more priests in the Mexico City area who deplored the corruption of the clergy, the hypocrisy of the upper classes and the idolatry of the Indians.[64] A very telling letter from Bermúdez dated 1865 described the onset of this group and his own personal journey. It clearly describes the connections between political liberalism and its critique of Roman Catholicism, enlightened Christianity and their nascent movement, later known as Church of Jesus.

Manuél Bermúdez was motivated by the persecution he suffered from the Roman Catholic Church for thirteen years for his "liberal opinions," indicating that he had associated himself with the Liberal causes at least since 1852. He eventually began to study for himself the doctrines and conduct of the Catholic Church, coming to the conclusion that it was without "the spirit of Jesus," "without the pure customs of the primitive times," and full of superstitions and vices. For him it was a mercantile agency pretending to sell "heaven for gold"—it "sacrifices the happiness of nations, it impedes their enlightenment and their progress, to forbid to humanity the rights it has received from God, and to exercise upon men a horrible despotism of conscience: all crimes before God, and before enlightened Christianity."[65]

It is important to note his emphases in this letter, perhaps one of the earliest and from one of the original leaders of what would become the Church of Jesus. More than other subsequent documents it connects the movement with the agenda of the Liberal Catholics and the Enlightened Catholics a century earlier.[66] Bermúdez notes that the Roman Catholic

64. Greenland, "Religious Reform," 12.

65. Manuel Bermúdez, Letter to Horatio Potter, March 13, 1865. Archives of the Episcopal Church, Austin, Texas.

66. Many later documents would come from the next generation of leaders like Manuel Aguas or from representatives of the Episcopal Church in Mexico adding their perspective on the movement in order to garner support from the United States.

Church, upon inspection, was without the "spirit of Jesus," full of superstitions and *"without the pure customs of the primitive times."* Like the Enlightened Catholics, the Constitutionalist Fathers looked to the early Church as a more innocent era as yet uncorrupted by the accretions of later centuries—perhaps referring to Baroque theatricality and the perceived superstitions of the masses. While Catholic in their theology and administration of the sacraments, the Constitutionalist Clerics and their group sought to reform themselves according to the Bible and primitive Christianity, a set of priorities that will reverberate throughout the history of the movement. They so looked to the early Church as their model that they claimed to have rediscovered the form of vestments used by the apostles (alb with cincture and stole).[67] Bermúdez attacks the Church for having stooped to sell "heaven for gold," most likely a reference to the fees charged for the administration of sacraments, and emphasizing that instead of serving humanity, it impedes human beings from exercising the innate gifts received from God, indicating the inward work of grace we encountered with the Jansenists and the moral gift of conscience seen in Liberals such as Ocampo. These, for Bermúdez, were crimes against God and "against *enlightened Christianity.*"

The Constitutionalist Fathers not only attacked the morals and questionable practices of the Catholic Church but in line with the Liberal emphasis on Reason, questioned the roots of Catholic authority. It was not enough that practice and theology be founded upon custom or tradition—an appeal to papal authority or divine mission. Rather, religion should be reasonable—the antipathy of the superstition they so vigorously attacked. Reasonable faith, based upon the Bible, should strive to benefit society rather than hinder its progress into modernity. Concretely speaking then, true Christian faith is not only compatible with the Constitution of 1857 but should also endeavor to support it. Bermúdez, Orestes and the others were Liberal Catholics in the tradition of eighteenth-century Enlightened Catholicism. Despite all its deficiencies they saw the Roman Catholic faith as integral to Mexico—an important part of the nation's history and its people's spirituality. The Constitutionalist Fathers only sought to correct what they perceived as abuses in the Church, or traditions that were not based upon the gospel, such as the issue of clerical celibacy. They did not perceive of Liberalism as antithetical to the Catholic faith but as a viable tool through which

---

67. Bechtel, "The Mexican Episcopal Church," 6 n.9.

a reform of the Church might be enacted. In other words, they might have conceived of the Conservative captivity of the Catholic Church by which the Christian message had been compromised by the colonial *status quo*—a Church that had lost sight of the fundamentals of the faith as it sought to retain its traditional power, prestige and wealth. The Juárez Reforms then, could serve as a means by which the Church could be purged of its conflicts of interest, freeing it from the interests of its own power and outdated traditions to better serve the Mexican people.

The Constitutionalist Clergy left the Roman Catholic Church as soon as "the Republic initiated the reformed religion, of which neither I nor my companions can authorize the abuses." This is perhaps a reference to the Liberal separation of Church and State and the abuses committed by the Liberal army during the War such as the desecration of churches.[68] Bermúdez continues: "Since the work of restoring the Mexican Roman Church to its first purity would have been very difficult and fraught with opposition. Therefore, it appeared better and of quicker fruit to admit and plant in the capital the Mexican Apostolic Catholic Society instituted in 1853 in New Mexico and Chihuahua by Rev. Dr. Nicholson"[69] Thus in order to best work towards the reform of the Church the Constitutionalist Fathers sought to ally themselves with the Mexican Apostolic Catholic Society. This organization was no more than a group of Christians who believed in God according to the Scriptures and used the Book of Common Prayer as a guide or basis of union for their worship. It was begun, first in New Mexico in the early 1850s, by E. C. Nicholson of the Methodist Episcopal Church (MEC) in the United States. He was unable to found a Methodist congregation in the West so instead began Bible study groups.[70] Finding success thusly, he established the Society in the northern state of Chihuahua. It is difficult to conceive of this seedling movement as the planting of a church as Nicholson did not seem concerned with the founding of an institution with the structures to propagate itself beyond providing local leaders. The opposition towards establishing independent churches was overwhelming during his tenure in New Mexico.[71] The establishment of

68. Cf. Meyer and Sherman, *Course*, 383.

69. Manuel Bermúdez, Letter to Horatio Potter, March 13, 1865. Archives of the Episcopal Church, Austin, Texas.

70. Cf. Martínez, *Sea La Luz*, 56–57.

71. Ibid., 56–58.

a rival Church, particularly one without resources from abroad could prove disastrous and dangerous for its members. Since the local leaders were not ordained priests then, it is inconceivable that the Society could constitute a Church in the sense of preaching the Word and the administering the Sacraments by a priest in the apostolic succession. Most likely it seems that the Mexican Apostolic Catholic Society was meant to serve as a mutual support group for persons who wanted to meet, pray, and study the Bible and encourage one another in good works. There seems to be no effort underway other than to make better Christians rather than create Methodists.[72]

Nicholson himself confessed that he had desired to work among the people in Central or South America but that the time was ripe to initiate missions in Mexico, particularly to English-speaking residents there.[73] However, the political reforms instituted by Juárez had made it possible to work among the Mexicans. In a fit of hyperbole he stated, "Juárez seized upon the pillars of the papal edifice and Sampson-like pulled down the mighty structure, overwhelming the priesthood and sweeping away their consecrated places together with treasure and images of silver and gold."[74] For Nicholson, the Episcopal Church was better suited to the needs of Latin America than any other denomination. For one, the liturgy of the PECUSA had much in common with the Catholic Mass, evangelical and yet containing all that was scriptural and catholic (universal) in the Mass. Further, since the Episcopal Church had its roots in antiquity it would be received better by the Mexicans as age and antiquity, a pedigree, were respected qualities. He goes on to note that his efforts in New Mexico had come to naught until he introduced morning and evening prayers, something people accustomed to the monastic hours and the accompanying tolling of the bells may have found familiar.[75]

It is unclear how and when the Constitutionalist Clerics became familiar with Nicholson's work but once acquainted, they began to use an adaptation of services from the Book of Common Prayer for their services. It is at this point that the movement began to transform and

72. Cf. E. C. Nicholson, Letter to Dr. Craik, January 31, 1864. Archives of the Episcopal Church, Austin, Texas.

73. Ibid.

74. E. C. Nicholson, Letter to Rev. Dennison, January 1, 1865. Archives of the Episcopal Church, Austin, Texas.

75. E. C. Nicholson, Letter to Dr. Craik, January 31, 1864. Archives of the Episcopal Church, Austin, Texas.

evolve—from a support group composed almost entirely of reforming clerics to a religious movement that sought to provide to the general population a related, yet alternative chord to the dominant Church.

The group of Constitutionalist Clergy were opposed by Lázaro de la Garza y Ballesteros (1785–1862), the Archbishop of Mexico, and others through publications that denounced them as a "synagogue of Satan," a "Protestant Church," and tellingly, "an invention of Jansenism," for their support of the Constitution. Any official who swore allegiance to the document would be excommunicated.[76] The Constitutionalist Clergy were displaced from their positions, so they sent a letter of appeal to the pope, signed by seventy-two priests.[77] This missive never made its destination, but it did reach the Liberal government in Veracruz. Juárez had Melchor Ocampo, the Secretary of State write to Rafael Martínez, who had previously, in 1857, led a statistical survey of the Church for the Liberal government.[78] In a letter dated October 25, 1859, he assures Martínez of the interest and appreciation of the government and that the State would assist in the matter of church reform and reward those clerics who would assist the progress of the nation given that clergy would lose their means of support if they came out in favor of the reformed Church.[79] "The government will take care that your efforts shall be rewarded in proportion to their usefulness to the country, and the government will take equal care to recompense all those worthy priests who, believing theirs is a mission of peace, yield their assistance in giving it to the Republic."[80]

Thus the Liberal clergy were to win over their congregations as well as other priests, and demonstrate that the Constitution of 1857 was consistent with Christian principles. The Liberal priests and those who joined them could help improve the quality of public education so that instead of learning "rancid silliness and ultramontanism, the young would imbibe morality."[81]

---

76. Bastian, *Disidentes*, 33, Bechtel, "The Mexican Episcopal Church," 13.

77. Bechtel, "The Mexican Episcopal Church," 14–15.

78. Nesvig, *Religious*, 84.

79. Rice, "Evangelical Episcopalians," 28.

80. Greenland, "Religious Reform," 13; cf. Bastian, *Disidentes,* 33; It is unclear though in what nature or under what justification this support would be forthcoming as Juárez's government was dedicated to the separation of Church and State.

81. Nesvig, *Religious*, 84.

Benito Juárez entered Mexico City victoriously on January 11, 1861. The government granted Martínez and nine other priests three centrally located churches, La Merced, La Santísima and San Hipólito.[82] Later, Ignacio Ramírez, the justice minister, would bequeath to them four more churches: Santo Domingo, La Jesús María, La Profesa and Bethemitas.[83]

The Church hierarchy, some of whom had been exiled by the Liberals before and during the Wars of Reform, along with Conservative papers attacked the renegade priests and their renegade parishes. Defenders of the Church would stand at the churches of the Constitutionalist Fathers, before the Mass, urging parishioners not to attend as the priests had been excommunicated. The papers published lists of deacons and priests who had joined the group and left the Catholic Church. In the end the Constitutionalist Clergy had to leave their parishes for several months.[84] A Liberal law issued in 1861 decreed that clerical supporters of the Constitution should take over churches confiscated from the regular orders, but both the numbers of these priests was too small and the local officials dragged their feet in executing the order in the classic colonial tradition of "*Obedezco pero no cumplo*" (I obey but do not comply).[85] The Constitutionalist Fathers, however, could count on the support of the Liberal newspapers, particularly from *El Monitor Republicano* which was led by one of their own, Enrique Orestes.[86] It was through the Liberal press that the clerics would continue their attacks on their opponents and seek to win the minds and hearts of the public.

Pamela Voekel keenly observes in her article detailing the early years of the Constitutionalist Clergy that this was a time when politics and religion were intricately interwoven and passions for one easily bled into the other. Thus when in December 1860 the Liberal government prohibited the public procession of the Eucharist to the sick, Enríquez Orestes mocked the scene in his newspaper, comparing those kneeling on the street as the Host passed as Israelites worshipping the golden calf. He himself would take the Eucharist to the dying but under his robes.[87] This is not too unlike the attacks on excessive displays of devotion or

---

82. Bastian, *Disidentes,* 33, Callcott, *Liberalism,* 23–24.
83. Kirk, "Mysterious Way," 6.
84. Nesvig, *Religious,* 85–86.
85. Ibid., 89.
86. Ibid., 90–91.
87. Ibid., 87.

piety that Enlightened Catholics made in the eighteenth century, but the interweaving of the politics of the Liberal/Conservative struggle appears to have pushed the combatants further into their respective corners with little common ground for understanding or reconciliation. Conservative clergy became more vehement in their stances and beliefs while Liberal priests became equally angry and despairing of any hope for reform in the Catholic Church. Each side, convinced that theirs was the battle for the soul of the Church, dug their heels in, and with the tinder of political loyalties added to the fire, it is no wonder that more heat than light was generated. With that context in mind, the movement that began advocating for reform ended in schism.

THE MEXICAN APOSTOLIC CHURCH OF 1861

Ramón Lozano was a parish priest and hacienda owner in Santa Barbara in the northeastern state of Tamaulipas. In March, 1861, following the Reform Laws, he sought to legitimize his three children. In the process he brought down the ire of the Conservative newspaper *El Pajaro Verde* as well as the condemnation of the bishop of Linares. He declared Lozano's sacraments invalid and prohibited any communication with him. Lozano defended himself, declaring loyalty to the Reform Laws and pointing out that he was far from being the only priest in the town to have reneged on his vows of celibacy. With growing resistance from the church hierarchy Lozano issued a declaration of the new *Iglesia Apostólica Mexicana de Santa Barbara de Tamaulipas*. This document, composed of twelve articles, was signed by over seventy people, including a number of priests, and called for a Church that was reformed, national, and founded on the Bible and the apostolic foundations.[88] The manifesto stated that true Catholicism and liberty of conscience would form the foundation of the Church, but that Church canons that contradicted the Reform Laws would be banned. Here we note that this body has the makings not only of a dissident religious group but by its allegiance to the Reform written into its declaration has the intention of being a truly national Church. The manifesto referred to the Church as being Catholic, Apostolic, and Mexican. The faith, sacraments, and ceremonies would go unchanged from those of the Roman Catholic Church; though it went on to condemn the celibacy of the priesthood, a sticking point over which the church reformers struggled long and hard

88. Bastian, *Disidentes*, 33; Nesvig, *Religious*, 92; Greenland, "Religious Reform," 14.

in light of the sudden legitimacy given to the fruits of clerical concubinage under the Reform Laws.[89]

Both church hierarchy and Liberals reacted to the establishment of this Mexican Apostolic Church. The Archbishop of Monterrey, for example, wrote a pastoral letter urging parishioners to go elsewhere for the sacraments. The Constitutionalist Clerics, however, invited Lozano to Mexico City, where, in Aguilar's house they decided to organize an independent church according to the principles laid out by Lozano. Through this move the Constitutionalist Clergy went further than their Enlightenment predecessors. Whereas the Enlightened clergy and others of the eighteenth century sought to renew the Church from within (through educational initiatives, the improvement of the parish priest, and by attacking religious opulence), the Constitutionalist Fathers took reform further into schism. They took the primitivist impulses in Enlightened religion that sought to base the faith in the early Church and went further. Since the Catholic Church of their time revealed its "despotism" over conscience by opposing the Reform laws and since it proved too entrenched to change from within, it was time to begin anew, founded on the Bible (disseminated to a greater length through the Bible Societies) and the early Church fathers. Another factor that perhaps contributed to the decision to start a Church body was the fact that the Juárez government was dedicated to the separation of Church and State. Whereas the State had attacked the privilege and finances of the Church, it did not take an active hand in punishing clergy that opposed it. When Juárez came to power after the Wars of Reform, he took a more conciliatory attitude towards the Conservatives, giving amnesty to all but a few leading Conservative generals and bishops.[90] Despite the pledge of support from the Liberal government, all the dissident priests had received thus far were a few church buildings. Whatever his feelings, Juárez was not about to replace the leaders of the Roman Catholic Church in Mexico with the few priests who had lent him support. He was not about to risk another whole-scale war over religion after having struggled for three years to gain the presidency. In effect, the Constitutionalist Father's own loyalty to the Reform may have cost them the ecclesiastical victory they desired. Unable to effect true church renewal through legislation as the Enlightened Catholics did, they decided first to plant a version

---

89. Rice, "Evangelical Episcopalians," 29–30; Kirk "Mysterious Way."
90. Meyer and Sherman, *Course*, 385–86.

of the Mexican Catholic Apostolic Society, a parachurch organization in modern parlance, and having failed at gaining much support in the midst of opposition, they then chose the further step of establishing a parallel Church following Lozano's example.

The next several years proved precarious for the alternative Church. The government had ceded to them the church Santísima Trinidad in Mexico City, but the people continued to stay away in droves. Political support was not forthcoming as Conservative forces and the Catholic Church redoubled their efforts, no doubt reinforced by the expulsion of the seven bishops accused by the government of collaborating with the Conservatives during the Wars of Reform. To add further injury, in the beginning of June, Melchor Ocampo, the Constitutionalist Clergy's advocate in government, was assassinated.[91] In addition, the Juárez government was now involved in a costly war with the French, British, and Spanish over unpaid debts since December 1861/ January 1862. Though the Spanish and British would eventually settle their differences with Mexico and leave, the French would occupy the country from 1863–67.[92] The fact that in 1862 Enrique Orestes and other clergy sought the financial help of the PECUSA gives evidence to their precarious existence, which by this time was not much more than a dozen priests and a few others, meeting in Bermúdez's home.[93]

UNDER THE FRENCH FLAG

Having received extraordinary powers and a strong vote of confidence from Congress, Benito Juárez, his Cabinet and what was left of the Mexican army, in the face of the advancing French military, evacuated to San Luis Potosí in the north-central region of the country. Meanwhile, battle lines had been drawn clearer between the State and the Church in the summer of 1862 when, upon hearing that priests were encouraging people to collaborate with the oncoming French against the government, Juárez issued a presidential decree condemning any clergy of any cult to three years imprisonment or deportation for inciting rebellion. He also suppressed the cathedral chapters and forbade the wearing of clerical garb in public.[94]

91. Bastian, *Disidentes*, 34.
92. Meyer and Sherman, *Course*, 387–401.
93. Nesvig, *Religious*, 93; Bastian, *Disidentes*, 33.
94. Meyer, *Course*, 390–91.

The Church had found its champion in the Tricolor. On their arrival in the Mexican capital, the French were celebrated in the National Cathedral with a Te Deum. A monarchist minority had convinced Emperor Napoleon III in France that Mexico would welcome a king. The Hapsburg Ferdinand Maximilian (1832–67), the Austrian archduke, was offered the crown and told disingenuously that the majority of the Mexican people clamored for a European king. Maximilian reached the outskirts of Mexico City on June 12, 1864, stopping by the Basilica of Guadalupe to pay homage to the Mexican Virgin before making his way into the city to a less than exuberant welcome by the people. Eleven Mexican prelates issued a pastoral letter celebrating the end of godless radicalism.[95]

Maximilian's first troubles came not from Liberals but from the Conservatives who had labored to place him on the throne. Much to their surprise and chagrin he would not revoke the Reform Laws and when the papal nuncio arrived with his list of demands, Maximilian all but ignored him. He would not return church lands confiscated by the government (and in fact levied several forced loans against the Church), and refused to re-establish the spiritual monopoly of the Catholic Church to the exclusion of all other religions.[96] It soon became obvious to the Conservatives that they had chosen the wrong man to spearhead their desires. Maximilian was a study in contradictions. A royal Hapsburg and the Emperor of Mexico, Maximilian sought to rule as an enlightened monarch and allow the Mexican people a greater voice in their affairs. A devout Catholic he nonetheless made provisions for religious liberty.

In this more permissive atmosphere the church of the Constitutionalist Fathers continued to operate with Maximilian's consent, who allowed the group to distribute Bibles and literature. Already in 1863 a group of evangelists in Nuevo León had received permission from the Emperor to sell Bibles. Once Maximilian promulgated the freedom of worship, the Society of Christian Friends was formed in which the Constitutionalist Fathers participated.[97] Maximilian also allowed the Constitutionalist Clerics to solemnize marriages. By allowing this the Emperor effectively put the dissident clergy on an equal footing with the Catholic

---

95. Ibid., 393.
96. Ibid., 395–96.
97. López and Guerra, *Protestantismo*, 67.

priests on all things but pay.⁹⁸ Led by Bermúdez, they met at Calle San José #21, adopting as a basis for doctrine the Bible as interpreted by the creeds and general councils, including the right of the clergy to marry and the establishment of services in Spanish rather than Latin.⁹⁹

Díaz Martínez succeeded Bermúdez in 1864. By this time no bishop had joined the movement, and for these renegade Catholic priests, apostolic succession through a bishop would be necessary in order to ordain priests. To procure this and the support the Mexican Society so desperately needed, it was decided to appeal to the leadership of the Protestant Episcopal Church of the United States.

Evangelical Episcopalians in the Nineteenth Century

Whereas modern observers may notice the diversity within the Episcopal Church—from conservative to liberal in theology, contemporary to Anglo-Catholic in liturgy, and all points in between—in the mid-nineteenth century the Episcopal Church was very much a product of the American religious environment, best characterized by its revivalist/evangelical strains. American revivalism was a product of its Puritan forbears that emphasized the conversion of the individual. Originally conceived from within a Calvinist framework, the evangelists and theologians of the First Great Awakening (1734–41) called upon individuals to search their consciences and to respond to the supernatural work of grace that God was working within them. Individuals were to reject all efforts of their own to attain salvation and to believe God's message in the Bible that promised redemption to those who trusted in Christ alone. This message carried within it a revolutionary spark as it placed the ultimate matter of salvation not within the community or in church leaders but within the conscience of the individual herself. It appealed to the rural and those disenfranchised by established churches, as seen in the reactions to the itinerant ministry of George Whitefield.

After the independence of the United States from Great Britain the flames of revival surged once again in the 1830s, particularly in rural New York and the Ohio Valley. Under Charles Grandison Finney (1792–1875), the Second Great Awakening took on a different tone. Whereas Whitefield and Jonathan Edwards emphasized the role of the

98. E. C. Nicholson, Letter to Rev. Dennison, January 1, 1865. Archives of the Episcopal Church, Austin, Texas.

99. Greenland, "Religious Reform," 20, Bechtel, "The Mexican Episcopal Church," 16.

Spirit in the individual's regeneration, Finney and his contemporaries focused on the individual's emotional reaction to the Gospel message. Thus, for Finney, revivalism became a stage opportunity—the music, the "mourner's bench," the message, were created to evoke a reaction in favor of salvation. In this context, salvation turned from an act of God to an act of the individual's will. This was a particularly attractive and relevant interpretation for the newly independent American people. Having freed themselves lately from the tyranny of England they could free themselves from Satan's bondage. As a people who could vote for their political leaders, they could now cast their vote for God. It is a message that went hand-in-hand with American progress. Seeing themselves as specially chosen by God or Providence they spread westward. Under this Manifest Destiny, they would convert the peoples they encountered with the good news of (political and religious) freedom and, if resisted, would resort to conquest for the good of the nations they encountered. It was in this spirit that the young nation flexed its muscles and spread west, and, desiring the lands belonging to their neighbors for their own economic and national progress, instigated the Mexican War of 1847.

The darker side to American evangelicalism was its virulent anti-Catholicism. This took two forms: religious and political. On the one hand was the traditional Reformation condemnation of the Catholic Church as idolatrous and unbiblical. The papacy was seen as tyrannous and even as antichrist for declaring itself the Vicar of Christ. Some Protestants equated Rome with the Whore of Babylon of Revelation 17–18. Political anti-Catholicism came from religious and irreligious alike as they perceived of the Catholic Church as a dangerous entity, set upon subjecting consciences and nations to the papacy's dictates. People saw it as a threat to democratic institutions and public schools. The influx of immigrants during the nineteenth century from Catholic countries such as Ireland and Italy alarmed some. The anti-Catholic nativist movement achieved prominence in the 1840s and its fears and hostilities resulted in mob action and violence against Catholics. The nativists found their political voice in the Know-Nothing Party of the 1850s (named as such because its members claimed to "know nothing" when questioned about it).[100] These kinds of sentiments and beliefs, present in the air since the founding of the American colonies, were present in the Episcopal

---

100. For a recent treatment of anti-Catholicism in the United States see Jenkins, *New Anti-Catholicism*.

Church of the mid-nineteenth century and affected how they viewed the Mexican reformers.

In the decades preceding contact made between the Mexican dissidents and the PECUSA, the Episcopal Church was caught up in its own struggles. The "Low Church" party—a term used synonymously with "evangelical" by this time—emphasized justification by faith, a personal conversion experience, and the authority of the Bible against that of tradition. They rejected the Real Presence of Christ in Communion, holding it to be a subjective exercise for the believer, and took part in some aspects of American revivalism. The "High Church" party, eventually associated with John Henry Newman and the Tractarian movement in England, focused on tradition and the importance of apostolic succession. The Tractarians read the Thirty-Nine Articles of the Church of England through a Catholic lens and sought to revitalize medieval traditions including the use of elaborate vestments, candles, incense and the Real Presence of Christ in the Eucharist, which they often referred to as the Mass. The High Churchmen thought the evangelicals too sentimental, eschewing rich and time-honored traditions in favor of simplistic emotional revivalism. For the evangelical party, the High Church movement was nothing less than an attempt to infuse the Anglican/Episcopal Church with Roman Catholic beliefs and practices.

In the United States conflict between the High and Low Church parties was not as extreme as in England. However, in 1839 the Oxford tracts that had given rise to the Tractarian movement were published in the United States. Some evangelical leaders within the PECUSA were alarmed, thinking that the Oxford Movement threatened the belief in justification by faith. To this was added the pressures of a generation gap. Older church leaders, in general, identified with Protestant faith and doctrine. Younger churchmen, however, were more willing to experiment with practices and ideas associated with Roman Catholicism including monastic orders and the veneration of Mary. Between 1840 and 1873 the evangelical party made efforts to minimize the influence and role of the High Churchmen, or Anglo-Catholics, as they were also known. Struggles over the interpretation of the Thirty-Nine Articles, the Prayer Book, and relationships with other Protestant denominations tossed the denomination back and forth, even resulting in the evangelical schism of 1873 that formed the Reformed Episcopal Church.[101]

---

101. For a detailed exposition of this period see Rice, 36–52. Cf. Prichard, *History*, 137–56.

Of Mexicans and Episcopalians

Having maintained contact with the Episcopal Church in the United States on several fronts, Díaz Martínez, Francisco Domínguez, and Enrique Orestes made their way to New York to have a bishop consecrated and to see if they could obtain financial support.[102] The meeting in New York was fraught with tension. Though greeted warmly by the Episcopal leaders, the Mexicans refused to say Mass with their hosts, perhaps due to unfamiliarity with the Episcopal order or, in this writer's opinion because the Mexicans did not want to appear that they were becoming part of the Episcopal Church. Orestes, after all, had defended the Catholic sacraments as essential for salvation and that the Host was not merely symbolic of the Body and Blood of Christ but was the sacrifice itself. For their part the Anglos wondered whether their visitors would elevate the Host and declare that it was Christ.[103] A letter from Elijah Guión—rector of St. Paul's Church in New Orleans who, with his associates, intended to serve as recommendations for the Constitutionalist Fathers—states that Orestes and Domínguez were on their way to New York and that they held to the Thirty-Nine Articles and the discipline and worship of the PECUSA. There is no further context to this letter to give us the perspectives of Orestes and Domínguez, so it is difficult to ascertain whether this was a misunderstanding on Guión's part, whether the Mexicans had overstated their commitment to the PECUSA so they could receive the ordination and support they required or whether Guión exaggerated their position to assist their endeavor. Given Orestes' commitment to the Catholic interpretation of the sacraments it is difficult to reconcile the facts on this declaration.[104]

As for the matter of ordination, the Right Reverend Henry Hopkins pointed out to the visitors that there were some canonical difficulties as to why a bishop could not be ordained but did not detail his objection.[105] It is quite probable that the Episcopal Church, since they recognized the sacraments and ordinations of the Roman Catholic Church, was uncom-

---

102. Bechtel, "The Mexican Episcopal Church," 17, Bastian, *Disidentes*, 36.

103. E. C. Nicholson, Letter to S. Dennison, May 1, 1865, Archives of the Episcopal Church, Austin, TX. Cf. Nesvig, *Religious*, 93.

104. Elijah Guión et al., Letter to the bishops, clergy, and laity of the Protestant Episcopal Church in the United States, October 17, 1864, Archives of the Episcopal Church, Austin, TX.

105. Bechtel, "The Mexican Episcopal Church," 17; Bastian, *Disidentes*, 36.

fortable with the idea of ordaining a bishop to a parallel body.[106] Of course, given the contemporaneous struggles in the PECUSA over the High and Low Church approaches to the liturgy and doctrine, Hopkins and the others could have also observed that the Mexican body had no intention of becoming Protestants and indeed may have suspected that the priests did not yet hold to the belief in justification by faith alone, a bulwark of American evangelicalism (including that wing of the Episcopal Church).

> At a council held in 1861, they (the Constitutionalist Clergy) adopted two main ideas, on which they could agree, namely, their independence from Rome, and the right of the clergy to marry. Besides, they believe that the Bible should be placed in the hands of all who are able and desire to read it; they all repudiate the worship of the Virgin Mary, and some of their representatives, at least, seem to lay fast hold on the doctrine of "Justification by Faith" as the only way to salvation. These people claim to be the reform*ing*, and not the reform*ed*, Church of Mexico; which implies perhaps that all are not yet sincere believers, and may need winnowing to separate the chaff from the wheat.[107]

To help assess the situation there, a delegate, E. C. Nicholson (now an Episcopal clergyman), who had worked in New Mexico and Chihuahua, was sent to Mexico to investigate the nascent Church in late 1864.

Nicholson's letters and reports are a glimpse into the life of the reformed Church during this period. He described the incompetence of Maximilian, who because of his waffling between Liberal and Conservative positions on issues, left a "bad odor" in the noses of the Liberals and the priests. During his time in Mexico, about six months, Nicholson formed a congregation with Episcopal polity and gave it the name he had previously used in Chihuahua, The Mexican Catholic Apostolic Society.[108] Nicholson notes that upon his arrival at Veracruz he met with people, all liberals adverse to the Emperor and administered the sacraments. He held services in people's homes as churches had been closed or used as stables or barracks by imperial troops. Nicholson especially notes the reaction to the services, held from the Book of Common

---

106. Since the times of St. Cyprian of Carthage (third century) and St. Augustine of Hippo (fourth century) the validity of the sacraments does not rest upon the worthiness of the officiant but upon the promises of God.

107. "Mexico," *The Spirit of Missions* 30 (April 1865), 158, quoted in Rice, "Evangelical Episcopalians," 61.

108. Rice, "Evangelical Episcopalians," 59.

Prayer. People inquired about the service book, saying it was "unlike the mockery of the Mass." He made sure that in his addresses he connected the antiquity and catholicity of the Prayer Book with the progress and prosperity of both England and the United States.[109]

Nicholson met with the Constitutionalist Fathers in Mexico City. As a result of his experiences with the Prayer Book and his conferences with Nicholson, Bermúdez became convinced that the Episcopal Church was the True Church. Bermúdez was also "admitted" as an evangelist of the Society based upon his prior Catholic credentials. Bermúdez stated, "Once united to the Episcopal communion . . . I believed I ought to associate my feeble services to the noble apostleship of Dr. Nicholson. We have advanced somewhat in proselytizing since already we reckon persons who will be our colaborers (sic) in Mexico, Toluca, Queretaro, Michoacán, Orizaba and other points."[110]

Bermúdez, by this time, seems to have given up the hope of Church reform from within and that Mexico as a nation would turn from the Roman Catholic Church so long as it was the monopolizer of religious worship. To this end he attached himself to a rival Church body. Bermúdez looked to the Church in the United States to continue to give the Mexicans "so great good," both now and in the future.[111] Bermúdez in this letter never states why exactly he decided to attach himself to the Episcopal Church. Up until this time the Constitutionalist Fathers had maintained their identity and mission as a reform movement with Catholicism, even if they had separated from that body. In an unsigned letter from 1865 that was witnessed by Bermúdez, the author (Nicholson?) noted that the leaders of the Mexican Apostolic Christian Church, as the Constitutionalist Fathers now called themselves, are "true catholics," assuring his audience that that they were moral people who believed in religious freedom, dedicated to God and humanity. They had renounced the pope and conformed their doctrine and liturgy according to the

---

109. E. C. Nicholson, Letter to Rev. Dennison, January 1, 1865, Archives of the Episcopal Church, Austin, Texas. Cf. William Tatlock, Mexican Episcopal Church Letter of the Four Bishops and Statement of the Provisional Committee, New York: Board of Missions of the Protestant Episcopal Church, November 11, 1894, Archives of the Episcopal Church, Austin, TX.

110. Manuel Bermúdez, Letter to Horatio Potter, Bishop of New York, March 13, 1865, Archives of the Episcopal Church, Austin, Texas.

111. Ibid. He does not elaborate on what constitutes the "great good" but it can be surmised from the letter that it has to do with financial and/or moral encouragement.

Book of Common Prayer and the PECUSA, practicing the sacraments and exercising morning and evening services.[112] It is quite possible that in the political atmosphere of the mid-1860s, when Juárez was still in exile as President, the future was uncertain and pressure from Conservatives continued, that the support of the Episcopal neighbor to the north seemed like a godsend to this vulnerable group.

A NATIONAL CHURCH?

As the struggle for Mexico continued between Juárez and Maximilian into 1866, radical Liberal leaders began to take on a more anticlerical stride. The French offensive had convinced them that the Catholic clergy, themselves allegedly composed of foreigners, were disloyal to the nation and were subversive, supporting a foreign power—even celebrating French victories. Additionally, Vatican centralization that would climax in the First Vatican Council in 1868 cemented views that the Roman Catholic clergy responded first to the pope and were potential traitors.[113]

Juárez returned to Mexico City in 1867 and with the fall of Maximilian and the dissolution of his empire anticlerical views would disseminate even further through newspapers and pamphlets. Juárez's return was favorable to the dissident priests as the government again set forth the idea of establishing a national Church. This time, having experienced the weak support among clerics for the movement, the Church was led by a committee of laypeople: Mariano Zavala, Magistrate of the Supreme Court of Justice, Marcelino Guerrero, José Maria Iglesias, and Manuel Rivera y Río. They sought to create a body that was national, liturgical, and based on the Bible, which they saw as the key to religious reform and sought to distribute to the masses.[114]

Juárez's motivations for supporting the Church are murky. On the one hand, he believed that Protestantism, with its focus on the Book, could effect educational reform, especially among the Indians. "I should

---

112. Unknown author, Letter to unknown recipient, 1865, Archives of the Episcopal Church, Austin, TX. There seems to be, in this letter, an overt campaign to establish the Episcopal credentials of the Mexican Church. If this letter was written by Nicholson, then it shows how much further he had moved in his advocacy of the movement and his desire that it come under the auspices of the PECUSA.

113. Bastian, *Disidentes*, 37.

114. Bechtel, "The Mexican Episcopal Church," 15; Bastian, *Disidentes*, 37.

like Protestantism to Mexicanize itself and win the Indians; they need a religion that obliges them to read and that does not force them to spend their savings in tapers for the saints."[115] Greenland surmises that whereas Juárez may have preferred the Catholic Church, as it was Mexican in identity, he may have lent support to other church groups so as to incite the Catholic Church to reform itself.[116] This may have been part of the motivation behind his support of the Constitutionalist Clerics as they had emerged as a native reform movement that was still Catholic and not yet quite Protestant. We see, though, how the movement has progressed this far from being a renewal movement within the Church led by dissident priests to forming a parallel church body in 1861 to, after the Second Empire, moving towards being either a national Church or coming under the protection of the PECUSA. The circumstances and personalities of this next phase of its existence would determine that direction.

In 1867, the year of Juárez's return to power, Manuel Aguilar Bermúdez died. Shortly before his death Bermúdez addressed a letter to Reverend Dennison of the PECUSA lamenting that they have not received answers from the foreign committee regarding requests for financial aid. The author believes Jesuits, "secret agents of Antichriste (sic)" may be employed by the post office and intercepting letters.[117] The theme of financial support, even desperation is evident in Rafael Martínez's letter to the Reverend Bishop J. D. Wilmer of New Orleans. He describes his work in establishing the Directive Committee of the Mexican Reformist Church. As president of this committee he was able to oversee the planting of the church in some other Mexican states. Those churches would work in conjunction with the committee. Because the work was difficult, however, he would need to know the extent of the support from the brethren in the United States, the "prosperous and glorious American Church." Martínez states that he wanted to send two speakers to tour the United States to drum up support, but not having the funds necessary he appeals to Wilmer for aid. Among other things, the Mexican Church needed money to purchase one or more churches as they had been meeting in private homes to the

---

115. Quoted in Greenland, "Religious Reform," 21.

116. Ibid.

117. Manuel Aguilar Bermúdez, Letter to Rev. Dennison, August 8, 1867, Archives of the Episcopal Church, Austin, TX.

ridicule and scorn of Roman Catholics.[118] Furthermore, they required funds to publish Christian books, to establish Sunday Schools, to send out missionaries, and to support poor and converted priests who were now without income. Martínez requested that any monies forwarded be sent under his name so that they could be distributed as needed, and promised to send the American Church monthly reports to be disseminated in letters and pamphlets. His rancor towards the Catholic Church is evident in his parting words, a combination of political, religious, and economic diatribe: They are "worthy representatives of Satan, traitors toward God and their native-land, rebels and seditious, who pretend to sell the eternal blessings in the church and have forgotten the savior's words 'Render into (sic) Caesar &c.'"[119] The Bishop, in turn, forwarded a copy of the letter to the representatives of the Church of the Foreign Committee. He laments that the (post-war) condition of the churches of the American South prevented giving aid to the Mexicans, and implies that the Northern, more prosperous churches should take their cause under consideration. Wilmer compares the Mexican Reformation to that in sixteenth-century England and how the latter would never have succeeded without the aid of the reformers on the continent. In short, if the Americans do not help them, the Mexican cause might perish. He does not believe the movement is a temporary flash-in-the-pan one, but one that has potential to assail "that hoary patriarch of superstition."[120]

THE MAKINGS OF A PROTESTANT CHURCH

Also that year, 1867, Manual Aguas (d.1872), a Dominican preacher and priest, embraced the reform movement. A prodigious man, Aguas was a physician and had served as professor of philosophy and theology. He ministered in Cuautla in the state of Morelos before going on to Atzcapatzalco in Mexico City. He also served as confessor to the canons of the Metropolitan Cathedral and preacher to the archbishop

---

118. We are never told what happened to the church buildings given the movement by Juárez before the Maximilian Empire. Were the Constitutionalist Fathers forced to abandon them during that interim?

119. Rafael Díaz Martínez, Letter to Rev. Bishop J. D. Wilmer of New Orleans, October 5, 1867, Archives of the Episcopal Church, Austin, TX.

120. Bishop J. D. Wilmer, Letter to the Church of the Foreign Committee of the Protestant Episcopal Church, NY, 1867, Archives of the Episcopal Church, Austin, TX.

and chapter. He even ministered at San José before its secularization.[121] However, even as a Catholic priest Aguas had his idiosyncrasies that placed him within the reform-minded clergy. He would omit references to saints and to indulgences, for example. After a protest by members of the Franciscan Order for his failure to mention their founder's name on the day of his feast Aguas resigned.[122] In an autobiographical pamphlet translated into English and distributed to the Episcopal Church, Aguas describes himself as having attacked the Protestant churches, "a pestilence that was coming to make us, in Mexico, more unfortunate than ever. I, consequently, opposed its doctrines with all my power. I sincerely thought that, in so doing, I not only did good service to my native land, but also gained merits to aid me in obtaining everlasting glory."[123] He continues to say: "I was in this sad state when there reached me the pamphlet called 'True Liberty.' I read it most carefully; and, notwithstanding that I tried to find, in the arsenal of my Romish subtleties, arguments with which to answer the clear reasoning that I found in this publication, a voice within, the voice of my conscience, told me that my answers were not satisfactory, and that perhaps I was in error."[124]

Aguas dedicated himself to reading Protestant books and to the Bible. "This study, from the moment that it was accompanied by earnest prayer, led me to true happiness. I commenced to see the light. The Lord had pity on me, and enabled me to clearly understand the great troths (sic) of the Gospel."[125] Aguas stated his conversion differently in the newspaper, *El Monitor Republicano*, in April 1871. After having studied Protestant works, he came to the conclusion that there were three types of religion: that of God, that of the priest, and that of human beings. He chose what he perceived as the path of God as revealed to him in the Bible. "It is true that Rome tells us that there is danger in reading the Bible without notes; do not believe them, no such danger exists, a thousand times no. It is not possible that a God of goodness and love

---

121. Bechtel, "The Mexican Episcopal Church," 21.

122. Greenland, "Religious Reform," 28.

123. Manuel Aguas, Letter of Manuel Aguas, 1871, Archives of the Episcopal Church, Austin, TX.

124. Ibid.

125. Ibid.

should leave to us a dangerous book where in place of life we would find poison and death."[126]

In late 1867 Aguas, to whom the leadership of the dissident church had fallen, reorganized the movement. According to Bastian, the movement was divided into two groups. One the one hand, there were the ex-priests who were more conservative in ritual and theology and enjoyed some of the support of the Juárez government. On the other, were lay-led groups composed mainly of government workers, artisans, and former Liberal soldiers.[127] Aguas sought to bring these two divisions together. Led by lay members it was renamed the Mexican Church of Jesus (*Iglesia Mexicana de Jesús*), without an official state mandate but with its well-wishes. The government placed at its disposal the churches of San José de la Gracia and San Francisco. Several other priests joined the movement including Maximilian's former chaplain, Agustín Palacios and Ignacio Arellano, another ex-Dominican.[128] Aguas also organized a synod charged with guarding the faith and discipline of the Church and appointed a commission towards the formation of a seminary.[129] The divisions between the Masons and the clerics still simmered underneath however.

In 1868 the Mexican Church sent two delegates to New York to request the consecration of a Mexican bishop. Presiding Bishop Hopkins refused the request. While in New York the delegation met Henry C. Riley who was serving as the pastor of a Spanish-American Episcopal Church. Riley had been raised in Chile and was familiar with Latin American culture. As the Episcopal Board of Foreign Missions would not involve itself in the Mexican affair, Riley, who was independently wealthy, went as a representative of the American and Foreign Christian Union, a nondenominational evangelical mission organization whose mission it was to convert Roman Catholics to Protestantism.[130]

Not long after his arrival, Riley became active in the dissident Church, preaching publicly and going house to house to hand out literature and let people know about the Society. He established friendly

---

126. Quoted in López and Guerra, *Protestantismo*, 69.
127. Bastian, *Disidentes*, 38.
128. Ibid., 38.
129. Bechtel, "The Mexican Episcopal Church," 21.
130. Rice, "Evangelical Episcopalians," 63; Dussel, *Tomo V*, 301.

relations with Secretary of the Treasury, Matías Romero. Romero later stated his motivations:

> I strongly favored the implantation of a Protestant community to restrain the abuses of the clergy . . . I had to send for Protestants and bring them here, because only a few foreigners professed any religion at all . . . I then favored a Protestant community presided over by Mr. Riley, who wished to establish a National Mexican Church in competition with the Roman Catholic . . . with the cordial cooperation of President Juárez who shared my sentiments and was perhaps more radical than I in these matters . . . I sold them the Church of San Francisco, one of the most beautiful in Mexico.[131]

Because of his financial resources Riley was able to facilitate the purchase of San Francisco and San José de Gracia.[132] The purchase of the two buildings added enthusiasm to the movement. Benito Juárez and other leading politicians even attended services in the two churches.[133] Nonetheless, this was still a loose aggregation of independent congregations composed of both Liberal ex-clerics who conserved the Catholic ritual and doctrine and worshipped in the buildings obtained from the government and lay societies composed of government workers, artisans and many masons, including soldiers of the Wars of Reform. These latter tended to be more democratic ("the people here are in charge and not the bishop, as in the Roman sect."), met in homes or rented properties, were exclusive to men and by invitation only. Their ceremonies were more Masonic in style and anti-Catholic.[134] According to Bastian, religious dissidence was weakly diffused throughout the country through three networks of organization and influence: the schismatic clergy and seminarians, who concern us most here, of whom there were never

---

131. Quoted in Baldwin, *Protestants*, 17.

132. San José was built in 1659–61 for a woman's order gathered under the patronage of St. Monica, and was later used by the Order of the Holy Conception. After the government confiscated it, it served as a warehouse and barracks. Today it is still the cathedral of the Anglican Church of Mexico.
San Francisco is centrally located in Mexico City and was formally part of the convent of the Franciscan order. As late as 1878, visitors reported large congregations attending services. Bechtel, "The Mexican Episcopal Church," 19. Cf. Gray, *Mexico As It Is*, 137–38.

133. Bechtel, "The Mexican Episcopal Church," 27.

134. Bastian, *Disidentes*, 39–40.

very many in number but who had the tacit support of the government, the liberal, Masonic groups led by some ex-military under the name of "evangelical societies," and independent, lay-led religious movements whose growth in rural areas went hand in hand with agrarian reform and some forms of anticlericalism.[135] Riley himself noted that because of the Roman Catholic Church's collusion with Maximilian, many, ecclesiastics and laypeople, had been driven away from that body. They converted mainly for two reasons, according to Riley, because they lamented the wars raged upon the patriots (Liberals) and because they became convinced of the errors of the Catholic Church.[136]

According to some American sources, Manuel Aguas was converted when, as a Catholic priest, he was recruited to discredit Riley. After reading extensively of Riley's works and those of the Society, he was convinced of the errors of Catholicism and embraced the Mexican Catholic Apostolic Society. This supposedly occurred in the winter of 1871.[137] However, the timeline for this interpretation not only appears too convenient, giving much of the credit to Riley, but also does not fit into Aguas' own testimony that places his conversion prior to his meeting with Riley and who, in a letter to Bishop Nicholas Arias dated April 10, 1871, affirms his decision and describes his work with the reformed Church.[138]

Having rejected the "errors of Romanism" Aguas:

> commenced to attend the Provisional Protestant Church, which had been established in a large hall situated in the street of San Juan de Letran. Being short-sighted, I there began to know my dear brother, the Rev. Henry Chauncey Riley, solely by his voice. It filled me with comfort to hear him speak of Jesus and his precious blood, the liturgy and hymns, which the congregation used, enchanted me, as they were full of the pure faith of the primitive Christian and I anxiously desired the arrival of Sundays, because in our church services, I enjoyed delicious

---

135. Ibid., 41–42.

136. H. Riley, Works of the Church Paper #1, 1882, Archives of the Episcopal Church, Austin, TX.

137. Creighton, *Church in Mexico*, 4, cf. Rice, "Evangelical Episcopalians," 63.

138. Bastian, *Disidentes*, 38. Cf. Manuel Aguas, Letter of Manuel Aguas, 1871. Archives of the Episcopal Church, Austin, TX.

moments of peace and joy—Christian emotions that I had never felt in the Roman sect.[139]

Soon thereafter, Aguas was introduced to Riley and together they worked to establish a YMCA, begin classes for young men interested in ministry, and hold services in San José de la Gracia. Aguas goes on to describe the opposition and violence he and other members of the Church faced from Roman Catholics. Riley himself faced tensions with fellow missionaries as regards his Episcopalian background and his desire to establish a reformed Catholic Church rather than a thoroughly Protestant one.[140]

Aguas threw himself into the work of the Church of Jesus with all the zeal of a convert. Here we see how the tone of the debate has shifted from a reform effort to a confrontation with Catholicism, perhaps fuelled in part by the anti-clerical and anti-Catholic feeling in the air after Maximilian's reign. Aguas accepted the challenge of a Roman Catholic priest, Don Javier Aguilar y Bustamante, to debate on the topic, "Is the Church of Rome Idolatrous?" on Sunday, July 2, 1871. The church was filled, but Aguilar did not show as his superiors feared a disturbance. Aguas assumed he won by forfeit and addressed the gathered crowd, attacking the doctrines and practices of the Roman Catholic Church.[141]

Aguas not only disassociated himself from the Catholic Church but also from the Liberalism to which the Constitutionalist Fathers had been attached. For him, the Liberal policies were insufficient to address the challenges facing Mexico. Only a religious transformation in favor of Protestantism would help. "Our society is divided between 'Liberals' and 'Conservative Romanists.' . . . The 'Liberals' have plunged into the dark horrors of infidelity, and are the slaves of their evil inclinations; The Romanists are the slaves of the tyrant Rome. In a word, true religion has not been the foundation of our society. The results of this want have been fratricidal wars, insecurity, avarice, poverty, and misery. Scenes of wickedness have been the schools where our Mexican children have been educated."[142]

139. Manuel Aguas, Letter of Manuel Aguas, 1871, Archives of the Episcopal Church, Austin, TX.
140. Bechtel, "The Mexican Episcopal Church," 19.
141. Ibid., 21.
142. Manuel Aguas, Letter of Manuel Aguas, 1871, Archives of the Episcopal Church, Austin, TX.

In a reply to the Bishop of Mexico over his excommunication, Aguas criticized the practices, wealth, and abuses of the Catholic Church. He vividly imagined a visit from Saints Peter and Paul to the National Cathedral. They are shocked with the practices they encounter, including clerical celibacy and the cult of saints and veneration of relics. They are even more shocked when, in a dialogue with the Bishop, they discover that these practices are associated with the Gospel and their teachings in Scriptures.[143] In addition to his theological convictions that reveal a much more Bible-based, anti-Catholic thought ("that title [archbishop] does not exist in the Bible."), Aguas defends his patriotism, perhaps under scrutiny for affiliating himself with the religion of the United States.

> Just in case, may the God of the Nations forbid it, that the North American Nation should resolve to annex our country and should formally invade us, the Mexican people, despite the traitors, would exert unheard-of efforts to preserve the integrity of our territory. Of the Protestants it can be said with surety and truth that we would occupy whatever place the Supreme Government would appoint us in the campaign . . . If we Mexican people should emancipate ourselves from Rome, becoming free then of that enormous weight that hangs over our consciences, then we will attempt to affirm with every certainty that the danger of losing the homeland would no longer remain. In said conflict, the victory would be ours and ours alone, as we will no longer be divided, and only unity—which gives strength and breath to the nations—would exist.[144]

Protestantism not only would liberate the Mexican people from Rome, but would also unify the people in the face of any real or imagined threats. Protestants, affirms Aguas, were not un-Mexican, but rather, it was the Roman Catholic Church that posed a danger to the nation. Here he invokes the anticlericalism simmering in Mexican memory as a result of the Church hierarchy's refusal to come to the economic aid of the nation during the U.S.-Mexican War. "All Mexicans of good faith should convince themselves that the Roman Church is, and always has been, antipatriotic and traitorous. Remember the indolence with which

---

143. Manuel Aguas, Letter of Manuel Aguas to the Bishop of Mexico, 1871, Archives of the Episcopal Church, Austin, TX. In all honesty, this open letter attacking the sacrifice of the Mass, purgatory, and communion under one kind, among other things, is a tract worthy of any sixteenth-century Protestant Reformer.

144. Quoted in López y Guerra, *Protestantismo*, 70.

that church perceived the North American invasion of 1847: being, at that time, immensely wealthy they refused to aid the government which sought resources to preserve national independence."[145]

This document was published broadly throughout Mexico and even translated for distribution in the United States. Soon after the publication of Aguas' pamphlet, the Catholic Church reacted to Aguas' theological positions without mentioning the matter of nationalism.

However, for our purposes, the reaction of Juan Orestes is more relevant as it reveals the variety of opinion and positions within the Church of Jesus. Orestes, it will be remembered, was one of the original Constitutionalist Fathers that supported the 1857 Constitution. He stated that in 1867, upon Juárez' return to power and with the hopes that under the restored president, peace and unity might be restored to the nation, "in common accord all of the reformist ecclesiastics entered into a profound silence and retreat, following the conciliatory policies of the government."[146] But Aguas' antagonistic tone forced Orestes to break his silence, warning that the conflict would help neither Catholics nor Protestants. Calling upon his own nationalistic option for the poor, he accused Aguas of having forsaken "poor and weary" Mexican Catholicism for the "rich and powerful" Protestantism of the United States. Orestes remained a Catholic Liberal at heart and advocated for religious liberty, affirming that in the end it would be good for the Catholic Church as it would reveal to her the great number of faithful children she held.[147] This manifestation of ideological differences highlights the extent to which the movement of the Constitutionalist Clerics had changed since 1859. Orestes and his fellow reformers were Liberal Catholics in the tradition of eighteenth-century Enlightened Catholicism. Despite all its deficiencies they saw the Roman Catholic faith as integral to Mexico—an important part of the nation's history and its people's spirituality. The Constitutionalist Fathers only sought to correct what they perceived as abuses in the Church, or traditions that were not based upon the gospel, such as clerical celibacy and the ultramontane perception of papal authority. In other words, Orestes was content with the tree but sought to prune it of some of its deficiencies. For Aguas, however, pruning was not enough; the entire tree had to go. Aguas, under Riley's influence,

---

145. Quoted in ibid., 70–71.
146. Quoted in ibid., 71.
147. Ibid., 72.

had decided that the problem lay with Catholicism itself and only the Protestant faith could lay claim to being biblically sound and ensuring salvation. Orestes's accusation of Aguas's having forsaken "poor and weary" Catholicism for the "powerful" Protestant religion of his friends is one that would be leveled and repeated against Protestants and evangelicals throughout Latin America from that time forward. In this case, however, it reveals the differences that had arisen between the old guard of the Church of Jesus and its new charismatic leadership. Not only so, but it also portended the direction in which the Church of Jesus was headed, and not everyone was happy about it.

Orestes was not the only Constitutionalist Father to call into question the direction in which the Church of Jesus was heading. Rafael Díaz Martínez and Francisco Domínguez, who had been part of the original envoy to the PECUSA in New York in 1864, were living in South Texas by 1869. Martínez in particular had fallen out of favor with Riley and was in close contact with Bishop Wilmer of Louisiana. Riley wrote to Wilmer, seeking to discourage Wilmer from advancing Martínez as Bishop of Mexico, telling him that Martínez was not to be trusted.[148] While the exact reasons for the division between Martínez and Riley are unknown, it is not far-fetched to say, given Martínez's connections to Wilmer and Riley's opposition to Martínez as Bishop, that part of the issue may lie with the leadership of the Church of Jesus and the increasing conjunction between the Mexican Church and the PECUSA. Martínez and others may have rightly perceived that control of their movement was spinning away from local control and into that of the wealthy and influential American, Henry Riley.

Orestes' critique of Aguas demonstrates that the Church of Jesus was multiform and that there remained within it a core group that continued to see itself as a reform movement from within the Roman Catholic Church. These people had no intention of leaving the Church and becoming Protestants. They had sought out the Episcopal Church for financial assistance and, most importantly, for apostolic succession, without which they could not ordain priests. For Orestes, and conceivably for many others, leaving the Mother Church was unthinkable. As a reform movement they nonetheless sought out an improvement in the faith and practices of the only Church any of them had known

---

148. Henry C. Riley, Letter to Bishop Wilmer of Louisiana, October 5, 1869, Archives of the Episcopal Church, Austin, Texas. Rice, "Evangelical Episcopalians," 68 n.163.

and loved and that had provided them with an identity and mission. However, with the active hand and resources of Henry Riley, including his connections to the Episcopal Church, and with the native role of charismatic leaders such as Manuel Aguas, the axis of the Church of Jesus had begun to move inexorably from Reform Catholicism to North American Protestantism.

Towards the end of 1871 this movement gained speed when Manual Aguas was appointed bishop by the consulting body of the Church of Jesus. By 1872 the PECUSA had entered into a covenant with the Church of Jesus whereby the former would guide and assist the latter until it could sustain its own affairs.[149] Unfortunately, Aguas passed away on October 18, 1872, before he could be consecrated bishop by the PECUSA. Earlier that year Benito Juárez had died, bringing an end to an era in the history of Mexico and of the Mexican Churches. Aguas had named Luis Canales as an episcopal delegate and his successor. He presided over the synod and council and set up a system of lay readers in charge of congregations as there were few ordained clergymen. In 1872 the Church of Jesus was undergirded by funds from the American Church Missionary Society, which supported it for five years.[150]

In January 1873, members of the Church of San Francisco and the Convent of San José wrote to Riley in New York expressing their appreciation for his work on their behalf. Despite this there seemed to have been a loss that had overcome the Church with the death of Aguas and a frustration over missionaries from rival Protestant denominations; they had always viewed themselves as being the only Protestant church in the nation. Additionally, they complained about Canales, stating that he was unable to exert any church discipline over members who sought to usurp the ministers' authority.[151]

---

149. Baldwin, *Protestants*, 16.

150. Bechtel, "The Mexican Episcopal Church," 23. This funding assisted the church as the American and Foreign Christian Union discontinued financial support in 1872 once the Church of Jesus came into formal association with the PECUSA. Rice, "Evangelical Episcopalians," 68.

151. The Congregations of San Francisco and San José de Gracia, Letter to Henry Riley, January 24, 1873, Archives of the Episcopal Church, Austin, Texas. Cf. Rice, 66.

A CHURCH IN LIMBO

As mentioned above, not everyone was pleased with the efforts of Aguas and Riley to connect the Church of Jesus with the PECUSA. The transition from an independent church to a type of dependent mission church was troublesome to some Mexican ministers. Agustín Palacios, Sóstenez Juárez, and Arcadio Morales opposed the effort and broke away to continue as an independent body. This effort was frustrated by Palacios' aggressive anti-Catholic activity which led Morales to depart. He, in turn, was approached by the Presbyterians in 1874 and became an effective minister and preacher. Palacios and Juárez eventually joined the Methodists. Juárez, in particular, became a minister and preached actively until his death in 1891.[152]

In 1874, the Church of Jesus sought out assistance from the General Convention of the PECUSA for the consecration of bishops. This led to discussion in the House of Bishops over whether the PECUSA had the right to infringe upon the jurisdiction of the Catholic episcopate in Mexico and whether the Church of Jesus was a legitimate reformed Church. A commission was formed and Bishop Lee and Henry Dyer were sent to Mexico to evaluate the situation. Noting the need for leaders, Lee ordained seven deacons. This comprised the first official act of the PECUSA in Mexico.[153]

Since the Board of Missions of the PECUSA was not interested in a direct relationship with the Church of Jesus, the Mexican Commission created The League in Aid of the Mexican Branch of the Church. This League dedicated itself to promoting the Church of Jesus, collecting donations and establishing dioceses. By 1880 it success was apparent. In the 1870s the Church of Jesus was composed of fifty-four congregations with 3,500 members and 7,000 attendees, focused in Mexico City, the Valley of Mexico and Cuernavaca. It could boast of two seminaries, ten mission schools and an orphanage for girls. It was also aided by the beginnings of the Old Catholic Church movement in Europe which came about from the First Vatican Council's affirmation of ultramontanism and papal infallibility in 1870. The Church of Jesus became associated with these

---

152. Baldwin, *Protestants*, 17.

153. Rice, "Evangelical Episcopalians," 72. See also Creighton, *Church in Mexico*, 4–6.

newly independent churches in the eyes of the Episcopal Church, their success justifying further support of the Church in Mexico.[154]

By 1879, the Church of Jesus had elected three bishops, Tomás Valdespino as Bishop of Mexico City, Prudencio Hernández of Cuernavaca, and Henry Riley as Bishop of the Valley of Mexico. The candidates were submitted to the Mexican Commission for approval but of these three, only Riley was consecrated, the others rejected for technical reasons.[155]

With Riley's elevation in 1879 hopes were high that the Church of Jesus was on the path to autonomy. Riley, however, was unable to fulfill his responsibilities as bishop and soon after his consecration he was summoned to assist an Episcopal/Anglican Church in Spain. In 1884, Riley was forced to resign for negligence and incompetence, despite the fact that it was his presiding bishop who had ordered him to Europe. Riley was perceived to be something of a maverick, refusing to follow guidelines established for the election of church leaders and for being overly critical of American attempts to impose a Spanish translation of the U.S. Prayer Book upon the Mexican Church.[156]

Disorganization and dissent followed. The Church of Jesus split into two camps—the *Cuerpo Eclesiástico* (Ecclesiastical Body), primarily from the Valley of Mexico, who insisted that the Church of Jesus come under the direct authority of the PECUSA, and the Independent Mexican Church from Mexico City who continued to lobby for autonomy. Interest in an independent Mexican Church on the part of the PECUSA waned with the failure to establish any concrete relationships with the various Old Catholic Churches of Europe. In 1886, the House of Bishops recognized the *Cuerpo Eclesiástico* as the official Church of Jesus, thus making that body more dependent on foreign leadership.

Another blow to whatever dreams of independence that lingered in the Church of Jesus occurred during the latter quarter of the nineteenth century as businessmen and laborers from the United States and Great Britain immigrated to Mexico under the encouragement of President Porfirio Díaz, who sought to attract foreign investors. A small, English-speaking congregation was established in Mexico City by Bishop Eliot of Western Texas that grew in size and identified itself with other English-speaking congregations throughout the country. The discovery

---

154. Ibid., 74–75.
155. Ibid., 75–76.
156. Ibid., 76–78.

of oil in Mexico only increased the number of American residents as railroads were built, mines and oil wells were established and industry proceeded apace. In 1904, the General Convention recognized the need for an English-speaking mission and Henry Aves of Houston, Texas, was consecrated as Bishop of the Missionary District of Mexico in December of that year.

In 1901, the Church of Jesus once again sought the consecration of three bishops in order to attain independence but this came to naught. In 1906, the small remnant of the Church of Jesus that remained was absorbed into the mission of the Episcopal Church under Bishop Aves, whose primary responsibility remained with ministering to the English-speaking residents and foreigners in Mexico.[157]

SUMMARY AND CODA

Those who have dealt with the Church of Jesus in some manner—Bastian, Greenland, Bechtel, Rice, and Voekel, have all emphasized the failure of the movement in face of Conservative opposition, financial troubles, and a lack of support from the Juárez government. Only Rice has found fault with another factor, the divisions occurring among the evangelical and Anglo-Catholic segments of the PECUSA.[158]

This writer has a somewhat more nuanced opinion of the fate of the Church of Jesus. Upon reading the primary and secondary sources I have noticed two overwhelming themes that seem to go hand-in-hand: the shift in emphasis, goals, and even message of the nascent Church and the role strong personalities have played in it. These factors indicate the painful evolution of the movement that was subject to the convictions and agendas of people like Bermúdez, Lozano, Nicholson, Aguas, and Riley.

The shift in emphasis becomes easy to see when we compare Bermúdez and Aguas. Whereas Bermudez's letter expresses a frustration and even anger with the Roman Catholic Church, there is no indication that he desires to establish an alternate Church. Bermudez, to use him as an example, consciously or unconsciously taps into the reservoir of the Enlightened Catholics of the eighteenth and Catholic Liberals of the nineteenth century. He sees the Catholic Church as having departed

---

157. Rice, "Evangelical Episcopalians," 78–81.
158. Ibid., 91ff.

from "Enlightened religion" and become too obsessed with pecuniary matters to the point that they exploit the people. In the tradition of Enlightened Catholicism, Bermúdez and the Constitutionalist Fathers believe that reform is possible if the Church would look to the Bible and the teachings of early Christianity. Bermúdez is the still, small voice that has joined itself with other dissident priests who believe that Christianity is compatible with the democratic principles and the 1857 Constitution. Their numbers would never be large but perhaps like the bit of leaven in the dough they aspire to effect some change.

Manuel Aguas is the storm that breaks apart the rocks and trees. With the fury of a convert, this man, come to the movement almost a decade after the gathering of the Constitutionalist Fathers, is different in tone and message from Bermúdez. For Aguas there is little redeemable in the Catholic Church. He attacks and mocks the sacraments, rites, and beliefs of that body in the hopes of converting people from it. The Catholic Church for Aguas is not something in need of reform. It is a religion one must leave in order to find true salvation in the Christ of the Bible. Aguas, at least as we encounter him in his Letter, differs markedly in tone and conduct from the expressions of reform we encountered earlier. His language and experience is reminiscent of the evangelical revivalist experience; a man who was lost in papal idolatry but through the Bible experiences salvation in Christ. This language and interpretation of events of his conversion either came about as a result of careful editing to make his experience palpable to evangelical readers or the theology of the Mexican Church had by then shifted from reform to revival, perhaps as a result of further contacts with the Episcopal Church and local anti-Catholicism post-Maximilian.

Between these two extremes we can perceive the subtle and not so subtle changes that occurred within the movement. From Bermúdez and the Constitutionalist Fathers we have Lozano who believed in reform to the point of establishing a parallel body—still Catholic in its beliefs and sacraments but also wedded to primitivist instincts of the Bible and the early Church. He believes, out of personal and theological convictions, that the Church must be shorn of its practices and beliefs that are inconsistent with the Bible and early Church, such as clerical celibacy.

Having found little support from Juárez, who was then in exile, the Fathers appealed to the PECUSA who sent E.C. Nicholson. He perceived in the movement a potential for true reform in Mexico. While only an observer of the Church and not a leader, his presence and advocacy moved the clerics closer towards a relationship with the PECUSA. By this time the group is recognized (even by Maximilian) as a parallel church body alongside Roman Catholicism.

Upon Juárez's return the Church received encouragement from the government in the form of two church buildings. They still struggled financially and so continued their appeal to the United States. Manuel Aguas, the former Dominican, experienced a conversion and became a stalwart firebrand, attacking the Roman Catholic Church while attempting to organize the Church of Jesus, as it was now called. He was joined in this by Henry Riley, who had the financial resources the Constitutionalist Fathers never had. His connections with the PECUSA alongside Aguas' denunciations of the Catholic Church edged the Church of Jesus even closer to their North American cousins. By 1872, the year of Juárez's and Aguas' deaths, the Church of Jesus was an autonomous Church body, more Protestant than Catholic though beset by divisions over polity and the relationship of the Church to the PECUSA.

In this writer's opinion this does not denote failure but evolution. By the 1870s the Church of Jesus had twenty-three congregations in the Valley of Mexico and a few others elsewhere in the country. It had also begun publishing its own newspaper, *La Estrella de Belén*. Additionally, the Church of Jesus served as a seedbed for the Protestant leaders of the burgeoning movement in the nation. John Butler, agent of the London Biblical Society, Arcadio Morales, one of the first Mexican Presbyterian leaders, and Sóstenez Juárez, a former soldier converted by a French chaplain and who later became the first Methodist minister ordained in Mexico, all counted themselves members of the Church of Jesus.[159]

As early as 1867, when Benito Juárez made his triumphal return to Mexico City, interest in dissident groups appeared to have risen in the wake of anti-Catholic feeling. The Church of Jesus itself had difficulties with its heterogeneous nature. Because of the Masonic members within the overall organization, their services reflected Masonic ceremonies and were open only to men. In 1872 these lay societies petitioned the government for church buildings, calling themselves Congregationalists that were distinct from the Church of Jesus because "here the people are in charge and not the bishop, as in the Roman sect."[160] Meanwhile,

---

159. Dussel, *Tomo V*, 228, 289.
160. Bastian, *Disidentes*, 40.

by 1870 Juárez appeared interested in the propagation of Protestantism as a means to expand literacy among the poor and the Indians and perhaps provide a competitive market for the Roman Catholic Church. To that end he assisted in the construction of a church building in Tizapán whose congregation was composed of factory workers and tradesmen.[161] So by the time Manuel Aguas and Henry Riley arrive on the scene we have a situation where the Church of Jesus was more of an umbrella organization than a cohesive denomination. Between the clerics and the laypeople, the Catholics, the Masons, and those whose religious expression can be described as a nascent evangelicalism, the Church appeared to be in the midst of an identity crisis which, rather than trouble, can, like the varied and multiple forms of colonial Catholicism, be considered a sign of growth and development.

The Church of Jesus, like Mexican Catholicism in general, reflected the pluralist tints and hues that came with the establishment of Christianity in Latin America. What Voekel, Greenland, Rice, and others interpret as failure this writer sees as vitality. The Church of Jesus did not effect renewal within Catholicism as Bermúdez and Lozano desired. It did not become a national Church as others had hoped would happen with the patronage of Juárez. It did not even pose a serious evangelical challenge to the Catholic Church as Juárez and Aguas may have wished. Financial and organizational struggles within and a lack of support from without brought the movement to a crisis point. By the time of Aguas' death the Church of Jesus was experiencing birth pangs as it sought to express the variety of dissident movements and beliefs that emerged out of the Wars of Reform and the Liberal victory under Juárez and develop its own identity.[162]

However, with the ordination of Riley in 1879 the PECUSA demonstrated its interest in the Church and subsequent contact would further strengthen that relationship as sympathetic bishops in the United States sought to drum up support, including financial aid, for the Mexican Church. Nonetheless, the Church of Jesus continued to experi-

161. Ibid., 39.

162. It was at this time (1871) that Protestant missionaries began entering Mexico from the United States. The Society of Friends were the first to arrive, establishing themselves in San Luis Potosí and Tamaulipas. In 1872, Presbyterians are Congregationalists begin to work in the northern states of Nuevo León, Zacatecas, Chihuahua and Sonora. Methodists reach Mexico City in 1873, establishing schools and other social institutions. Dussel, *Tomo V*, 290.

ence difficulties and inconsistencies. Apparently, figures on membership and numbers of congregations varied during the period, making the Episcopal Church suspicious. According to one account there were over seventy congregations scattered from the states of Guerrero to Veracruz. The independent, congregational nature of the Mexican Society and the Church of Jesus made it very difficult to determine the full extent of its membership or associations. The *Spirit of Missions*, in 1864, reported 150 ex-priests involved in the reform movement. A year later that number was "over 100." In 1867 the *Spirit of Missions* estimated eighty priests and congregations. By April 1870 there were apparently forty congregations in Mexico City and the surrounding valley and 120 in the entire nation.[163] The PECUSA never quite understood the complex political and religious realities of the situation in the Mexican Church. One commentator expressed frustration and accounted it to a stereotypical Latin character:

> No Latin people have ever conducted to a successful revolt against Rome. The Teuton sharply separates in thought between his religious and political life and arranges the machinery of the one without reference to the other. The Latin steadily confuses the two. Thus the "new Christian Church in Mexico" felt every shifting current of political air. It dissolved and recombined in a way which first bewildered and then exasperated the American church, who tried to make businesslike terms with it. Concerning no portion of the Church's missionary work have there been such contradictory reports as concerning the Church in Mexico. It is possible that all the reports were true, for the reason that they were made about a contradictory body.[164]

Even as late as 1876 the PECUSA and its Evangelical constituents harbored suspicions regarding the appropriation of portions of the Mozarabic Rite by the Mexican Church and its sincere conversion from Roman Catholic "errors" and sought to control or guide the development of the Mexican liturgy.[165]

---

163. Rice, "Evangelical Episcopalians," 67–68.

164. Quoted in Bechtel, "The Mexican Episcopal Church," 24, cf. Creighton, *Church in Mexico*, 4.

165. Rev. Charles R. Hale, A.M., The Mozarabic Liturgy and the Mexican Branch of the Catholic Church of Our Lord Jesus Christ Militant upon Earth: A Liturgical Study, 1876, Archives of the Episcopal Church, Austin, TX. It would be interesting to conjecture what the approach of the Episcopal Church would have been towards the

In the end, this relationship, unequal and dependent for money and legitimacy (apostolic succession), is what finally nudged the Church of Jesus under the auspices of the Episcopal Church over and against any other options, including extinction. In 1906 the Church of Jesus officially became part of the Mission Church of the Episcopal Church. It would not be until 1995 that the Mexican Church would earn its place as an autonomous branch of the Anglican Communion.[166]

Church of Jesus, its theology and liturgy, had the Episcopalians been better represented by the Anglo-Catholic branch of the Church.

166. It is significant to note, in light of the historic struggles over autonomy and identity undergone by the Church of Jesus, the name they chose upon attaining independence. They did not echo their benefactors and call themselves the *Episcopal* Church of Mexico, but rather affirmed their autonomous place within the worldwide Anglican Communion as the *Anglican* Church of Mexico.

8

Conclusions

Yet as late as the eighteenth century Indians in both the Spanish-dominated Valley of Mexico and the farther-flung regions like rural Michoacán, San Luis Potosí, and Oaxaca continued to celebrate pre-Hispanic, autochthonous religious ceremonies. The Black Christs of Michoacán, which the faithful kissed in Yuriria, are black because people believe they drink the venom of poisonous animals like scorpions, snakes, and beetles in order to protect whoever offers them propitiation.

—Martin Nesvig, *Local Religion in Colonial Mexico*[1]

The Latin Church requires liturgical worship, combined with artistical (sic) and architectural taste in church buildings, and good music and singing . . . other denominations . . . appear more like secular public assemblies without ceremonies.

—Bishop Henry Lee, PECUSA, 1879[2]

OUR STUDY OF THE origins of Mexican Protestantism as expressed in the Church of Jesus movement has taken us from the immediate context of Benito Juárez's Mexico to the very origins of Mexican identity in the early sixteenth-century encounter of cultures. Throughout this study we have emphasized the continuing dialectic between strands and schools of religious expression (the Baroque, the Enlightenment, etc.)

---

1. Nesvig, *Local Religion*, xviii.
2. Bishop Henry Lee, Commission of the House of Bishops of the Protestant Episcopal Church in the United States, 1879, Archives of the Episcopal Church, Austin, TX.

as part of the great Latin American social fabric wherein races, cultures, worldviews and identities interacted in a back-and-forth manner and thereby created, and are creating, the diverse cultures of the region.

In the introduction to this study I used two works of art as touchstones in order to describe the processes by which the very Protestant Church of Jesus emerged from the very Catholic Baroque. The first painting, the *Fusion of Two Cultures*, epitomizes one perspective on the formation of Mexican (and it can be argued, Latin American) identity. In this point of view, Mexican identity comes out of violence and upheaval—the Spanish against the Indian, the American against the European. The death-embrace between these two figures can also be taken as illustrative of the continuing struggle and search for Mexican identity, perhaps best described by Ocatvio Paz in his *Labyrinth of Solitude*. According to Paz, the violent crushing of the Mexican indigenous spirit began with its own extremely authoritarian rulers, who were overthrown and replaced by the equally authoritarian Spanish conquerors of the colonial period. These then transitioned to the oligarchies of the nineteenth century (accompanied by intimidation by the United States). A result of this legacy of violence and suppression is a tension between violent resentment and passivity. The sense of oppression is not, however, without a feeling of inferiority and results in a sense of solitude, as Paz explains.

> Our sense of inferiority—real or imagined—might be explained at least partly by the reserve with which the Mexican faces other people and the unpredictable violence with which his repressed emotions break through his mask of impassivity. But his solitude is vaster and profounder than his sense of inferiority. It is impossible to equate these two attitudes: when you sense that you are alone, it does not mean that you feel inferior, but rather that you feel you are different. Also, a sense of inferiority may sometimes by an illusion, but solitude is a hard fact. We are truly different. And we are truly alone.[3]

Consequently, the history of Mexico is a search for historical origins, a nebulous search for a prelapsarian epoch before the "catastrophe" of historical time—the mythical Aztlan called forth by Mexican-American activists in the 1960s and '70s, for example. The Mexican experience is an "orphanhood, an obscure awareness that we have been torn from the

---

3. Paz, *Labyrinth*, 19.

All, and an ardent search: a flight and a return, an effort to re-establish the bonds that unite us with the universe."[4]

In historical and religious terms this experience of Conquest and oppression resulted in what Latino historian and theologian Justo Gonzalez terms a non-innocent reading of history that acknowledges the violent, ugly side of history as opposed to innocent Anglo-American versions of history. The latter proposes a metanarrative that begins with Columbus, continues to the First Thanksgiving, 1776, and the Westward Migration with little or no reference to the decimation of native peoples, the appropriation of their lands, the enslavement of millions of Africans or the violence committed against ethnic or religious minorities. On the other hand, Mexican children learn from an early age that their history was "born out of an act of violence of cosmic proportions in which our Spanish forefathers raped our Indian foremothers" and the ruins of pre-Columbian cities and towns stand in silent testimony to that catastrophe.[5] The authoritarian and violent nature of Spanish rule and the imposition of Christianity, according to Paz, led to an aversion to the distant and powerful God the Father and drew Mexican Christians to the maternal Virgin of Guadalupe (and the Suffering Christ one might add). To put it another way, while the national and personal experience of rape and desolation experienced during the Conquest led to an identity crisis in search of the missing father-figure or a nodding acknowledgement of the distant God (and his equally distant and benevolent representative the King of Spain) it primarily fostered an affection and attachment to the divine Mother and an identification with the beaten and crucified Christ. This paradigm of the clash of cultures, while historically valid in many points, fails to explain the emergence of divergent religious forms throughout Mexico and the rest of Latin America.

A different perspective on Latin American history and particularly the history of religion in the region is illustrated by the *casta* paintings of the colonial era. Like the paintings that sought to illustrate the various racial mixtures present in Latin America, the concept of *castizaje* that I proposed earlier posits an active interaction between ideas and cultures that result in new admixtures and expressions. Rather than a monolithic Catholicism or the binary opposition of popular/elite religion present in many descriptions of Latin American Christianity, the

4. Ibid., 20.
5. González, *Mañana*, 77.

concept of *castizaje* as I have described it emphasizes the continual processes of give-and-take between religious ideas and expressions. While not discounting the powers and immense impact of violence and empire upon the historical development of Latin American culture, identity and religion, *castizaje* takes into account the everyday and in-between relationships between individuals, institutions and ideas as they created new definitions, new identities and new expressions that not simply combined but also redefined traits from the originals.

CASTIZAJE AND THE CHURCH OF JESUS

In the beginning was the Conquest. The heritage of the Conquest, including the colonization of the Americas, the planting of the Church, and the importation of African slavery would become the pluralistic mix of people groups inhabiting the continents including their progeny. As we discussed in chapter two, this pluralism is basic to Latin American society and indeed, to Latin American Christianity as the Christian faith was interpreted and accommodated to and by the many people groups (with all that implies, geographically, culturally, socio-politically, etc.) across the continent. The ascendancy of Tridentine, Baroque Catholicism only aided that process by giving space to the varied religious expressions that were part and parcel of pluralistic Latin American Christianity. Cults of the saints, religious festivals, and art and architecture, produced by all social levels, both locally and over a greater expanse, multiplied and contributed to the tapestry that was colonial religion.

Enlightenment Christianity in the eighteenth century in no way departed from this trend as it was both a movement in reaction to and in continuity with Baroque Catholicism. This form of Christianity, espoused by a more educated and elite group of reformers both in Spain and in Mexico sought to correct abuses, exaggerations, and superstitions as they perceived them. They attacked the proliferation of saints, relics, and supposed miracles as well as the ostentation that went into the sensual display of Baroque spirituality. In its place they offered a religion that was more rational, so they believed, based upon the Bible and the early Church. It would be affected through the improved education of the parish priest as well as royal control of the Church over and against papal domination as expressed in the royal patronage, which forms half of the framework of this schema.

The Church of Jesus movement, the umbrella term for the dissident movement of the Constitutionalist Clerics, in turn emerged from some of the priorities and ideas inherent in Enlightened Catholicism and Catholic Liberals. Along with these two they sought to bring about change in the Catholic Church through a renewed emphasis upon the Bible and the early Church. As their political backdrop they had the debates over national patronage that occurred shortly after the independence of Mexico and which found their echo in the Reform Laws of Benito Juárez and the Constitution of 1857. Like the Enlightened Catholics they saw no contradiction between the mission of the Church and the State's control over some of the temporal aspects of the Church such as finances and properties. Under Juárez's administration some elements within the Church of Jesus sought to gain government favor, but when that came to all but naught, they sought the aid of the Episcopal Church in the United States (something they may have had to do eventually as it would have been beyond the State's power to provide for apostolic succession).[6]

With the introduction of evangelical Episcopalian elements into the Church of Jesus the nature of the body began to change. Like a branch grafted onto another tree the evangelical emphasis brought about through contacts with the PECUSA would transform it and bring the Church of Jesus closer to that body's traditions including, as we saw with Manuel Aguas, a virulent anti-Catholicism that was also fueled by anticlerical elements within Mexican society after the Maximilian occupation. The Church of Jesus as a dissident movement, as we noted, had its roots in the pluralistic milieu of Mexican Catholicism and Enlightened religion. Its already present commonalities with evangelical Episcopalians, such as the focus on the Bible and the criticism of perceived Catholic abuses such as clerical celibacy, would draw that body closer to the PECUSA until, under its auspices it morphed into a body reflective of institutional and theological evangelical Protestantism. A crude diagram would picture the emergence of the Church of Jesus in this way:

---

6. The Protestant Episcopal Church in the United States was the most logical source for apostolic succession. The emergence of Old Catholic Churches in Europe was decades away and the Orthodox bodies were not, at this time, a significant presence in either the United States or Latin America.

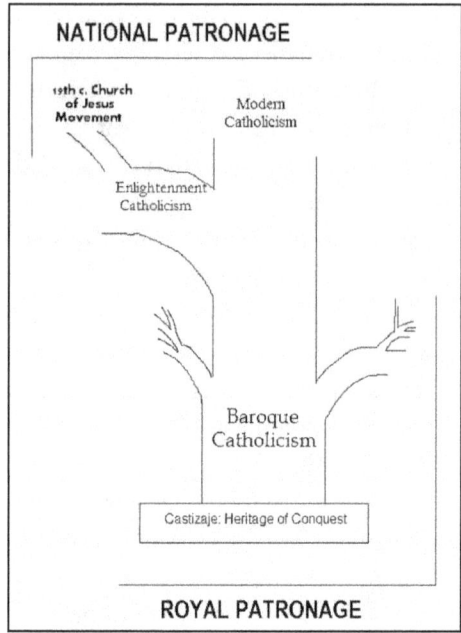

Figure 5: The Emergence of the Church of Jesus

The notion of *castizaje*, that protean pluralism evident in Latin American society from its beginnings, best expresses, in this writer's opinion, the process by which the Church of Jesus and nascent Protestantism came about. Whereas many writers treat the emergence of Protestantism as a separate chapter, almost appendix-like to the majority story of Roman Catholicism (perhaps due to assumptions as to the nature or place of Protestantism in Latin American society), this writer sees nascent Protestantism, at least as expressed in the Church of Jesus, as being part of the baroque pluralism that dominated, and arguably dominates the ethos of Latin American Christianity.[7] On a larger scale, Protestant religion, rather than dismissible as an invading species at worst and a marginal aberration at best, is part of the ongoing religious conversation between the peoples, traditions and institutions of Latin America, drawing upon and interacting with and sometimes against, the worldviews and traditions of the larger culture and in the process, becoming a part of the Latin American fabric of identity. In other words, though some

---

7. Prien, *Religiosidad*, 12.

forms of Protestantism have been home-grown (the Church of Jesus, *Assembleia de Deus do Brasil*) and others introduced from the outside (Presbyterian Church, Lutheranism) Protestant bodies, as a whole, have been successful in contextualizing themselves into the social, cultural and ideological matrices of Latin America. As a result, they have become part of the cultural and theological give-and-take, the continuing process of *castizaje* as they interact, adapt and change according their surrounding needs.[8]

THEOLOGICAL CODA

The late historian of African Christianity, Ogbu Kalu, stated that the study of history is used to relate the past with the present and the future in all aspects of life. It is not just the bare accumulation of facts that makes history important, but rather, its interpretation as it affects the priorities and needs of the present moment.[9]

Thus whereas historians who profess Christianity are guided by the techniques and procedures of the historian's craft, a scientific endeavor as it used to be called, the Christian faith imposes a perspective of its own in the interpretation of history that forces a theological perception on historical events that not only attends to the here and now but also to the "not yet," the eschatological hope of Christian faith. In other words, Christian historiography interprets facts for an understanding of what God was doing in Jesus Christ linked together with God's future actions in establishing God's Dominion among God's people.

A Christian historiography should not only be theologically coherent—by which I mean grounded upon an understanding of the life and mission of Jesus based upon the Bible and the Tradition (the creeds, liturgy, etc.)—but must also be ecumenical. Gone are (or should be) the

---

8. Obviously some denominational bodies and traditions have been more successful at inserting themselves into the needs and ideologies of the surrounding culture than others. As an example, can it be argued that the success of Pentecostalism vis-à-vis other Protestant faiths in Latin America derives in part from its commonalities with Baroque Catholicism, the dominant form of Catholic expression in Latin American history? Both emphasize the sensory and emotional, both seek an immanent experience of the transcendent God through music and art (and in the case of Pentecostalism, rhetoric) and both see the Divine in the everyday events of life—through healings and miracles that manifest themselves in the here and now and in the concrete.

9. I am indebted heavily to Kalu, *Historiography*, for the introductory concepts in this chapter.

days when X denomination or Church self-identified as the only or true Body of Christ, linking its institutions with the prophets and apostles to the exclusion of all other traditions. This "gap theory" presupposing a gap between the end of the New Testament era and the inception of X tradition is historically and theologically unsound and implies that God left Godself without a pilgrim people for Y number of years. Similarly, Church bodies that maintain a historical link to the first Christians, such as some of the Orthodox bodies and the Roman Catholic Church, should (and in many cases do, as seen in Vatican II) recognize that "the Spirit blows wherever It wishes" and that Christian faith is not exclusive to their own institution.

An ecumenical historiography, based on the notion of God's *oikumene*, recognizes the working out of God's acts and will throughout all of creation and human history. Thus this kind of historiography must look to a broader definition of the Church, rejecting all elitism, nationalism, and denominationalism and respecting every period, community, and aspect of culture. In his book, Kalu continues to critique several historiographical approaches. I will adopt those critiques and apply them to the writing of Latin American Christian histories.

Some historiographies take up an institutional approach to the writing of Christian history. They focus on the Church as an institution and often differ little from political histories; missionary X from Y tradition arrives and plants the Church. This approach is particularly visible in the early histories of Latin American Christianity written by Motolinía and others that emphasized the extirpation of native religions and the establishment of Catholicism. Such histories reinforce the notion of the Church as vehicle of salvation and custodian of grace and even equate the progress of the Church with salvation history. It is a perspective that is also seen in some of the writings of the PECUSA when dealing with the Mexican Church when they equate the gospel with the diffusion of Protestant missions in order to rescue the people from "papal idolatry."

Such denominationalism tends to focus on the role of foreign missions in the land. By neglecting the role of indigenous religion (be it Nahuatl or Catholic) they impose the image of God as foreigner, a stranger that is imported rather than native to the people. It can easily lead to a triumphalist notion of the Church as conqueror over other competitors and is common in medieval historiographies (for example, the story of St. Benedict over the Germans or St. Patrick in Ireland). This approach, and which comes close to equating the Church to a civilizing power, be it Spanish or British, runs against the biblical conception of the Church as a dynamic, prophetic voice that succors the poor and rebukes the mighty.

Another approach that is seen in the writing of Latin American Christian histories is the missionary history. A popular genre, they are usually written by missionaries or their protégés and are designed to tell how the missionary and missionary societies have crossed cultural barriers to communicate the gospel to such-and-such a people. Many of these are uncritical hagiographies that do not include cultural context or historiographical methods. Their histories are not related to secular history and the recipients of the message are seen as objects to undergo conversion rather than agents in their own right. The role of the missionary history is often propagandistic and is intended to drum up support for the mission in the home country or to provide an edifying tale of faith and heroism in the name of Christ for its readers. In this respect the popularization of the story of Nate Saint and Jim Elliot among the Waodani people of Ecuador is not too different from the hagiographies of the Middle Ages or the missionary biographies of the nineteenth century.

Another kind of history that has gained prominence in the last few decades is the sociological approach. Jean-Pierre Bastian's works on Latin American Protestantism and dissident religion and those edited by Martin Nesvig focusing on popular religion in colonial and modern Mexico, for example, have proven useful, even indispensable in bringing forth the stories of the subaltern or those groups usually marginalized in more institutional histories. However, these histories often fail to explain or deal with the inward, purely religious dimension of the historical actors. There must be a balance between the inward and outward factors; explanation of religious change must address purely religious factors and motivations as well as outward (ecological, economic, political, cultural) factors.

An ecumenical historiography would stress that the organizational structure of any given Church tradition does not constitute the total character of the Church. As the pilgrim people of God and their experiences of God's redeeming grace in Jesus Christ, the Church is expressed in its various cultural, ecological, and political milieus. Further, while the role of missionaries is undeniable, the idealization of missionary agents and structures distorts the history of the Church and ignores a wider understanding of evangelistic strategies as well as the inner life of the Church, including the role of people from the recipient culture in spreading the new faith such as lay evangelists, catechetical instructors and ordinary people in their day to day dealings.

Such a historiography must take into account the continuities and discontinuities between the native (indigenous, Catholic, African, etc.) and the adopted religion. In the Latin American context this means acknowledging the complexities of the continent—the cultural stew composed of indigenous, Africans, and Europeans (primarily Spanish and Portuguese but also other parts of Europe and even Asia). It must also account for the complexity of religious faith and pluralism in Latin America from the official pronouncements of hierarchy and church leaders to popular religious expressions to syncretistic religions such as *santería* and *candomblé*.

In the United States it has appeared popular of late to focus on the role of popular religion in Latin America, usually sociological glimpses into the faith expressions and experiences of the subaltern. Historians of a liberation theology persuasion have emphasized the theological side of this—the study of the religion of the poor and marginalized to whom Christ proclaimed the gospel as authentic expressions of religious faith rather than as syncretic aberrations of a barely-Christianized people.

Enrique Dussel and Maria Alicia Puente Lutteroth have both overseen or edited works that have sought to detail the history of Latin American Christianity and Mexican Christianity, respectively, from a liberationist perspective.[10] Dussel has explained in his introductory volume (Vol. I) that the project has sought to reconstruct the history of the Church in Latin America as both a scientific task and a theological task, affirming the Church's role as the Sacrament of Salvation particularly through the Church of the Poor.

The editor of the Mexican volume, however, differs in this assessment, affirming that the historian should seek to reconstruct the best possible approximation to what occurred in the past through the study of the available documents. He also states that the historian should not be guided by interpretive ideologies, be they theological, political, social, or cultural. In other words, while Dussel sees the task of history as encompassing a theological imperative, the Mexican team of scholars, led

---

10. See Dussel, *Tomo V* and Lutteroth, *Hacia,* for their works on Mexican Christianity. Enrique Dussel served as the General Coordinator for the eleven-volume series produced by CEHILA on the general history of the Church in Latin America.

by Alfonso Alcalá Alvarado, defines its task as an institutional history using historical methodology.[11]

Similarly, Maria Lutteroth defines her studies as encompassing the dominant religious entity from the conquest of Tenochtitlán to our present day. She affirms a history of the Church as the people of God who, from time to time, have allowed the liberating Word to sound forth and other times have not. Lutteroth admits though, that this kind of history was unable to be written as conceived due to the difficulty in obtaining the conditions necessary for such a task. She laments that the contributors to the book are merely "academics" and not historians with the vision necessary to fulfill the task.[12] As a result, while the chapters she contributes seek to deal with the history of the Church among the original inhabitants of the land in keeping with her focus on the marginalized, the remaining sections follow a more customary account of the Church as an institution.

One of the priorities in the writing of Christian history from a liberationist perspective is to draw out the stories of the poor and marginalized. Theologians on both sides of the border have, in the last few decades, plunged into the world of popular religion in order to rediscover the ways in which the gospel is present in the devotions and rituals of these poor such a Virgilio Elizondo's work on the Virgin of Guadalupe. The underlying thesis or assumption is that the religion of the marginalized not only expresses the gospel in some manner different from that of official or elite religion but that it can be a more authentic expression of such as the Good News received by the poor. The study of popular religion has been aided in a great way by sociological studies

---

11. Alvarado, "La enseñanza," 151–70. cf. Alcaide, "La historiografía recente," 319–34.

12. Lutteroth, *Hacia*, 9; cf. Alcaide, "La historiografía recente," 326. I believe that Lutteroth's distinction between "academics" and "historians" not only belittles the practitioners of the academic historian's trade but it is an unnecessary dichotomy. Lutteroth seems to believe that "academics" are dictated by accepted historiographical practices whereas "historians" have an ideology (a "vision") that guides their task. All historians, professional/academic and the so-called amateur historians must be guided by accepted and tested procedures and research techniques in order for their works to hold water, as it were. At the same time it is being recognized that the task of writing an objective history is a mirage and that all historians are guided in the selection and interpretation of their materials by their own contexts and agendas, be they conscious or unconscious. The validity of their interpretations is determined by how well their conclusions line up with the available evidence.

into the area with the caveat that sociologists, following anthropological studies into tribal religions, seek to study the religious expressions of the subaltern whereas liberationists seek the Church of the poor in its theological definition as those who are excluded from the bases of power and towards whom God expresses a "preferential option."

One of the difficulties and challenges of this kind of methodology is that it sets up an artificial dichotomy between the poor/elite, uneducated/educated, powerless/powerful. Carlos Eire, the Cuban historian, has noted that during late antiquity and the Middle Ages, "the relation between what was Christian and non-Christian could be fluid and uncertain and somewhat variegated according to time, place, and social class . . . Syncretism and antagonism were as intertwined as were the clergy and the laity, the elites and the nonelites, the towns and the countryside, zeal and indifference, the sacred and profane."[13] Hence, for example, in our Latin American context we must note that aspects or devotions attributed to popular religion are not exclusively held by the poor or subaltern. The devotion to the Virgin of Guadalupe, to take an example, crosses across social, political, and economic lines. Further, it is a testimony to the often confused state of Latin American Church historiography when works such as those of CEHILA and Lutterworth, while maintaining their intention to write a history of the Church from the perspective of the poor, nonetheless spend the majority of ink and paper describing the actions of the institutional Church, not only because primary documents by and about the subaltern or poor may be scarce but also because the Church as institution intersects the Church of the poor and in some ways defines it through its liturgy, charities and devotions. In other words, the dividing line between official religion and popular religion (or whatever way that dichotomy is expressed) is blurred.

Eire describes the confused state of defining popular religion when he observes that the concept of popular religion in itself has various polar opposites—official/unofficial, clerical/lay, and so on. And whereas liberationists may accentuate the category of the poor one must question as to whether that genre has been unduly defined by Marxism and whether the biblical concept usually translated "poor" encompasses a greater definition than deprivation and powerlessness.[14]

13. Nesvig, *Local*, 9–10.

14. In the Hebrew Bible there are no less than nine words that are rendered as "poor" in modern translations, each with different connotations. Cf. Hoppe, *There Shall*

Coming at it from a theological perspective we reaffirm that an ecumenical history of the Christian Church, while recognizing the priority of the gospel to the poor must be cognizant that the relationships and institutions of power and privilege go beyond physical or socio-political deprivation. It must encompass the impoverished and the wealthy, the powerless and the powerful, all the while noting that systematic evil affects all levels of a society. The canonical Gospels, after all, state that Jesus said both "Blessed are the poor in spirit" as well as "Blessed are the poor."[15] Our historiographical perspective must take into account both this theological point-of-view and, no less importantly, be able to account for the evidence before us in the history of the Latin American Church in a manner consistent with historical methodology.

Hans-Jürgen Prien, the German historian of Latin American Christianity, has been critical of some Latin American Christian historiographies, particularly those set forth by CEHILA.[16] Prien notices, in the volumes produced and edited by CEHILA, that despite their ecumenical structure, these tomes cannot arrive at a definition of the history of Christianity in which all church bodies perceive themselves as part of a whole. He observes that in this series, the Catholic Church is seen by many of its authors as an authoritative entity while the various protestantisms are posited as intruders incapable of acting out of purely theological motivations. In response, Prien sought to put forth an ecumenical historiography of the Latin American Church by focusing on the notion of the invisible Church as the agent that is created by and proclaims God's Word.[17] This approach has its benefits. An emphasis upon the invisible Church would naturally lead the historian to a study of the marks of the Church, however they are defined—the presence of Word and Sacrament, the work of the people of God on behalf of the poor, etc. The fault with Prien's description is that it in emphasizing

---

Be. Ogbu Kalu has suggested that the concept of the poor must encompass a given culture's definition of poverty, such as the lack of familial connections. Kalu, *African Christianity*, 15.

15. Cf. Matthew's and Luke's respective versions of the Sermon on the Mount. Though scholars agree that Luke's version may indeed be the more original one, nonetheless both versions are accepted as authoritative canon by the Christian Church and each reveals depth and meaning in the obligations and priorities of the gospel.

16. *Comisión de Estudios de Historia de la Iglesia en América Latina* (Commission on the Study of the Church in Latin America), edited by Enrique Dussel.

17. Prien, *Religiosidad*, 89.

the spiritual nature of the Church the institutional nature of the Church can be shortchanged. In contrast, I propose another set of theological principles that address both the Church Visible and Invisible in Latin America; a set of ideas that hopefully persons across traditions can agree upon that may be useful in forming an ecumenical historiography and interpretation of the Church in Latin America and that will serve as a theological companion to the notion of *castizaje* described above.

First, there is the notion of the Church as *simul iustus et peccator*. The Church, in all its incarnations—Protestant, Catholic, Orthodox, visible and invisible—stands under the cross and not over it, always under its grace or judgment.[18] As a mixed body it is composed of saints and sinners, an idea rooted in the Bible but expressed in Augustine as well as mystics of all stripes and the Protestant reformers. The same Church, in its institutional, local, and individual expressions is capable of great good and great evil—of establishing hospitals and Inquisitions, of immense care and charity towards some and violence, homophobia, and racism towards others. Similarly, on a microcosmic level the members of the Church have to live within the tensions of this principle. As children of grace who have been, are in the process of, and look forward to redemption, each baptized individual is a *corporum mixtorum* of sinful and grace-filled impulses. Throughout the centuries in Latin American Christianity (and in the Church in general) we have seen individuals and institutions act in manners that are horribly exploitative of "the Other" and in ways that demonstrate supernatural grace and Christian love. These traits are not exclusive to one group over another—the Church of the Poor, for example, can act in sinful ways just as the hierarchical members of the Church can act virtually. To be both sinner and saint is common to all according to Christian theology and the honest Christian historian, while maintaining an eye upon the manifestation of the gospel among and towards the poor, must relate the events, thoughts and lives of the whole Church, all of whom are agents of sin and grace, of their identity as sons and daughters of Adam and Eve and children of Christ.

18. Witness, for example Luther's own theology of the cross that emphasizes the role of Jesus' self-giving unto death in delineating and forming theology or the ubiquitous place of the Suffering Christ in Catholic Churches throughout Latin America and Passion Week performances that point to the believer's identification with the Crucified God (and vice versa) rather than the Victorious King. In Orthodoxy there is the parallel notion of the Savior who, through his suffering, reigns from the cross instead of being its passive victim.

Linked intimately to this concept is that of the *ecclesia reformata, semper reformanda*—the Church that is reformed and always in the process of reforming itself as its theologies, liturgies, and pieties interact with culture after culture, generation after generation, as it struggles to interpret the gospel. Aware of its mixed nature as saints and sinners and the need to transmit the living gospel to each culture and generation the Church must always be in movement, seeking ways in which to communicate the gospel as a living message in ways that are faithful to that message. In the words of G. K. Chesterton (and echoed by the late scholar Jaroslav Pelikan), Tradition is the "democracy of the dead."[19] It is the handing over of the content of faith to each new constituency and the constant back and forth between culture and interpretation as each group appropriates the message of Jesus. Anything else is not Living Tradition but dead antiquarianism—a holding on to the past for its own sake rather than a living transmission and subsequent ownership. This finds its rough Catholic parallel in John Cardinal Newman's concept of dogma developing from seed form in the Scripture throughout time. On a larger scale, the history of the Church is an unfolding of the gospel message through time. An ecumenical history of the Church in Latin America recognizes this and does not hallow any one period or expression over another, noting that the Church must always be in process of reforming itself, re-enculturating itself and reincarnating itself among different people groups. To quote Cardinal Newman, "To live is to change; to be perfect is to have changed often."

Liberation theologians have emphasized the gospel message to the poor as the locus of the Church's identity. This, as it has been stated above, has the potential of setting forth the false dichotomy of the poor vs. the wealthy, the powerless vs. the elite, and so on. Given the fact that oppressive and sinful systems are exploitative of both the victims and the victimizer, I would like to propose a larger interpretive key when assessing the locus of the Church that nonetheless includes the Scriptural preferential option for the poor.[20] Following Luther's own priority for a "canon within the canon" when faced with contradictory messages in the Bible, he posited that one should look for where Christ is revealed.

---

19. Chesterton, *Orthodoxy*, 48. Cf. "Kluge Prize Winner–2004: Jaroslav Pelikan."

20. "When human beings sin, they create structures of sin, which, in their turn, make human beings sin." In Faus, "Sin," 537.

> [In this way] all the correct holy books agree, in that every one of them preaches and drives Christ home. That is also the correct touchstone for evaluating all books: to see whether they drive Christ home or not, since all Scripture shows Christ, Rom. 3[:21], and Saint Paul desires to know nothing but Christ, 1 Cor. 2[:2]. Whatever does not teach Christ is not apostolic, even if Saint Peter or Saint Paul teaches it. Once again, whatever preaches Christ, that is apostolic, even if it were to be presented by Judas, Annas, Pilate, and Herod.[21]

Theologians of all Christian confessions can agree upon Martin Luther's notion that *crux sola est nostra teologia* (the cross alone is our theology)—namely that the sacrifice of Jesus is the measuring stick by which all theological endeavor is judged. The theology of the cross affirms that the nature and purposes of God for God's people and all creation were revealed in the self-giving of Christ on the cross. A historiographical reflection guided by the theology of the cross would assert God's preferential option for the poor—yet not only the socially, politically, and economically disadvantaged poor but all who have become victims of a theology of glory—worldviews and systems that enthrone power, control, fear, and oppression towards others in whatever manner. It is the recontextualization of Christianity's first-century social, theological, and political matrix that set Jesus and his followers against the Roman Empire in its theological pretensions and its own "gospel" of peace through violence. One recognizes that Good Friday and Easter are inseparable: one is not a theology of suffering while the other of glory. The victory of Jesus is seen in the cross while His suffering with and for humanity is bound up in his resurrection where his scars are still visible. Similarly, one can answer the question, "Where is the Church?" by looking for where Christ is present, where he gives "life and that in abundance" (John 10:10). While one may hold, quite biblically, to God's preferential option for the poor as the direction towards which the *missio Dei* is enacted, by placing priority upon the centrality of the cross, the Christian historian's attention can encompass the entire people of God as they seek to witness to the Christian message in confessions as well as charities, in poverty and through privilege, through liturgy and private devotion. It is recognizing once again that the cross stands in judgment over all peoples, groups, and institutions. This theological consideration overcomes the dichotomy between official and

---

21. Luther. "Preface to the Epistles of St. James and St. Jude, 1522," 35:395–98.

popular religion, between Protestant and Catholic in Latin America, as the shibboleth that proves and points to the working forth (or not) of the mission of God in the life of the Church.

Bibliography

PRIMARY SOURCES

Aguas, Manuel. *Letter of Manuel Aguas.* New York: Whittaker, 1871. Archives of the Episcopal Church, Austin, Texas.

———. *Letter of Manuel Aguas to the Bishop of Mexico.* New York: Whittaker, 1871. Archives of the Episcopal Church, Austin, Texas.

Bermúdez, Manuel. Letter of Manuel Bermúdez to Horatio Potter, Bishop of New York, March 13, 1865. Archives of the Episcopal Church, Austin, Texas.

Bermúdez, Manuel Aguilar. Letter of Manuel Aguilar Bermúdez to Rev. Dennison, August 8, 1867. Archives of the Episcopal Church, Austin, Texas.

Congregations of San Francisco and San José de Gracia. Letter from the Congregations of San Francisco and San José de Gracia to Henry Riley, January 24, 1873. Archives of the Episcopal Church, Austin, Texas.

Guión, Elijah, Shaves, Daniel & Vallas. A Letter of Elijah Guión, Daniel Shaves and Vallas to the bishops, clergy and laity of the Protestant Episcopal Church in the United States, October 17, 1864. Archives of the Episcopal Church, Austin, Texas.

Hale, Rev. Charles R., A.M. *The Mozarabic Liturgy and the Mexican Branch of the Catholic Church of Our Lord Jesus Christ Militant upon Earth: A Liturgical Study.* Reprinted from the *American Church Review* (April 1876), Privately Printed 1876. Archives of the Episcopal Church, Austin, Texas.

Hooker, Josephine. "Mexican Leaflets, Mexico. Letters from a Lady from our own Correspondent in the City of Mexico," 1875. Online: www.anglicanhistory.org/mx/index.html.

Lee, Bishop Alfred, Dyer, H. and Riley, Henry Chauncey. "Origin and Outline History of 'The Mexican Branch of the Catholic Church Militant upon Earth.'" 1877. Online: www.anglicanhistory.org/mx/index.html.

Lee, Bishop Henry. *Commission of the House of Bishops of the Protestant Episcopal Church in the United States.* (1879). Archives of the Episcopal Church, Austin, Texas.

Martínez, Rafael Díaz. Letter of Rafael Díaz Martínez to Rev. Bishop J. D. Wilmer of New Orleans, October 5, 1867. Archives of the Episcopal Church, Austin, Texas.

de Mier, Fray Servando Teresa. "Borradores del sermón que predicó el padre doctor fray Servando Teresa Mier el día 12 de diciembre de 1794," Online: http://www.filosofia.org/aut/001/17941230.htm.

———. *Memorias. Ed. por Oscar Rodríguez Ortíz.* Caracas: Biblioteca Ayacuho, 1994.

———. *Apologia*. ed. por Guadalupe Fernández Ariza. Rome: Bulzoni Editore, 1998.

———. *The Memoirs of Fray Servando Teresa de Mier*. Translated by Helen Lane, edited by Susana Rotker. Oxford: Oxford University Press, 1998.

Nicholson, E. C. Letter of E. C. Nicholson to Dr. Craik, January 31, 1864. Archives of the Episcopal Church, Austin, Texas.

———. Letter of E. C. Nicholson to Rev. Dennison, January 1, 1865. Archives of the Episcopal Church, Austin, Texas.

———. Letter of E. C. Nicholson to S. Dennison, May 1, 1865. Archives of the Episcopal Church, Austin, Texas.

Riley, H. *Works of the Church Paper #1* (1882). Archives of the Episcopal Church, Austin, Texas.

Riley, Henry C. Letter of Henry C. Riley to Bishop Wilmer of Louisiana, October 5, 1869. Archives of the Episcopal Church, Austin, Texas.

Unknown Author. Letter of unknown author. 1865. Archives of the Episcopal Church, Austin, Texas.

Tatlock, William. *The Mexican Episcopal Church Letter of the Four Bishops and Statement of the Provisional Committee*, New York: Board of Missions of the Protestant Episcopal Church, (November 11, 1894). Archives of the Episcopal Church, Austin, Texas.

Wilmer, Bishop J. D. Letter of Bishop J. D. Wilmer to the Church of the Foreign Committee of the Protestant Episcopal Church, NY, 1867. Archives of the Episcopal Church, Austin, Texas.

SECONDARY SOURCES

Alberola, A., and La Parra, E. *La Ilustración Española*. Alicante: Instituto Juan-Gil Albert, 1986.

Alberro, Solange. *El águila y la cruz: Orígenes religiosos de la conciencia criolla. México, siglos xvi–xvii*. México: Fondo de Cultura Económica, 1999.

Alcaide, Elisa Luque. "La historiografía reciente sobre la historia de la Iglesia en México (1984–1994)." *Anuario de La Historia de la Iglesia* 5 (1996) 319–34.

Alvarado, Alfonso Alcalá. "La enseñanza de la Historia de la Iglesia en América Latina." *Anuario de La Historia de la Iglesia* 5 (1996) 151–70.

Anderson, Allan. *An Introduction to Pentecostalism*. Cambridge: Cambridge University Press. 2004.

Andrien, Kenneth J. *Andean Worlds: Indigenous History, Culture, and Consciousness under Spanish Rule, 1532–1825*. Albuquerque: University of New Mexico Press, 2001.

Ángel, Vicente, and Palenzuela, Álvarez. *Historia de España de la Edad Media*. Barcelona: Ariel, 2002.

Appolis, Émile. *Les Jansénistes Espagnoles*. Bordeaux: SOBODI, 1966.

Aston, Nigel. *Christianity and Revolutionary Europe c.1750–1830*. Cambridge: Cambridge University Press. 2002.

Baldwin, Deborah J. *Protestants and the Mexican Revolution: Missionaries, Ministers and Social Change*. Urbana: University of Illinois Press, 1990.

Barnett, David B., Kirian, George T. and Johnson, Todd M., eds. *World Christian Encyclopedia*. New York: Oxford University Press, 2002.

Bastian, Jean-Pierre. *Historia del Protestantismo en América Latina*. México: CUPSA. 1986.

———. *Los Disidentes. Sociedades Protestantes y Revolución en México, 1872–1911.* México: Colegio de México/ Fondo de Cultura Económica. 1989.

Bastian, Jean-Pierre. *Protestantes, Liberales y Francomasones. Sociedades de Ideas y Modernidad en América Latina, siglo XIX.* México: CEHILA/Fondo de Cultura Económica. 1990.

Bayer, Oswald. *Martin Luther's Theology: A Contemporary Interpretation.* Grand Rapids: Eerdmans, 2008.

Bechtel, Alpha Gillet. "The Mexican Episcopal Church: A Century of Reform and Revolution." MA Thesis, San Diego State College, 1966.

Beezley, William H., and Curcio-Nagy, Linda A. *Latin American Popular Culture.* Wilmington, DE: SR Books. 2000.

Begg, Ean. *The Cult of the Black Virgin.* New York: Penguin, 1997.

Blank, Rodolfo. *Teología y Misión en América Latina.* St. Louis: Concordia, 1996.

Bonino, José Míguez. *Faces of Latin American Protestantism.* Grand Rapids: Eerdmans, 1997.

Borges, Pedro. *Historia de la Iglesia en Hispanoamérica y Filipinas.* 2 Vol. Madrid: Biblioteca de Autores Cristianos, 1992.

Bosch, David J. *Transforming Mission: Paradigm Shifts in Theology of Mission.* Maryknoll, NY: Orbis, 1991.

Brading, D. A. "Tridentine Catholicism and Enlightened Despotism in Bourbon Mexico," *Journal for Latin American Studies* 15 (1983) 1–22.

———. *The Origins of Mexican Nationalism.* Cambridge: Cambridge University Press, 1985.

———. *The First America: The Spanish Monarchy, Creole Patriots and the Liberal State, 1492–1867.* Cambridge: Cambridge University Press. 1991.

———. *Church and State in Bourbon Mexico.* Cambridge: Cambridge University Press, 1994.

———. *Mexican Phoenix: Our Lady of Guadalupe: Image and Tradition Across Five Centuries.* Cambridge: Cambridge University Press, 2001.

Bradley, James E., and Van Kley, Dale K. *Religion and Politics in Enlightenment Europe.* South Bend, IN: University of Notre Dame Press, 2001.

Burkhart, Louise. *Holy Wednesday.* Philadelphia: University of Pennsylvania Press, 1996.

Cairns, Earle E. *Christianity through the Centuries.* Grand Rapids: Zondervan, 1981.

Callahan, William J. *Church, Politics, and Society in Spain, 1750–1874.* Cambridge: Harvard University Press, 1984.

Callcott, Wilfred Hardy. *Liberalism in Mexico 1857–1927.* Stanford: Stanford University Press, 1931.

Cardaillac, Louis. *Toledo, Siglos XII–XIII. Musulmanes, Cristianos y Judíos: La Sabiduría e la Tolerancia.* Translated by José Luis Arántegui. Madrid: Alianza Editorial, 1991.

Carr, Raymond. *Spain: A History.* Oxford: Oxford University Press, 2000.

Charbonnier, Jean-Pierre. *Christians in China: A.D. 600 to 2000.* San Francisco: Ignatius, 2007.

Chejne, Anwar. *Historia de España Musulmana.* Translated by Pilar Vila. Madrid: Catedra, 1974.

Chesterton, G. K. *Orthodoxy.* New York: Doubleday, 1936.

Chestnut, R. Andrew. *Born Again in Brazil: The Pentecostal Boom and the Pathogens of Poverty.* New Brunswick, NJ: Rutgers University Press, 1997.

Christian, William A. Jr. *Local Religion in Sixteenth-Century Spain*. Princeton: Princeton University Press, 1986.

———. *Apparitions in Late Medieval and Renaissance Spain*. Princeton: Princeton University Press, 1989.

———. *Visionaries: The Spanish Republic and the Reign of Christ*. Berkeley: University of California Press, 1999.

Cleere, Henry. *Approaches to the Archaeological Heritage*. Cambridge: Cambridge University Press, 1984.

Collins, Roger. *Early Medieval Spain: Unity in Diversity, 400–1000*. New York: St. Martin's Press, 1983.

Connaughton, Brian. "The Enemy Within: Catholics and Liberalism in Independent Mexico, 1821–1860." In *The Divine Charter: Constitutionalism and Liberalism in Nineteenth-Century Mexico*. Lanham, MD: Rowman & Littlefield, 2005.

Costeloe, Michael P. *Church and State in Independent Mexico*. London: Royal Historical Society, 1978.

Creighton, Frank Whittington. *The Church in Mexico, by the Rt. Rev. Frank Whittington Creighton, d.d., Bishop of Mexico*. Philadelphia, 1929.

Cross, F. L., and Livingston, E. A., eds. *The Oxford Dictionary of the Christian Church*, 3rd ed. Oxford: Oxford University Press, 1997.

Curcio-Nagy, Linda. *The Great Festivals of Mexico City: Performing Power and Identity*. Albuquerque: University of New Mexico Press, 2004.

Damboriena, Prudencio. *Protestantismo en América Latina*. Friburgo: Feres, 1962.

De la Hera, Alberto. *Iglesia y Corona en la América Española*. Madrid: Editorial MAPFRE, 1992.

De Rivadeneira, Antonio Joaquin. "America for the Americans." In *Latin American Revolutions, 1808–1826: Old and New World Origins*. Norman, OK: University of Oklahoma Press, 1994.

Deiros, Pablo Alberto. *Historia del Cristianismo en América Latina*. Buenos Aires: Fraternidad Teológica Latinoamericana, 1992.

Dodds, Jerrilynn D. et al. *The Arts of Intimacy: Christians, Jews and Muslims and the Making of Castilian Culture*. New Haven: Yale University Press, 2008.

Dussel, Enrique. *Historia General de la Iglesia en América Latina, Tomo I: Introducción General*. México: Paulinas, 1984.

———. *Historia General de la Iglesia en América Latina, Tomo V: México*. México: Paulinas, 1984.

Dussel, Enrique, *The Church in Latin America 1492–1992*. Maryknoll, NY: Orbis, 1992.

Edwards, David L. *Christianity: The First Two Thousand Years*. Maryknoll, NY: Orbis, 2001.

Elizondo, Virgilio P. *Galilean Journey: The Mexican-American Promise*. Revised and Expanded Edition. Maryknoll, NY: Orbis, 2000.

Elliott, J. H. *The Spanish World*. New York: Abrams, 1991.

Estévez, Rosa M. Pérez. *La España de la Ilustración*. Madrid: Actas Editorial, 2002.

Faus, José Ignacio González. "Sin." In *Mysterium Liberationis: Fundamental Concepts of Liberation Theology*, edited by Ignacio Ellacuría and Jon Sobrino, 532–42. Maryknoll, NY: Orbis, 1993.

Fraginalis, Manuel Moreno. *Africa in Latin America, Essays on History, Culture and Socialization*. New York: Holmes & Meier, 1984.

Gilabert, Francisco Martí. *Carlos III y la Política Religiosa*. Madrid: Rialp, 2004.

Giles, Mary E. *Women in the Inquisition: Spain and the New World*. Baltimore: Johns Hopkins University Press, 1998.

González, Justo L. *The Story of Christianity*. 2 vols. New York: HarperOne, 1984.
———. *Christian Thought Revisited: Three Types of Theology*. Nashville: Abingdon, 1989.
———. *Mañana: Christian Theology from a Hispanic Perspective*. Nashville: Abingdon, 1990.
———. *Historia del Cristianismo, 2 tomos*. Miami: Unilit, 1994.
Gonzalez, Michelle A. *Sor Juana: Beauty and Justice in the Americas*. Maryknoll, NY: Orbis, 2003.
González, Ondina E. and González, Justo L. *Christianity in Latin America: A History*. Cambridge: Cambridge University Press, 2007.
Goss, Robert E. "The Gospel of John." In *The Queer Bible Commentary*, edited by Deryn Guest, Robert E. Goss, Mona West, and Thomas Bohache, 548–65. London: SCM, 2007.
Gossen, Gary H. *South and Meso-American Native Spirituality: From the Cult of the Feathered Serpent to the Theology of Liberation*. New York: Crossroad, 1997.
Gray, Albert Zabriskie. *Mexico as It Is: Being Notes of a Recent Tour in That Country*. New York: Dutton, 1878.
Graziano, Frank. *Cultures of Devotion: Folk Saints of Spanish America*. New York: Oxford University Press, 2006.
Greenland, Fay Sharon. "Religious Reform in Mexico: The Role of the Mexican Episcopal Church." Unpublished M.A. thesis, University of Florida, 1958.
Gruzinski, Serge. *Images at War: Mexico from Columbus to BladeRunner (1492–2019)*. Durham, NC: Duke University Press, 2001.
Hall, Gwendolyn Midlo. *Slavery and African Ethnicities in the Americas: Restoring the Links*. Durham: University of North Carolina Press, 2006.
Hall, Linda B. *Mary, Mother and Warrior: The Virgin in Spain and Latin America*. Austin: University of Texas Press, 2004.
Hastings, Adrian. *A World History of Christianity*. Grand Rapids: Eerdmans, 2000.
Hoppe, Leslie J., O.F.M. *There Shall Be No Poor among You: Poverty in the Bible*. Nashville: Abingdon, 2004.
Hsia, R. Po-Chia. *The World of Catholic Renewal 1540–1770*. Cambridge: Cambridge University Press, 1998.
Irvin, Dale and Sunquist, Scott. "*History of the World Christian Movement, Vol. 2 (1450–the Present).*" No pages. Online: http://www.hwcmweb.org/.
Jaffary, Norah E. *False Mystics: Deviant Orthodoxy in Colonial Mexico*. Lincoln: University of Nebraska Press, 2008.
Jenkins, Philip. *The New Anti-Catholicism: The Last Acceptable Prejudice*. Oxford: Oxford University Press, 2003.
Kalu, Ogbu. *Historiography of African Christianity: An Ecumenical Perspective*. Bern, Switzerland: Arbeitsstelle Oukumenische Schweiz, 1988.
———. *African Christianity: An African Story*. Pretoria: University of Pretoria, 2005.
Katzew, Ilona. *Casta Painting*. New Haven: Yale University Press, 2004.
Kirk, Daniel. "Mysterious Way: Protestant Reformation in Nineteenth Century Mexico." *Encounters Mission Ezine* 10 (February 2006) No pages. Online: www.redcliffe.org/uploads/documents/mysterious_way1_10.pdf.
Lafaye, Jacques. *Quetzalcóatl and Guadalupe: The Formation of Mexican National Consciousness 1531–1813*. Chicago: University of Chicago Press, 1976.
Larkin, Brian. *The Very Nature of God: Baroque Catholicism and Religious Reform in Bourbon Mexico City*. Albuquerque: University of New Mexico Press, 2010.

Latourette, Kenneth Scott. *A History of Christianity*. 2 vols. Rev. ed. New York: HarperOne, 1975.
Leon-Portilla, Miguel. *Tonantzin Guadalupe: Pensamiento Náhuatl y Mensaje Cristiano en el "Nican Mopohua."* México: Fondo de Cultura Económica, 2000.
López, Laura Espejel and Guerra, Rubén Ruiz. *El Protestantismo en México (1850–1940). La Iglesia Metodista Episcopal*. México: Instituto Nacional de Antropología e Historia, 1995.
López-Portillo, Carmen Beatriz. *Sor Juana y su Mundo: Una Mirada Actual*. México: Fondo de Cultura Económica, 1998.
Lovejoy, Paul E. "Context of Enslavement in West Africa: Ahmad Baba and the Ethics of Slavery." In *Slaves, Subjects and Subversives: Blacks in Colonial Latin America*, edited by Jane Landers and Barry Robinson, 9–38. Albuquerque: University of New Mexico Press, 2006.
———. *Transformations in Slavery*. Cambridge: Cambridge University Press, 2000.
Lowney, Chris. *A Vanished World, Medieval Spain's Golden Age of Enlightenment*. New York: Free, 2005.
Luther, Martin. "Preface to the Epistles of St. James and St. Jude." In *Luther's Works*, American Edition, 35:395–98. Philadelphia: Fortress, and St. Louis: Concordia, 1955–1986.
Lutteroth, María Alicia Puente. *Hacia Una Historia Mínima de la Iglesia en México*. México: Jus, 1993.
Mackay, John A. *The Other Spanish Christ*. London: SCM, 1932.
Magister, Sandro. "Benedict XVI's First Visit to Latin America." *Chiesa Espresso* (April, 2007). No pages. Online: http:// http://www.chiesa.espresso.repubblica.it/articolo/135981?eng=y.
Mann, Charles C. *1491: New Revelations of the Americas before Columbus*. New York: Knopf, 2005.
Mann, Thomas et al. *Convivencia: Jews, Christians and Muslims in Medieval Spain*. New York: Jewish Museum, 1992.
Martin, David. *Tongues of Fire: The Explosion of Protestantism in Latin America*. Oxford: Blackwell, 1990.
Martínez, Juan Francisco. *Sea la Luz: The Making of Mexican Protestantism in the American Southwest, 1829–1900*. Denton: University of North Texas Press, 2006.
Martínez, Rosa M. Capel & Gómez, José Cepeda. *El Siglo de las Luces: Política y Sociedad*. Madrid: Síntesis, 2006.
Matute, Álvaro et al. *Estado, Iglesia y Sociedad en México. Siglo XIX*. México: Miguel Ángel Porrua, 1995.
Mecham, J. Lloyd. *Church and State in Latin America*. Chapel Hill, NC: University of North Carolina, 1966.
Menocal, María Rosa. *The Ornament of the World: How Muslims, Jews, and Christians Created a Culture of Tolerance in Medieval Spain*. Boston: Little, Brown, 2002.
Meyer, Michael C. & Beezley, William H. *The Oxford History of Mexico*. Oxford: Oxford University Press, 2000.
Meyer, Michael C. & Sherman, William L. *The Course of Mexican History*. 5th ed. Oxford: Oxford University Press, 1995.
Michael, Christopher Domínguez. *Vida de Fray Servando*. México: Era, 2004.
Miller, Marilyn Grace. *Rise and Fall of the Cosmic Race: The Cult of Mestizaje in Latin America*. Austin: University of Texas Press, 2004.
Morales, Francisco. *Clero y Política en México (1767–1834)*. México: Sep/Setentas, 1973.

Nebel, Richard. *Santa María Tonantizin Virgen de Guadalupe.* México: Fondo de Cultura Económica, 1995.
Nesvig Martin Austin, ed. *Local Religion in Colonial Mexico.* Albuquerque: University of New Mexico Press, 2006.
———. *Religious Culture in Modern Mexico.* New York: Rowman & Littlefield, 2007.
O'Callaghan, Joseph. *A History of Medieval Spain.* Ithaca: Cornell University Press, 1975.
———. *Reconquest and Crusade in Medieval Spain.* Philadelphia: University of Pennsylvania, 2002.
Oleszkiewicz-Peralba, Malgorzata. *The Black Madonna in Latin America and Europe: Tradition and Transformation.* Albuquerque: University of New Mexico Press, 2009.
Olson, Christa Johanna. "Casta Paintings: The Construction and Depiction of Race in Colonial Mexico." No pages. Online: http://hemi.ps.tsoa.nyu.edu/archive/student-work/colony/olson/Casta1.htm
Pardo, F. Osvaldo. *The Origins of Mexican Catholicism: Nahua Rituals and Christian Sacraments in Sixteenth-Century Mexico.* Ann Arbor, MI: University of Michigan Press. 2006.
Paz, Octavio. *The Labyrinth of Solitude and Other Writings.* Translated by Lysander Kemp, Yara Milos, and Rachel Phillips Belash. New York: Grove, 1985.
———. *Sor Juana, or the Traps of Faith.* Cambridge: Harvard University Press. 1988.
Peláez, Agustín Churruca, S.J. *Historia de la Iglesia en México.* México: Buena Prensa A.C., 2002.
Pelayo, Marcelino Menéndez. *Historia de los heterodoxos españoles, Tomo I.* 5th ed. Madrid: Biblioteca de Autores Cristianos, 2006.
Penyak, Lee M., and Petry, Walter J. *Religion in Latin America: A Documentary History.* Maryknoll, NY: Orbis, 2006.
Pérez-Torres, Rafael *Mestizaje: Critical Uses of Race in Chicano Culture.* Minneapolis: University of Minnesota Press, 2006.
Pessar, Patricia R. *From Fanatics to Folk: Brazilian Millenarianism and Popular Culture.* Durham: Duke University Press, 2004.
Petry, Ray. *History of Christianity: Readings in the History of the Church.* Grand Rapids: Baker, 1962.
Pike, Frederick B. *The Conflict between Church and State in Latin America.* New York: Knopf, 1964.
Prichard, Robert. *A History of the Episcopal Church.* Harrisburg, PA: Morehouse, 1991.
Prien, Hans-Jurgen. *La Historia del Cristianismo en América Latina.* Salamanca: Sígueme, 1985.
———. *Religiosidad e Historiografía: La irrupción del pluralismo religioso en América Latina y su elaboración metódica en la historiografía.* Madrid: Vervuert/ Iberoamericana, 1998.
Rappaport, Pamela Kirk. *Sor Juana Inés de la Cruz: Selected Writings.* Mahwah, NJ: Paulist, 2005.
Reilly, Bernard F. *The Contest of Christian and Muslim Spain 1031–1157.* Oxford: Blackwell, 1992.
———. *The Medieval Spains.* Cambridge: Cambridge University Press, 1993.
Ricard, Robert. *The Spiritual Conquest of Mexico.* Berkley: University of California Press, 1966.
Rice, John Steven. "Evangelical Episcopalians and the Church of Jesus in Mexico 1857–1906." Unpublished M.A. Thesis, University of Texas, 2000.

Rivera, Luis N. *A Violent Evangelism: The Political and Religious Conquest of the Americas*. Louisville: Westminster John Knox, 1992.

Rodríguez, Daniel R. *La Primera Evangelización Norteamericana en Puerto Rico 1898–1930*. México: Borinquen, 1986.

Rout, Leslie B. *The African Experience in Spanish America: 1502 to the Present Day*. Cambridge: Cambridge University Press, 1976.

Samson, C. Matthews. *Re-Enchanting the World: Maya Protestantism in the Guatemalan Highlands*. Birmingham: University of Alabama Press, 2007.

Sánchez, David A. *From Patmos to the Barrio: Subverting Imperial Myths*. Minneapolis: Fortress, 2008.

Sandoval, Moises. *On the Move: A History of the Hispanic Church in the United States*. Maryknoll, NY: Orbis, 2006.

Saranyana, Josep-Ignaci. *Teología en América Latina*. 4 vols. Madrid: Iberoamericana, 1999–2002.

Schroeder, H. J., O.P. *The Canons and Decrees of the Council of Trent*. St. Louis: Herder, 1941.

Schroeder, Susan. "Father José María Luis Mora, Liberalism, and the British and Foreign Bible Society in Nineteenth-Century Mexico." *The Americas* 50 (1994) 377–97.

Schroeder, Susan and Poole, Stafford. *Religion in New Spain*. Albuquerque: University of New Mexico Press, 2007.

Schwaller, John, ed. *The Church in Colonial Latin America*. Wilmington, DE: Scholarly Resources, 2000.

Sedgwick, Alexander. *Jansenism in Seventeenth-Century France: Voices from the Wilderness*. Charlottesville: University Press of Virginia, 1977.

Shiels, W. Eugene, S.J. *King and Church: The Rise and Fall of the Patronato Real*. Chicago: Loyola University Press, 1961.

Sorkin, David. *The Religious Enlightenment: Protestants, Jews and Catholics from London to Vienna*. Princeton: Princeton University. Press, 2008.

Stevens-Arroyo, Anthony M. "Marriage Made in America; Trent and the Baroque." In *From Trent to Vatican II*, edited by Raymond F. Bulman and Frederick J. Parrella, 39–59. Oxford: Oxford University Press, 2006.

Stoll, Martin. *Is Latin America Turning Protestant? The Politics of Evangelical Growth*. Berkeley: University of California Press, 1990.

Sullivan, Lawrence E. *Native Religions and Cultures of Central and South America*. New York: Continuum, 2002.

Taylor, William B. *Magistrates of the Sacred. Priests and Parishoners in Eighteenth-Century Mexico*. Stanford: Stanford University Press, 1996.

Thomas, Hugh. *Conquest: Montezuma, Cortés and the Fall of Old Mexico*. New York: Simon & Schuster, 1993.

Townsend, Richard F. *The Aztecs*. London: Thames & Hudson, 1992.

Van Kley, Dale. *The Jansenists and the Expulsion of the Jesuits from France 1757–1765*. New Haven: Yale University Press, 1975.

Vierira, David Guieros. *O Protestantismo, a maconaria e a questão religiosa no Brasil*. Brasília: Editora Universidade de Brasília, 1980.

Voekel, Pamela. *Alone Before God: The Religious Origins of Modernity in Mexico*. Durham, NC: Duke University Press, 2002.

Walker, Williston. *A History of the Christian Church*. New York: Scribner, 1985.

Ward, W. R. *Christianity under the Ancien-Régime 1648–1789*. Cambridge: Cambridge University Press, 1999.

Index

A

Africa, 53, 54, 57, 58, 60
African, 8–11, 16, 27, 29, 30, 31, 33, 52–54, 56, 59–61, 64–68, 190, 193, 196, 199
African-Americans, 16
Africans, 13, 27, 57, 60, 63, 189, 196
Afro-Caribbean, 64
Afro-Christian, 23
Aguas, Manuel, 10, 34, 151, 169, 170, 171, 173–79, 181–84, 191
Aguilar y Bustamante, Javier, 150, 158, 168, 174
Ajofrín, Francisco de, 109
Alcantará, José María, 137
Alegre, Francisco Xavier, 107
Alexander VI, Pope, 41, 42
Alexander VII, Pope, 88
Alexandrine Donations, 41
Alfonso X, 44, 54, 197
Alvarado, Alfonso Alcalá, 197
Alvarez, Juan, 140, 141
ambiguity, 32
ambivalence, 31, 32
Americas, 38, 42, 45–48, 54, 55, 60, 62, 63, 68–70, 80, 99, 106, 111, 114, 116, 118, 131, 190
Ancien–Regime, 78, 83, 84, 88
Anglican Church of Mexico, 2, 24, 25, 163, 172, 180, 186
Anglicanism, 2, 24
Anglo-Catholic, 161, 163, 181, 186

anti-Catholic, 4, 7, 10, 133, 162, 172, 174, 175, 179, 182, 183, 191
anticlericalism, 10, 89, 101, 128, 132–34, 145–48, 167, 173–75, 191
anti-Jesuit, 87, 94, 95, 96
antimonarchical, 122
anti-Pelagian, 84
antiquity, 27, 39, 110, 154, 166, 198
anti-regalist, 131
anti-religion, 134
antireligious, 14, 78, 132
apostles, 39, 74, 111, 117, 152, 194
apostolic, 10, 46, 47, 88, 111–15, 129, 144, 153, 154, 157–59, 161, 163, 165–66, 173, 177, 186, 191, 202
Arellano, Ignacio, 171
Arenas Conspiracy, 124
Arias, Bishop Nicholas, 173
Aristotle, 108
Arizpe, Miguel Ramos, 123
articles, 143, 157
Augustine of Hippo, 84, 85, 106, 133, 165, 200
Augustinian, 11, 95, 96
Augustinus, 84, 85, 88
authoritarianism, 22
authority, 10, 40, 47, 49, 63, 79, 80, 87, 92, 93, 96, 100, 101, 106, 117, 118, 129, 144, 146, 148, 152, 163, 176, 178, 180
Ayutla, Plan de, 140, 143
Aztec, 8, 9, 35, 38, 39, 53, 56, 61, 63, 64, 65, 108, 110, 114, 115

B

Baptist, 16, 72, 132
baroque, 5, 6, 72, 75, 79, 80, 81, 95, 96, 97, 102, 104, 192
Baroque Catholicism, 5, 6, 11, 12, 33, 34, 52, 68–76, 80, 84, 89, 93, 152, 187, 188, 190, 193
Bastian, Jean-Pierre, 15, 16, 19–22, 24, 26, 33, 121, 130, 137, 141, 142, 150, 155–57, 159, 164, 167, 171–73, 181, 183, 195
Bechtel, Alpha Gillet, 24, 152, 155, 161, 164, 167, 170–72, 174, 178, 181, 185
beliefs, 13, 20, 23, 39, 62, 85, 89, 101, 131, 138, 157, 162, 163, 182, 184
Bermudez, Manuél Aguilar, 166, 168, 181
Bible, 5, 6, 11, 13, 14, 18, 27, 34, 79–81, 95, 97, 111, 131, 132, 134–38, 152–54, 157, 158, 160, 161, 163, 165, 167, 170, 175, 182, 190, 191, 193, 198, 200, 201
bishop, 2, 10–12, 39, 40–46, 48, 49, 51, 52, 56, 58, 70, 80, 83, 86–88, 92,–94, 96, 101, 117, 121–24, 126, 127, 142, 143, 148, 149, 157–59, 161, 164–66, 171, 172, 178–81, 183, 184, 187
Bourbon, 11, 34, 40, 49, 79, 81, 83, 90, 91, 93, 95, 99, 103, 114, 120, 131
Bourbon Reforms, 11, 99, 101, 103, 131
Brading, D. A., 34, 109, 116, 142
Bustamente, Anastasio, 127

C

Calama, José Pérez, 108
Calixtus III, Pope, 44
Canales, Luis, 178
capitalism, 14
Casta, 30, 57, 61
casta paintings, 29, 32, 57, 61, 189
Castile, 37, 43, 44, 45, 55, 82
castizaje, 28–33, 189–92, 193, 200
catechesis, 62, 100
catechism, 56. 105, 134
cathedral, 35, 50, 71, 93, 104, 120, 126, 127, 148, 159, 160, 169, 172, 175
Catholic Enlightenment, 5, 6, 34, 52, 77–81, 84, 89, 95, 98, 99, 101, 102, 103, 107, 108
Catholic Monarchs, 41, 45, 91, 101
Catholicism, 2, 4, 5, 6, 10–14, 19, 20, 23–25, 34, 35, 50–53, 55, 57–59, 61–63, 65–71, 73, 75, 76, 79–81, 118, 134, 136, 138, 143, 145, 151, 152, 157, 162, 163, 173, 174–78, 182–84, 189–94
catholicisms, 11
Catholics, 25, 52, 76, 133, 138, 144, 151, 152, 157, 158, 162, 163, 169, 171, 174, 176, 181, 184, 191
CEHILA, 21, 28, 59, 196, 198, 199
celibacy, 152, 157, 175, 176, 182, 191
cemetery, 34, 50, 141
censorship, 108, 131
ceremony, 39, 63, 69, 75, 84, 102, 104, 107, 150, 157, 172, 183, 187
chaplaincies, 103
chaplain, 48
charity, 5, 48, 74–76, 80, 81, 86, 94, 97, 99, 102, 106, 133, 135, 138, 200
Charles II, 82, 91
Charles III, 79, 82, 83, 91, 93–95, 97–99, 101, 103, 114, 116, 130, 161, 185
Charles IV, 98, 99, 103
Chiapas, 121, 127
Christ, 1, 13, 20, 21, 26, 28, 40, 47, 62, 64, 65, 70, 71, 73, 75, 80, 85, 87, 88, 96, 97, 105, 106, 115, 130, 134–36, 161–64, 182, 185, 189, 193–96, 200–202
Christendom, 2, 43, 55, 56
Church Fathers, 5, 86, 106, 158
Church of Jesus, 4–6, 10, 12, 13, 23, 24, 33, 34, 49, 52, 151, 171, 174, 176–81, 183–88, 190–93; *see also* Iglesia de Jesús
churrigueresque, 69, 71
Clement XIV, Pope, 78, 88, 91
clergy, 4, 11, 25, 27, 42, 44, 47, 48, 56, 63, 72, 73, 76, 83, 86, 87, 89, 92, 93,

96, 98, 100, 107, 108, 116, 121–24, 126–28, 133–38, 141, 142, 145, 146, 148, 149, 151, 153, 155–61, 164–65, 167, 170, 172, 198
clergyman, 47, 117, 165, 178
clerical, 3, 27, 32, 91, 96, 97, 108, 121, 124, 125, 127, 142, 145, 147, 149, 152, 156, 158, 159, 174–76, 182, 191, 198
clericalism, 14
cleric, 5, 10, 12, 25, 34, 39, 41, 45, 49, 69, 78, 80, 84, 89, 96, 123, 124, 126, 146, 148, 150–52, 154–56, 158, 160, 167, 168, 171, 172, 176, 183, 184, 191
colony, 11, 51, 52, 75, 79, 100, 101, 103, 120, 121, 130, 150
Columbus, Christopher, 22, 38, 55, 189
communion, 59, 76, 81, 93, 108, 163, 166, 175, 186
community, 18, 70, 71, 81, 107, 134, 135, 143, 161, 172, 194
Comonfort, Ignacio, 141, 150
concordat, 83, 92, 124, 127, 128
confraternity, 11, 51, 71–76, 81, 104, 106, 107
Congress, 122, 123, 125, 126, 137, 144, 149, 159
conquest, 9, 13, 35–39, 49, 50, 58, 60–62, 66, 74, 110, 111, 112, 116, 117, 162, 189, 190, 197
conscience, 105, 106, 133, 135, 151, 152, 157, 158, 161, 170
consecration, 88, 171, 179, 180, 181
conservative, 16, 119, 121, 125, 126, 127, 145, 149, 161, 171
Conservatives, 12, 20, 121, 140, 141, 145, 150, 153, 156, 157, 158, 159, 160, 174, 181
Constantine, 117
Constitution of 1824, 109, 122, 127
Constitution of 1857, 10, 12, 34, 117, 119, 121, 123, 127, 135, 138, 139, 143, 144–50, 152, 155, 176, 182, 191
Constitutionalist Clerics/Fathers, 10, 12, 23, 24, 25, 34, 151–59, 164–66,
168, 169, 174, 176, 177, 182, 183, 191
constitutionaries, 88
convent, 65, 107, 125, 132, 150, 178
conversion, 14, 16, 26, 43, 55, 59, 62, 85, 89, 100, 161, 163, 170, 173, 182, 183, 185, 195
converso, 61, 112
converts, 19, 138
convivencia, 54, 55
Corpus Christi, 52, 70, 71
Cortazar, Alejandro, 138
Cortez, Hernán, 35, 38
council, 45, 50, 51, 72, 88, 124, 165, 178
Council of the Indies, 42, 45–48, 57, 66, 82, 104, 113, 116
councils, 41, 43, 46, 48, 49, 82, 90, 116, 161
Creole, 11, 34, 109–15, 117, 118–20, 123
crown, 4, 5, 11, 12, 37, 40–42, 45–49, 55, 79, 81, 83, 84, 90–92, 94, 96, 99, 100, 101, 103, 110, 120, 121, 131
Crusades, 14, 38
Cruz, Sor Juana Inés de la, 3, 65–68, 110
customs, 61, 98, 100, 114, 151, 152

D

decree, 23, 41, 48, 58, 68, 70, 73, 103, 144, 150
Delgadillo, Francisco, 147
democracy, 117, 134, 147, 201
Descartes, René, 107
devotion, 5, 10, 21, 23, 26, 28, 49, 61–63, 68–70, 72–76, 86, 90, 93, 95, 97, 98, 101, 104, 112, 156, 197, 198, 202
Diaz, Porfirio, 180
dioceses, 42, 43, 127, 179
dissidence, 172
dissident, 6, 7, 19, 20, 24, 26, 148, 149, 151, 157, 158, 160, 167, 171, 182–84, 191, 195
Domínguez, Francisco, 150, 164, 177

Dominicans, 47, 62
Dussel, Enrique, 21, 33, 59, 196

E
economics, 8, 14, 103
economy, 58, 95, 113, 122
education, 14, 21, 32, 48, 62, 72, 80, 89, 93, 95–98, 100, 107, 126, 136, 137, 138, 143, 146–49, 155, 190
El Monitor Republicano, 134, 156, 170
election, 41, 42, 44, 45, 51, 59, 117, 126, 180
Elijah, 164
emperor, 12, 91, 117, 120, 137, 142, 160, 165
Empire, 3, 22, 40, 43, 46, 82, 83, 99, 101, 122, 142, 167–69, 190, 202
encyclical, 117, 123, 124, 137
Enlightened Catholics, 4, 6, 11, 12, 25, 33, 34, 52, 76, 91, 98, 101, 107, 108, 133, 138, 147, 151, 152, 157, 158, 176, 181, 182, 191
Enlightenment, 5, 6, 34, 52, 61, 76–79, 80, 81, 83–85, 87, 89–91, 93, 95, 97–99, 101–3, 105–9, 111, 113–15, 117, 131, 139, 151, 158, 187, 190
Ensenada, Marques de la, 92, 94
enslavement, 53, 56, 189
episcopacy, 87
episcopal, 4, 6, 7, 10, 24, 25, 34, 41, 47, 48, 73, 95, 96, 100, 103, 130, 149, 151–55, 161–78, 180–82, 185–87, 191
Episcopal Church, 153, 154, 161, 163–67, 170, 171, 177–82, 185, 186, 191
episcopalian, 10, 24, 96, 155, 158, 161, 164, 165, 174, 191
episcopate, 117, 145, 179
epistemology, 52, 78
eschatological, 193
eschatology, 29
Esquilache, Marqués de, 95
Estrella de Belén, 183
Eucharist, 66, 70, 71, 80, 81, 93, 97, 130, 156, 163

Eucharistic, 69, 70, 101, 108
evangelical, 1, 2, 3, 7, 10, 14, 15, 16, 19, 22, 23–25, 60, 78, 132, 154, 155, 161, 163, 165, 171, 173, 177–79, 181, 182, 184, 185, 191
evangelicalism, 3, 22, 34, 162, 165, 184
expulsion, 3, 11, 78, 94, 98, 100, 101, 107, 108, 114, 127, 131, 149, 159

F
Fabian y Fuero, Francisco, 103,
faith, 2, 5, 7, 12, 13, 15, 16, 18–21, 23, 25–29, 32, 33, 39, 40, 42, 55, 59, 60, 61, 71, 74–76, 78, 80, 81, 84, 86–89, 91, 93, 97, 104, 105, 108, 135, 137, 152, 153, 157, 158, 163, 165, 171, 173, 175–77, 190, 193–96, 201
Farías, Valentín Gómez, 126, 127, 137, 149
federalist, 120–23
Fernando (Ferdinand) of Aragon, 42, 45, 160
Fernando III, 37,
Fernando VI, 3, 37, 55, 83, 90, 92, 93, 100, 110, 119
Fernando VII, 119
festivals, 52, 70, 71, 72, 74, 93, 104, 105, 135, 150, 190
Finney, Charles Grandison, 161, 162
First Great Awakening, 161
foreigners, 16, 139, 167, 172, 181
France, 2, 8, 12, 41, 52, 78, 81–90, 95, 99, 101, 116, 117, 121, 128, 131, 142, 147, 159, 160, 167, 183
Franciscan, 39, 45, 47, 62, 64, 93, 170, 172
freedom, 14, 65, 85, 89, 127, 132, 136, 139, 140, 143, 144, 146–50, 160, 162, 166
Freemasonry, 20
freemasons, 4
friars, 35, 36, 39, 45, 47, 73, 79, 115, 137
fundamentalism, 14
funeral, 50, 72, 74–76, 92, 102, 106, 125

G

Gallican, 49, 87, 88, 91, 96
Gallicanism, 87, 88, 91
Garza y Ballesteros, Archbishop Lázaro de la, 142, 155
God, 11, 17, 18, 21, 23, 25, 27, 34, 38–40, 45, 46, 49–52, 55, 57, 59, 62, 63, 66, 67, 69, 71–73, 75, 79–81, 84, 85, 87, 88, 98, 102–6, 107, 111, 112, 133–35, 139, 141, 142, 144, 151–53, 161, 162, 165, 166, 169, 170, 175, 189, 193–95, 197–200, 202, 203
gospel, 11, 15, 25, 26, 28, 86, 111, 139, 152, 194–96, 197, 199–202
grace, 25, 75, 81, 84–86, 102, 106, 116, 133, 135, 144, 152, 161, 194, 195, 200
Greenland, Fay, 24, 148, 151, 155, 157, 161, 168, 170, 181, 184
Gregoire, Henri, 116
Gregory VII, Pope, 43, 44, 47, 73, 126, 127, 149
Gregory XIII, Pope, 47
Guadalupe, Virgin of, 12, 26, 28, 51, 61, 64, 67, 71, 74, 109–15, 123, 160, 189, 197, 198
Guión, Elijah, 164

H

hagiographies, 26, 73, 195
Hapsburgs, 82, 91, 160
Hernández, Bishop Prudencio, 180
Haro y Peralta, Alonso Nuñez de, 103
Herrera, José Joaquin, 128
heterodoxy, 3, 81
Hidalgo y Costilla, Miguel, 78, 108, 120, 138, 149
hierarchy, 2, 6, 12, 14, 29, 33, 72, 84, 89, 94–97, 102, 124, 127, 134, 140, 143, 145, 148, 149, 156–58, 175, 196
Hipólito, San, 156
history, 8, 13, 14, 18–26, 28, 29, 33–35, 37, 40, 46, 49, 51, 57–59, 61, 63, 68, 70, 76, 78, 84, 89, 92, 93, 108, 110, 111, 113, 145, 152, 176, 178, 188, 189, 193–201
historiography, 13, 20, 25, 27, 28, 114, 193–96, 199, 201
Hobbes, Thomas, 101, 108
holiness, 15, 123
holy, 15, 17, 18, 38, 51, 63, 64, 87, 91, 101, 104, 105, 118, 130, 131, 135, 172
Hopkins, Right Reverend Henry, 164, 165, 171
Huerta, José de Jesús, 147
hybrid, 6, 31, 56, 63, 75
hybridity, 9, 29, 31, 37, 60, 63–65, 68
hybridization, 31

I

identity, 2, 7, 15, 23, 30, 31, 43, 55, 56, 70–72, 74, 114, 131, 166, 168, 178, 184, 186–90, 192, 200, 201
idolatry, 25, 100, 151, 182, 194
Iglesia de Jesús, 10, 21, 40, 42, 98, 100, 101, 107, 130, 131, 133, 135, 137, 139, 141, 143, 145, 147, 149, 151, 153, 155, 157, 159, 161, 163, 165, 167, 169, 171, 173, 175, 177, 179, 181, 183, 185, 199; *see also* Church of Jesus
Iguala, Plan de, 120, 121
image, 25, 50, 51, 61, 69, 72, 73, 75, 97, 102, 104–6, 111, 112, 115, 116, 154, 194
immigrant, 2, 10, 15, 51, 54, 61, 110, 162
imperialism, 3, 123
independence, 5, 11, 12, 14, 15, 24, 40, 47, 52, 78, 108, 115, 117–22, 125, 136, 144–46, 148, 161, 165, 176, 180, 181, 191
Indians, 10, 29, 30–32, 50, 51, 53, 56, 57, 61, 66, 72, 99, 100, 104, 105, 109, 110, 112, 113, 115, 120, 140, 151, 167, 168, 184, 187–89
indulgences, 13, 38, 45, 130, 170
Innocent VIII, Pope, 45
Inquisition, 3, 11, 45, 65, 91, 92, 93, 97, 101, 121, 130, 200
Inquisitor, 61, 97

institution, 25, 28, 55, 59, 62, 83, 101, 120, 125, 145, 146, 153, 194, 197, 198
insurgency, 116, 117, 120
insurrection, 52, 119, 131
intellectuals, 78, 82, 96, 98
Inter caetera, 41
Isabella (Isabel) of Castile, 3, 37, 42, 45, 55
Islam, 63, 112, 131
Ixtlilxochitl, Juan Fernando de Alva, 110

J
James, Saint, 38, 111, 132, 136, 202
Jansen, Cornelius, 84, 85, 106
Jansenism, 11, 49, 81–89, 95, 96, 116, 117, 133, 142, 155
Jansenist, 52, 79, 84–88, 91, 93, 95–98, 101, 102, 108, 116–18, 124, 133, 152
Jesuit, 11, 41, 71, 77, 78, 84–87, 89, 92–98, 100, 101, 107, 108, 113, 114, 131, 142, 168
Jesus, 4–7, 10, 12, 13, 21, 23, 24, 33, 34, 39, 48, 49, 51, 52, 59, 60, 65, 70, 73, 75, 77, 85, 87, 88, 93–95, 97, 100, 107, 134, 136, 151, 152, 171, 173, 174, 176–81, 183–88, 191–93, 195, 199–202
Jews, 3, 37, 54, 55, 57, 60, 61, 130
Joachim of Fiore, 62
Jovellanos, Gaspar Melchor de, 116
Juárez, Benito, 4–6, 10, 12, 16, 34, 49, 90, 108, 133, 140, 150, 156, 159, 172, 178, 183, 187, 191
Juárez, Sóstenez, 179, 183
juaristas, 150
Judaism, 63, 112
Julius II, Pope, 42
justification, 86, 116, 155, 163, 165

K
king, 45–49, 54, 57, 81–83, 87, 90, 92–95, 97–99, 111, 116, 117, 119, 121, 123, 160

L
La Merced, 156
Labastida y Dávalos, Pelagio Antonio, 142
Lancasterian Method, 136
Larkin, Brian, 69, 70, 71, 74, 75, 103, 104, 105, 106
Las Casas, Bartolomé de, 36, 110
Leo XII, Pope, 117, 123
Ley Iglesias, 141, 167
Ley Juárez, 141, 143,
Ley Lerdo, 141–43, 150
Liberal, 4, 6, 12, 14, 20, 24, 25, 119, 120, 121, 123–28, 132–36, 138–42, 145–47, 149, 150–53, 155–58, 165, 160, 161, 165, 167, 171, 172–74, 176, 181, 184. 191
liberalism, 4, 121, 144–47, 151, 152, 156, 174
liberation, 19, 21, 22, 27, 28, 59, 60, 196
Liberation Theology, 59, 60, 201
liberationists, 27, 198
limpieza de sangre, 61
Linares, 121, 127, 157
liturgical, 38, 39, 70, 71, 73, 108, 167, 187
liturgy, 28, 43, 68, 69, 70, 75, 80, 81, 86, 94, 103, 104, 154, 161, 165, 166, 173, 185, 186, 193, 198, 201, 202
Lizana y Beaumont, Francisco Javier, 106
Lorenzana, Francisco, 101, 103, 105, 106, 107, 108
Lozano, Ramón, 157, 158, 159, 181, 182, 184
Luther, Martin, 13, 34, 85, 200–202
Lutheran, 3, 13, 15, 16, 130, 131
Lutheranism, 131, 193

M
magistrate, 107, 167
Manifest Destiny, 3, 21, 55, 162
Martínez, Rafael Díaz, 91, 92, 95, 96, 150, 153, 155, 156, 161, 164, 168, 169, 177

martyr, 67, 70
Marxism, 27, 198
Marxist, 35, 58
Mary, *see Virgin Mary*
Masonic, 120, 133, 146, 172, 173, 183
Masons, 24, 121, 171, 172, 184
Mass, 5, 43, 70, 75, 76, 80, 81, 93, 97, 103, 106, 107, 154, 156, 163, 164, 166, 175
Matamoros, 38, 132
Maximilian, Emperor Ferdinand, 12, 142, 145, 160, 165, 167, 169, 171, 173, 174, 182, 183, 191
Meier, Fray Servando Teresa de, 79, 115–18, 123, 151
Memorias, 116
mendicant, 47, 94, 127
mercantilism, 14
mestizaje, 28, 29, 30, 31, 61
mestizo, 28, 29–31, 33, 61, 123
metanarrative, 189
Methodists, 16, 17, 153, 154, 179, 183, 184
methodology, 4, 27, 34, 59, 89, 197–99
Mexican Catholic Apostolic Society, 129, 153, 154, 157, 158, 159, 165, 166, 173
Mexican–American War, 17, 28, 140, 188
Mexico City, 8, 9, 35, 36, 50, 51, 56, 65, 71, 103, 104, 106, 120, 122, 134, 137, 140, 150, 151, 156, 158–60, 166, 167, 169, 172, 179, 180, 183–85
Michoacán, 108, 121, 127, 133, 166, 164, 187
millennium, 2, 62
miracle, 5, 15, 38, 80, 81, 113, 134, 190, 193
Miravete, Archbishop Pedro José de Fonte y, 122
mission, 3, 10, 14, 16, 21, 24–26, 38, 41, 42, 47, 56, 58, 59, 64, 70, 83, 94, 100, 114, 132, 143, 152, 154, 155, 166, 166, 171, 178, 179, 181, 186, 186, 191, 193–95, 203

missionary, 2– 4, 15–18, 24–26, 39, 45, 62–64, 73, 86, 111, 132, 169, 174, 178, 184, 185, 194, 195
Mocteuzoma, 39
Molina, Luis de, 85
monarch, 11, 40, 42, 43, 45, 46, 48, 49, 55, 82, 83, 90, 92, 99, 101, 114, 117, 119, 120, 121, 160
monarchist, 122, 160
monarchy, 45, 83, 90, 98, 117, 120
monastery, 74
monasticism, 85, 149, 150, 154, 163
monastics, 94
monks, 47, 127, 149
Moody, D.L., 14
Moor-Killer, *see James, Saint*
Mora, José María Luis, 126, 133, 134, 136–39
Morales, Arcadio, 108, 123, 179, 183
Mozarab, 43, 185
mulatez, 29
Muslim, 3, 37, 38, 43, 53–55, 57, 61

N
Nahua, 31, 61, 64, 65, 112
Napoleon III, 160
nationalism, 11, 34, 109, 111, 112, 115, 142, 176
nationalist, 142
neo-Marxist, 58
Nesvig, Martin, 23, 25–27, 33, 58, 59, 64, 71–75, 107, 132, 133, 135, 138, 155–57, 159, 164, 187, 195, 198
newspapers, 1, 123, 125, 126, 134, 144, 156, 167
Nican Mopohua, 61, 112
Nicholson, E.C., 153, 154, 161, 164, 165, 166, 167, 181, 182

O
Ocampo, Melchor, 133, 140, 152, 155, 159
Ordenanza, 42, 45, 47, 48
orders, 10, 33, 45, 47–49, 51, 56, 57, 62, 71, 72, 74, 75, 77, 83, 94, 100, 101, 108, 150, 156, 163

Orestes, Enrique, 150, 152, 156, 159, 164, 176, 177
orthodoxy, 5, 10, 58, 63, 75, 76, 78, 79, 86, 201
Orthodoxy, Eastern, 13, 191, 194, 200
Ovando, Juan de, 47

P

Pacheco, Juan Vicente Güemes, 51, 52, 104
papacy, 12, 40–43, 46, 76, 91, 96, 98, 116–18, 123, 127, 128, 134, 162
papal nuncio, 45, 91, 129, 160
parish, 11, 12, 48, 83, 93, 97, 98, 104, 107, 123, 124, 127, 138, 145, 147, 149, 157, 158, 190
Pascal, Blaise, 86, 87
patriotism, 109, 110, 114, 146, 175
patron, 34, 44, 49, 50, 51, 55, 71, 73, 74, 81, 113, 128, 134, 172
patronage, 4–6, 11, 12, 34, 39, 40, 41–49, 83, 91, 92, 100, 121–29, 146, 147, 149, 184, 190, 191
Patronato Real, 4, 35, 39, 45, 46, 48, 49, 119, 123, 149
Patronazgo, 42, 45, 47, 48
Paul III, Pope, 130
PECUSA (Protestant Episcopal Church in the United States of America), 6, 24, 154, 159, 163–65, 167, 168, 177, 178, 179, 180–85, 187, 191, 194; see also Episcopal Church
peninsulares, 109, 112, 114, 120
Pentecost, 1
Pentecostal, 2, 14, 15, 17, 18, 20, 21, 23, 32
Pentecostalism, 15, 17, 19, 22, 193
Philip II, 45, 47, 58, 82, 90, 91, 92, 99, 130
Philojansenists, 95
philosophy, 54, 67, 90, 101, 107, 169
piety, 5, 6, 11, 12, 33, 51, 52, 57, 67, 69, 70, 75, 76, 80, 81, 84, 93, 94, 95, 101, 102, 103, 105, 108, 149, 157, 201
pilgrimage, 69, 105

Pius IX, Pope, 128, 142, 144
Pius V, Pope, 45, 128, 142, 144
pluralism, 11, 12, 19, 27, 61, 64, 70, 139, 184, 190–92, 196
pope, 2, 38, 40, 41, 43–45, 47–49, 51, 69, 71, 78, 83, 86–89, 91, 92, 94, 95, 97, 98, 106, 112, 117, 118, 122–30, 134, 137, 142, 144, 149, 155, 166, 167
Portugal, 37, 39, 41, 54, 55, 82, 95
Portuguese, 2, 8, 27, 29, 53, 54, 78, 196
positivism, 14
post-colonial, 31
postmillennial, 21
post-Tridentine, 52
practices, 13, 23, 32, 39, 62, 89, 90, 152, 163, 174, 175, 177, 182, 197
predestination, 84
prelates, 45, 48, 103, 107, 108, 160
premillennial, 14
Presbyterian, 16, 132, 179, 183, 184, 193
president, 12, 16, 35, 47, 121, 123, 125–28, 137, 140, 141, 149, 150, 158, 160, 167, 168, 172, 176, 180
priest, 6, 10–12, 44, 47, 48, 50, 63, 72, 74, 75, 88, 93, 94, 96, 97, 100, 101, 103–5, 107, 108, 117, 123, 124, 126, 127, 133, 138, 144, 145, 147–51, 154–59, 161, 165, 167–72, 174, 177, 182, 185, 190
priesthood, 13, 85, 87, 94, 154, 157
Protestant, 1–4, 6, 7, 10, 13–25, 33, 58, 68, 78, 81, 85, 86, 89, 97, 121, 124, 130–32, 139, 155, 161–66, 168–70, 172–79, 183, 184, 187, 188, 191–94, 200, 203
Protestant Reformation, 4, 13, 14, 55, 68, 89, 162, 169
Protestantism, 2–4, 7, 10, 13, 14–24, 26, 55, 62, 68, 84–86, 121, 130–32, 134, 135, 139, 140, 142, 144, 150, 160, 167, 168, 171, 174–76, 178, 184, 187, 191–93, 195, 199
protestantization, 2
Puebla, 102–4, 108, 127, 141, 142, 144, 145

purgatory, 73, 74, 75, 76, 130, 175
Puritan, 161
Puritanism, 84

Q
Quetzalcóatl, 63, 111, 112, 114, 115

R
race, 10, 28–32, 53, 54, 57, 75, 189
Rávago, Francisco, 92
Real Presence, 70, 163
Reconquest, 37, 38, 41, 44, 55
reform, 6, 7, 10–13, 20, 43, 45, 49, 52, 68–70, 78, 80, 81, 83–87, 89, 90, 92–99, 101–3, 106–8, 114, 116, 119, 120, 126, 127, 130, 131, 132, 135, 137, 138, 140, 141, 143, 145, 148, 150–55, 157, 158, 166, 167, 168–70, 173, 174, 176, 177, 182, 185, 201
Reformed, 163
reformer, 43, 61, 69, 85, 96, 98, 101, 102, 105, 106, 108, 124, 125, 133, 157, 163, 169, 176, 190, 200
regalism, 96, 115
regalist, 46, 52, 91, 92, 95, 96, 98, 99, 101, 116, 117, 123–25, 127, 131, 147
Riego, Rafael del, 119
relic, 5, 11, 50, 69, 71, 73–75, 80, 84, 97, 106, 115, 175, 191
religion, 23, 25, 55, 58, 59, 62, 63, 66, 69, 71–75, 78, 91, 93, 96–99, 107, 143, 187
Remedios, Virgin of, 50, 63
republic, 5, 12, 16, 49, 56, 79, 94, 100, 115, 118, 122, 128, 145, 153, 155
revolution, 3, 16, 20, 24, 35, 78, 89, 95, 116, 117, 119, 121
Rice, John Steven, 181, 184
Riley, (Bishop) Henry C., 163, 164, 171, 173, 177–81, 183, 184, 187
rites, 75, 76, 102, 107, 111, 182
ritual, 26, 38, 39, 53, 65, 80, 81, 104, 106, 171, 172, 197
Rivadeneira, Antonio Joaquín de, 109, 110
Rocafuerte, Vicente, 139

Roman Catholic Church, 2–4, 12–14, 17–22, 40, 41, 43, 51, 60, 66, 67, 87, 91, 97, 118, 120, 123, 124, 128, 129, 133, 138, 139, 143, 151–53, 157, 158, 163, 164, 166, 167, 169, 171–77, 181, 183–85, 192, 194, 202
Romanism, 173
Romanists, 174
Rome, 5, 10, 12, 39, 40, 42, 43, 46, 47, 81, 88, 91, 92, 111, 117, 123–25, 128, 142, 151, 162, 165, 170, 174, 175, 185
Rousseau, 78, 101, 108
Royal Patronage, *see* Patronato Real
royalist, 63, 84, 145

S
sacrament, 68, 69, 84, 85, 141, 144, 152, 154, 157, 158, 164, 165, 167, 182, 196, 199
saint, 1, 11, 19, 39, 51, 52, 64, 69, 70–76, 81, 85, 89, 98, 102, 105, 106, 107, 111, 133, 134, 135, 168, 170, 175, 190, 200, 201
Salamanca, 56
salvation, 1, 13, 25, 40, 45, 69, 74–76, 85, 106, 107, 133, 144, 161, 162, 164, 165, 177, 182, 194
San Francisco, 171, 172, 178
Santa Anna, Antonio Lopez de, 122, 126, 127, 140, 142
Santiago (Matamoros), *see* James, Saint
schism, 25
schismatic, 88, 172
scholastic, 53, 107, 136
scholasticism, 84, 95
Scottish Rite (escoses), 78, 120, 121
Second Great Awakening. 161
seminarians, 72, 93, 172
seminary, 93, 94, 97, 141, 150, 171, 179
sermon, 38, 51, 98, 103, 112, 115, 116, 126, 147–49
Siete Leyes, 127
Sigüenza y Góngora, Carlos, 66, 110, 111, 113, 114
sin, 56, 60, 85, 200, 201

Sixtus IV, Pope, 45
slave, 9, 10, 53, 54, 57, 61, 63, 118, 174
slavery, 53, 54, 132, 190
Sorbonne, 86
Spain, 3, 5, 6, 11, 12, 14, 17, 23, 33, 37, 38, 41–45, 47–49, 51, 52, 54–56, 58, 61–64, 67, 68, 71–83, 85, 87, 89–93, 95, 97–103, 105, 107–13, 115–17, 119, 121–25, 128, 130, 131, 180, 189, 190
Spaniard, 26, 29, 39, 57, 60, 61, 62, 99, 109, 114
Spanish-American War, 17, 171
State, 4–6, 11, 12, 18, 27, 28, 34, 35–37, 39, 40–49, 52, 54, 55, 78, 79, 82, 84, 93–96, 98, 99, 100, 101, 104, 108, 118, 119, 121–29, 131–33, 136, 139–50, 153, 155, 158, 159, 169–71, 191, 198, 199
supernatural, 38, 85, 115, 161, 200
superstition, 11, 70, 80, 97, 133, 134, 138, 151, 152, 169, 190
syncretism, 8, 27, 196, 198

T

Tepeyac, 51, 64, 112
Teresa, Saint, 61, 90
Texas, 17, 24, 34, 128, 131, 151, 153, 154, 161, 166, 177, 178, 180, 181
theologian, 56, 59, 60, 63, 79, 80, 86, 161, 189, 201
theology, 19, 27, 40, 52, 59, 60, 62, 65, 69, 78, 81, 81, 84, 85, 87, 95, 103, 107, 108, 138, 152, 161, 169, 171, 182, 186, 196, 200, 202
Thirty-Nine Articles, 163, 164
Thomas, Saint, 111, 112, 114–16
tolerance, religious, 5, 14, 15, 54, 89, 138–40, 142, 148
Tonantizin/ Tonantzin, 61
tradition, 6, 12–18, 22, 23, 25, 27, 43, 45, 49, 56, 58, 63, 67, 79, 81, 84, 87, 95, 105, 144, 146, 147, 151, 152, 156, 163, 176, 182, 191–95, 200, 201
translation, 3, 27, 97, 131, 137, 198
transubstantiation, 70

Trent, Council of, 45, 46, 47, 48, 57, 68–70, 73, 82, 84–86, 89, 103, 104, 105, 116, 130, 142, 167, 179
Tridentine, 4, 5, 11, 52, 68, 69, 76, 81, 104, 105, 190

U

ultraliberalism, 146, 147
ultramontanism, 12, 88, 98, 118, 133, 142, 155, 176, 179
United States, 2–4, 6, 10, 15–19, 22, 23, 27, 33, 49, 78, 99, 123, 128, 131, 136, 139, 140, 145, 146, 151, 153, 161–64, 166, 168, 175, 176, 180, 183, 184, 187, 188, 191, 196
university, 54, 72, 74, 93, 95

V

Valdespino, Bishop Tomás, 180
Valdivielso, Ignacio, 128
Vasconcelos, José, 28
Vatican, 12, 14, 22, 142, 167, 179, 194
Vega, Luis Laso de la, 112
Veracruz, 122, 125, 150, 155, 165, 185
vicereine, 65, 66
viceroy, 46–48, 51, 52, 57, 65, 72, 82, 87, 99, 104, 110, 115, 119, 120
Vico, Giambattista, 114
Virgin Mary, 12, 26, 28, 51, 61, 63–65, 67, 68, 71, 73, 74, 75, 107, 112, 113, 115, 116, 160, 163, 165, 189, 197, 198
Vitoria, Francisco de, 56
Voekel, Pamela, 25, 34, 71, 75, 97, 101, 102, 106, 107, 133, 156, 181, 184

W

War, 17, 38, 82, 83, 91, 99, 128, 132, 140, 150, 153, 162, 175
Wars of Reform, 4, 10, 12, 24, 34, 138, 142, 144, 145, 148–51, 155–61, 168, 170, 172, 178, 184, 191
wealth, 38, 57, 72, 75, 81, 93, 103, 125, 128, 129, 131, 142, 146, 148, 153, 175
worldview, 34, 39, 52, 97

worldviews, 9, 18, 20, 34, 54, 133, 188, 192, 202
worship, 64, 86, 94, 97, 104, 105, 136, 139, 150, 153, 160, 164, 165, 166, 187
writers, 65, 90, 108, 133, 192

Y
York Rite (yorkinos), 19, 120, 161, 164, 166, 171, 177, 178

Z
Zavala, Mariano, 126, 167

www.ingramcontent.com/pod-product-compliance
Lightning Source LLC
Chambersburg PA
CBHW062022220426
43662CB00010B/1431